# NIKOS

# KAZANTZAKIS

# AND HIS ODYSSEY

## A Study of the Poet and the Poem

BY PANDELIS PREVELAKIS

Translated from the Greek by Philip Sherrard

With a Preface by Kimon Friar

SIMON AND SCHUSTER · NEW YORK · 1961

Library of Congress Catalog Card Number: 61-5845
Manufactured in the United States of America
By George McKibbin & Son, New York

# Contents

## PART III THE POET AND THE POEM 113

## EPILOGUE 163

## NOTES 171

EDITOR'S NOTE: *All references to Kazantzakis'* ODYSSEY *are to the Simon and Schuster edition, published in 1958 and translated by Kimon Friar.*

# Preface

When in August of 1951 I first met Nikos Kazantzakis in a student's hostel in Florence, he exclaimed after a half hour's conversation that I must surely have read all of his books, for I seemed to understand his thought completely. At that time I had read and translated into prose only a few pages of his *Odyssey,* but our subsequent correspondence of six years and our daily collaboration of some six months on my verse translation of his *The Odyssey: A Modern Sequel* and also of *The Saviors of God* confirmed in both of us a rapport which was unique, as between spiritual father and son. Only one other person, he told me then and often repeated, understood his temperament and thought so well, and that was Pandelis Prevelakis, his Cretan compatriot, the renowned novelist, poet and art critic. But I can only claim to have known and loved this great man of letters for a brief six years, whereas Pandelis Prevelakis knew and loved him and watched with fervor and admiration his titanic struggles ever since they met in November of 1926, when Prevelakis was a stripling of seventeen just out of high school and Kazantzakis a tormented man of almost forty-four who in the previous year had embarked on the fluctuating seas of his *Odyssey,* a voyage which was to take him some thirteen years and half around the world.

That author is extremely fortunate whose life and work, immediately after his death, is recounted and detailed with an inner and loving understanding and yet not with blind idolatry. To a great degree he becomes immune in the future to the perverted attacks or distorted hero worship of prejudiced reporters, and in this book Prevelakis has set down the true, sympathetic yet impartial measurements by which Kazantzakis must accurately be judged by coming generations. He began his book two years before, and finished it one year after, his friend's death. "You are the only man in the world," Kazantzakis wrote him less than a half year before his death, "who can judge me and whose word will have unspeakable value for me. God give you strength, and give me life that I may see what you write." Of critical importance is the fact, to which Prevelakis refers in this book, that for a short time he and Kazantzakis had been estranged. This period must have given Prevelakis the necessary detachment and power to reappraise his master with greater critical clarity, and their reconciliation enabled him to write his study not only with the loving dedication necessary to any deep understanding, but also with an impartiality which incisively illuminates but does not degrade.

[7]

He has therefore performed the critic's most exacting and honorable task: to present his subject in an affirmative light, yet to strip him of those idolatrous embellishments which obscure and do not reveal a man's true stature, because they fail to show him totally as a tormented human spirit with his deformations and his glories both. When, because of the great harmony-indifference between us, Kazantzakis once hesitantly told me that he looked toward me to complete some of his tasks after he had gone, I said to him, "But, Nikos, you must understand that to fulfill this I may perhaps have to do the opposite of what you intend, and even give you the Judas kiss of betrayal." His eyes lit up, he tossed his head in proud excitement, and he exclaimed: "Bravo! Bravo! You understand me fully! Such is the only worthy disciple. Destroy! Destroy! To destroy in this manner is only to rebuild." And in the *Odyssey,* when Odysseus says farewell to his disciple, Rocky, he blesses him and says: "Blessed be the bold, audacious daring of your youth, / steady your knees my friend, don't let my blessing throw you: / Now may that winnower God, who scatters age like chaff, / grant you the power to cast the disk of earth much further!"

Already, as a consequence of Prevelakis' detachment, passages from his book have been quoted out of context and distorted, in particular by Lily Zografou in her diatribe, *Nikos Kazantzakis: A Tragic Man,* 1959, but this in time can only validate Prevelakis' true interpretations and help to establish a just canon. In 1957 Kazantzakis' first wife, Galatea, published a novel, *Men and Supermen,* a thinly veiled account of her life with her former husband, and an astonishing misinterpretation of his work and motives from the point of view of a woman whose highly realistic nature compels her to interpret whatever is not materialistic and palpable as chimerical and false. In 1958, more in the spirit of disclosure than of tribute, she published *Letters to Galatea,* which her husband had written her between 1920 and 1924. In 1960 Yannis Anapliotis published *The True Zorba and Nikos Kazantzakis,* the first of what will become many attempts to correlate the imaginative work of an author with his actual source material. And a few months ago, a leading poet, Nikiphoros Vrettakos, published his own passionate and partisan account of the life and work of Kazantzakis. The flood gates have opened. The personality and work of Nikos Kazantzakis, especially in his native country, will be as much squabbled over and pulled apart as were the works and life of D. H. Lawrence by all who were seared by close proximity to such burning power, and even by those who did not know him at all. There are extraordinary similarities between the two men, which will become apparent as more of the works of Kazantzakis are made available in translation. Both were Dionysian, demon-driven men; both placed instinct and the promptings of the blood above the more ordered deductions of the mind; both celebrated the primitive and even atavistic origins of the human spirit; both were insatiable travelers who in landscape and inscape discerned the contours of God's or Nature's purpose (for Kazantzakis these two words are synonyms) ; both turned to the physical universe for their imagery and away from urban mechanics and subtleties; both extolled strife and crucifixion as the unavoidable and necessitous law of life, and even of love; both were impatient of refinements of craft, and entrusted themselves to the demonic outpourings of creative inspiration; both were disciples of Nietzsche's Zarathustra, valuing above all else the moment of cleaving insight given the man of vision; both placed the prophet above the man of letters; both were obsessed with messianic drives and dreams. And each soon became the untidy skirmish ground where friends blinded by love and foes blinded by hate fight not so much over his meanings as they squabble over his values as man and prophet.

To all this I must submit my own opinion that Prevelakis' book offers a corrective yardstick, for I find myself in accord with almost all of his deductions. Here, it seems to me, the reader will find a true account of Kazantzakis' attitude to good and evil, to praise or blame, to women and friendship, to ideas of spirit and ideas of blood, to Russia and Communist materialist philosophy, to violence and savagery, to created and creative nature, to Dionysus and Apollo, to the obsessive image of Christ, to heroic pessimism and Dionysian nihilism, to Man and men, to spirit and matter—indeed to all the fundamental passions and ideas which were the battleground on which Nikos Kazantzakis formed his character and his work. And in particular he will find what sources, struggles and ideas led Kazantzakis to the writing of what he considered to be the one work by which he must ultimately live or die in the memory of man: *The Odyssey: A Modern Sequel,* and of that book of spiritual exercises which the *Odyssey* best embodies, *The Saviors of God,* and which also underlies everything else he has ever written. Among Kazantzakis' posthumous papers, Prevelakis found this note: "Secondary works: [a list of his books follows]. *Obra* [i.e., The Work]: the *Odyssey.*" Part of the greatness of Nikos Kazantzakis may be judged by the quality and force of what he considered to be but "secondary works": *Zorba the Greek, The Greek Passion, Freedom or Death, The Last Temptation of Christ, The Poor Man of God,* and about fifteen poetic dramas, five books of travel, and innumerable poems, essays and translations.

I knew Nikos Kazantzakis only during the last years of his life, and what impressed me in his character and work was not so much the "Dionysian nihilism" which seems to have overwhelmed his contemporaries in their appraisals of him. He had stared into the eyes of the abyss and with resignation had accepted complete annihilation, whether that of the individual or the earth, in the ever churning and seething eruptions of nature in the throes of constant creation and re-creation. But what impressed me most, what I found exhilarating and tonic, was the heroic affirmation of life which he shouted into the maw of the obliterating void. What I recall most is the great Yes, and not the great No. Kazantzakis gives value and dignity to the human condition by asserting that man himself, with passionate affirmation, may create the structure of his life and work on the abyss itself. This work and this life become more precious and more worthy than any other comparable structure built on illusion, hope and dream, whether of heavenly recompense or personal or earthly immortality. When I voiced these, my only objections, to Prevelakis, he reminded me that I had known Kazantzakis at a time when the tormented struggles with himself had come to mellowed conclusion, and that he had known Kazantzakis at the height of his nihilistic struggles. There can be no doubt that Prevelakis is right, but I take consolation in his statements that the one positive idea which the *Odyssey* opposes to total nihilism is "the affirmation of life," and that "the only constructive element in his epic is the exaltation of life sensed to the point of lust." I would cavil only with the words "one" and "only." This, as Wordsworth says, makes all the difference, and I am certain that what a reader ultimately derives from the *Odyssey,* as from *The Saviors of God,* is not nihilistic despair but the exaltation of life and man's fate.

I cannot close this brief preface without praising the accuracy and style of Philip Sherrard's translation. Nikos Kazantzakis was fortunate in his appraiser and Pandelis Prevelakis in his translator.

*New York City*
*October 1960*                                          KIMON FRIAR

# PART I

# THE POET

Quis enim scit hominum quae sint hominis, nisi spiritus hominis, qui in ipso est?

Paul, I Cor. 2:11

. . . tamen est aliquid hominis, quod nec ipse scit spiritus hominis, qui in ipso est . . .

Augustine, *The Confessions*, X,v

## 1

For thirty-one years I have known him. Before setting out to describe him I have studied him from countless angles, in many different lights, indoors and outdoors, in his own country and against a foreign background. I have loved him, denied him and loved him again. I have known his habits, his likes and dislikes. I have read the books he wrote and those he admired, and he on his side has asked my frank opinion of both, in spite of the fact that I was twenty-six years his junior. We have traveled together, eaten bread and salt together, fasted together. We have shared success and disappointment. Some four hundred of his letters have traced for me his spiritual odyssey: in them his thought, thanks to the nobility of his purpose, is presented in its completion. I understood the greatness of his struggle and I have suffered for him. As a poet of the last century has said, the greater the difficulty a person has in achieving his deliverance, the more we are affected.

I could write a day-by-day memoir of him, taking occasional glances at him, hearing his voice, setting down his actions and his reactions. Bit by bit I could make known his integrity and his contradictions, page by page I could add some characteristic, I could correct and retouch. I could connect him with men and events, could make a drama of his life, weaving his being together with time. But this would be the labor of a biographer, or rather of a chronicler like Saint-Simon, who traces his hero's course through the bustle of a crowd, through the labyrinth of a palace: who does not miss the chance to record some impression, to seize hold of some word, some choice turn of phrase, to forge some epigram of his own.

Instead of making a portrait of this kind, broken up within a narrative, I shall try to express in the language of ideas the total impression I have of the Kazantzakis I first knew: I shall try to describe a "character." As every original life, so this one imposes the method by which it may be presented. External events here are very few, and few are those who take part in the action. The characteristic pose of my model is that which famous artists have established for that of "a man writing"—Botticelli in his "St. Augustine," Carpaccio in his "St. Hieronymus," or El Greco in his "St. Ildefonso": a holy man, in his cell, before a table and with pen in hand, confronts a blank sheet of paper . . . In the case of Kazantzakis, the cell walls fall from time to time, the world's panorama revolves behind him, the sedentary life gives place to an impetuous journey. In a sudden bout of piracy, the body sets forth to find fresh booty for the mind. Hunger rouses the motionless body: like the royal eagle, like the lion, my hero reveals his vitality in the chase.

In these circumstances, the biographer must describe the movement of thought and seek its causes according to its own inner laws, rather than by linking it to external events. Kazantzakis' life was motivated mainly from within: by a fever and loftiness of spirit, by a willfulness and an introverted frenzy. Let me add that it was also determined by that special sensibility of poets which Supervielle calls "vulnerability": that which attributes to the monster of society the most repulsive features and drives the poet into isolation. Nor must we omit the spur of ambition, of a boundless ambition peculiar to men deprived of the arena and reward of a legendary contest: Kazantzakis, on the morrow of the Cretan struggle for liberty, was as avid for glory as Julien Sorel after the Napoleonic Wars. Frustration was at the root of his ambition.

Kazantzakis was born at Herakleion, Crete, on Friday, February 18, 1883. His father was Michael Kazantzakis, a primitive peasant, unsociable and taciturn, and his mother, Maria, of the Christodoulaki family, a sweet, submissive and even saintly woman.[1] An equal diversity was present in Kazantzakis' upbringing. The chief school for a Cretan of that time was the titanic struggle of his fellow countrymen to wrest their freedom from the Turk: in lullaby and legend, in talk and song, the same educational spirit was present. The struggle had the quality and dignity of the Greek War of Independence of 1821 or of the Spanish *Reconquista*. Nowhere are extreme heroism, stubbornness and hardihood more united than in struggles like these, where peoples of two different faiths living side by side fight to destroy each other. The Rising of 1897, the climax of the struggle in Crete, forced the family of Michael Kazantzakis to take refuge in Naxos. The young Kazantzakis, familiar with scenes of violence and imbued with the heroic and savage spirit of his birthplace (represented by his father), now had the strange fortune to be educated from his fourteenth to his sixteenth year (1897–1899) at the French School of the Holy Cross, directed by Franciscan monks. This refugee boy from Crete was suddenly introduced to another world. He learned French and Italian and assimilated the rudiments of Western culture. After the first months of 1899 he continued his studies at the gymnasium of Herakleion.

His later education took him further away from the archaic civilization of his native island. He studied law in Athens (1902–1906), and philosophy in Paris (1907–1909). Before he came to Paris, Kazantzakis had already made his appearance in Greek letters with a work in which he dismisses "ideas of blood" in favor of "ideas of spirit," absorbed after the fashion of the period. The story, "Serpent and Lily" (1906), is irritatingly influenced by d'Annunzio, both in its flowery language and in the hero's view of the world: flaming passion, idealization of voluntary death, romantic self-adulation. His tragic play *The Master Mason* (published in 1910 but written two years earlier and dedicated to Idas),[2] despite the popular origin of the dramatic legend and various personal touches of the author, also expresses ideas—for the most part Nietzschean—cultivated in the West: the strong man molds his destiny like dough, sacrifices domestic happiness to his work and dedicates himself to purity for the sake of his ideal. This play does nonetheless mark a clear transition from rootless aestheticism to a more real world.

Nietzschean ideas also appear in another of Kazantzakis' early works, a monograph called "Frederick Nietzsche and the Philosophy of Right," written in 1908 in Paris and published in Herakleion the following year. In the ninety-three pages of this dissertation, Kazantzakis summarizes those parts of Nietzsche's philosophy which he himself has absorbed—ideas, precepts, utopias, which we shall meet again, remarkably un-

[ 15 ]

changed, throughout his later work and particularly in the *Ascetic* (or *The Saviors of God*) and *The Odyssey*. The great themes which were to occupy his whole life and to direct his creative effort—"optimistic or Dionysiac nihilism," the theory of the Superman, the bankruptcy of Western civilization—are from now on, thanks to Nietzsche's philosophy, clear in his mind.

"Ideas of blood" were stimulated by the Balkan war of 1912–13, in which Kazantzakis served as a volunteer although he never actually took part in the fighting. General historical conditions, combined with the teaching of Ion Dragoumis,[2] the activity of the "Educational Society"[3] and Barrès' theory of patriotism, led Kazantzakis back to his native gods. The whole Greek world was at that time dominated by the political genius of Eleutherios Venizelos.[4] Nationalistic fervor appears in the works of contemporary poets: in the sacrifice of Mavilis,[5] in the poetry of Palamas[6] and Sikelianos.[7] Sikelianos' sequence of rhapsodies, *Consciences,* was in fact written under Kazantzakis' own eyes: the two brother poets had undertaken in 1914 and 1915 a systematic pilgrimage to the holy places of Greece and had saturated themselves in the Greek-Christian spirit. Both had eagerly sought (to use the title of one of Sikelianos' rhapsodies) "the conscience of their land and of their race."

Kazantzakis' political view, as well as his world view, during the decade from 1912 to 1922 may be summed up as "aristocratic nationalism." Dragoumis, he writes, accompanied him as his own shadow.[8] The tragedies *Odysseus, Christ* and *Nikephoros Phocas* date from this period.[9] In these tragedies Kazantzakis, interpreting three subjects each separated from the other two by about a thousand years, expresses a large part of the experience he owes to his contact with the ancient and the Christian myth and at the same time reveals his intellectual curiosity and restlessness. As he himself wrote of Nietzsche, he truly bore in himself "all the struggle and antinomy of our tempestuous times and all the Tantalean thirst for truth." The springs at which he sought to quench this thirst were many. But the prophets and philosophers who most influenced him were, according to his own statement, Nietzsche and Bergson.[10] To these should be added William James, apologist of pragmatism, and—unexpectedly enough—the Buddha, prophet of total renunciation.

In 1920, when he was thirty-seven, Kazantzakis did not yet consider himself a writer, although he had published a number of literary works, had written four or five tragedies and the same number of school books (these latter in collaboration with his first wife), and had won awards for two of his plays. He did not consider himself a translator, in spite of the translations from Bergson, Nietzsche, William James, Darwin and Plato which for some years had provided him with his daily bread.[11] He did not consider himself to be a "political animal," although he had been Director General of the newly founded Ministry of Public Welfare from May 1919 to November 1, 1920 and had successfully undertaken a national mission, that of restoring the Greeks uprooted from the Caucasus to their native land (July–August 1919).[12] Out of excessive ambition as well as a sense of his own powers, Kazantzakis treated all these occupations as side lines. He had not yet decided what was his own destiny. Like Goethe when he set out for Italy, Kazantzakis set out to track down his fate on the roads of foreign lands. Was he a poet? A prophet? In the course of a forty-day stay on Mount Athos in 1914 in the company of Anghelos Sikelianos, he had become sadly aware of his own continuous lack of any definite purpose. The spectacle of Sikelianos calmly following his course had revealed to him, but not cured, his own tragic vacillation.[13]

Something must now be said of the messianic side of Kazantzakis' nature. His first wife, Mme. Galatea Kazantzakis, has, in spite of the derisive tone of her account in her transparent novel, *Men and Supermen,* described how Kazantzakis used to grapple with himself alone on the mountaintops (scene of prophetic inspiration) and try out the vitality of his expression on the simple minds of the shepherds.[14] This struggle was nothing new—he had known it since childhood.[15] Some daemon had entered him and would give him no rest. All his writing seemed vain, ineffective. Even the *Christ,* the tragedy in which he describes the resurrection of the Savior in the hearts of the disciples, is an oblique approach to the problem. "I work, struggle, am unhappy, unquiet. Nothing I write pleases me, I am inconsolable," he confessed to his wife on New Year's Eve, 1923. "The fleshless, philosophical, abstract idea," he wrote to her on another occasion, "can no longer satisfy the spirit of the carnivore. All is clear, whole in my mind, but I lack the power to leap the fence, to rise above what is ridiculous. Shall I ever have the power? If

[17]

not, my life will be one of the deepest, of the most incurable bitterness and effort. . . . I battle on, I look ahead like Odysseus, but I do not know whether I shall ever reach Ithaca. Unless the journey itself is Ithaca."[16]

The years 1922–24 were critical years. Kazantzakis carried his struggle to Vienna and later to Berlin.[17] In Vienna, he began to write a *Buddha* (which after various alterations and additions ended as the work published in 1956). In Berlin, he embarked on a strange book—"neither a work of art nor yet a philosophy"—entitled *The Saviors of God.**
These two works are witness to his effort to formulate the world view, or rather the religion, that he wished to announce to mankind. But the unrest of a defeated and starving Germany exceeded that of Kazantzakis. A "fiery circle" of Jewish men and women tore the world to bits with their hopeless reasoning in all-night discussions in which Kazantzakis participated. The prevailing political theory of the time was communism, the prevailing aesthetic theory expressionism. There was inflation, chaos. The faith of mankind? *Nullpunkt!* In this apocalyptic atmosphere, Kazantzakis renounced nationalism, one of his basic convictions, and began to doubt Christ and Buddha, the gods who in turn had conquered him. A new god rose in his mind, with the name of Lenin. Lenin's political theory, and still less its materialistic basis, never won Kazantzakis over completely. But Lenin's political activity attracted him as being an example, effective for our age, of how the prophet could be linked with the people.

The critical conditions of life and the violence of the class war in Germany brought Kazantzakis down to earth. The prophets were no longer speaking the language of revelation; they spoke that of logical argumentation and political propaganda. Kazantzakis considered joining the Russian revolutionary society and preaching his gospel there. "I have a presentiment that all my religious efforts will end in Russia. Now I know exactly what I want and am beginning to see and live the means of its realization." "I do not know how I shall get to Russia, how I shall act or communicate with others. Sometimes my mind fills with epic and crazy visions." "I have decided to go to Russia. I do not know when. I must prepare. Now I am learning Russian and am about to go to a craftsman here who has a shop in order to learn a craft—carpentry. In

* Published by Simon and Schuster, 1960; translated by Kimon Friar from the revised edition of 1945.

[ 18 ]

that way, I shall work three hours a day in Russia and shall visit the villages. There I shall try out the Word which I carry. . . . The need for action is violent in me: it cannot wait. My scheme of life seems so simple that once it is expressed it will enlighten and fortify the soul. . . . Oh, to lose oneself suddenly in the service of a purpose! What purpose? Have this earth, this starlight, a purpose? What does it concern us? Do not ask. Simply fight!"[18]

These outbursts, which are accompanied, it must be remarked, by incurable doubts, are taken from letters written in 1922 and 1923. The hour for his departure to the Soviet Union was not yet at hand. On January 18, 1924, Kazantzakis left Germany to wander in Italy. There was no "Messianic" object in this journey. But the story of St. Francis fascinated him and kept him at Assisi for two and a half months. The Poor Man of God had embodied thirst for the absolute, the triumph of spirit over flesh, and total deliverance. From July 1924 till the spring of 1925, Kazantzakis was in Crete. In the land of his birth he sought an outlet for his messianism: he took part in an unsuccessful illegal political action with the local Communists. All that remains of this enterprise is an "Apology"—"a note I addressed to the examining magistrate at Herakleion in 1924 when they had me up as a Communist." This is an important document—as yet unpublished—as it is a synopsis of Kazantzakis' political views. But if his thought is presented here in all its daring clarity, his part in the action appears to have been very slight. At the first opposition he took refuge in poetic creation, in the cure of a substitute: he shut himself up in a little out-of-the-way house by the sea at Tripiti, near Herakleion, where he began the writing of his *Odyssey*. He set down the first six rhapsodies, laying the foundation of his great consolation. During August and September 1925 he toured the Cyclades, exercising his senses, gathering material for his marine epic.

The journey to Russia took place in October 1925. It lasted about three and a half months. But Kazantzakis' utopian mania was restricted by circumstances—or rather by the conditions of the totalitarian regime —to journalistic investigation.[19] It is surprising to see how Kazantzakis forgets the violent tormenting "need for action," and like a sociologist or statistician methodically gathers the impersonal tokens of the conquests of the Revolution. Russian bureaucracy had succeeded in smothering the flame of the prophet beneath a mountain of statistics and papers.

[ 19 ]

The only one of his presentiments he found confirmed was the "Vision of the Unseen," that is, of the "cosmic force which uses us mortals as its bearers, as its beasts of burden, and hastens onward as if it had a purpose and as if it followed a definite path." Kazantzakis declares his "awe" before this seizure of man by the breath of the unseen, and describes this feeling, in the foreword to his "Travelogue," as the most significant that Russia gave him. Here we may discern a subconscious effort to maintain contact with his former convictions, leveled by the frightful Machine.

Kazantzakis' prophetic fury is at the same time quieted by the spectacle of the world. The chief distinction of poets is that, for them, the sensible world exists. For the time being Kazantzakis forgot his religious mission in order to undertake new journeys: to Palestine and Cyprus (April–May 1926), Spain (August–September 1926), Italy (October 1926), Egypt and Sinai (December 1926–January 1927). His pretended interest in political events was a concession to the newspaper organizations which were providing the funds for his travels.[20] But, to console his wounded spirit, he gazed insatiably at the countless sights of the world. In the pages he then wrote one senses the struggle concealed beneath the impetuous, elliptical and often excited style. He makes a strange narrator: his language is rough and pithy like that of a peasant. But the sense and the historical perspective betray the man of letters. Two different types of writer here work together: the one has gleaned from land and sea, the other has studied the literature of the ages. On the one hand there is exactness of observation and precision of expression, and on the other hand there is the quotation from a buried text, the verse of a forgotten poem. Into these strange travelogues more intellectual themes are introduced: mortality of civilizations, psychology of peoples, heroes of thought and action, monuments and landscapes; and besides these themes, love of beauty, yearning for universal justice, wrestling with the problem of existence—the endless daydreams of an ardent soul.

## 2

*Il fallait effort pour cesser de le regarder.*
—Saint-Simon concerning Fénelon

*On ne fut jamais si peu sentimental, avec plus de passion.*
—André Suarès concerning Cardinal de Retz

The reader of this book is already better informed about Kazantzakis than I was when I went to meet him at the house of his sister Eleni on Friday, November 12, 1926. All I knew of his life and work were his travel books. I was seventeen years old and had just left Rethymnon Gymnasium—to say a few words about myself. Number 59 Hermes Street was a dressmaker's shop, kept by his brother-in-law, Aristeides Theodosiades. On the landing where the stairs turned for the first floor was a little door with a plaster mask of Nietzsche hanging over the lintel: "sunken eyes, jutting forehead and drooping mustaches."[21] The room I entered was no larger than a bathroom, and its floor with two-colored tiles suggested one. There was a low ceiling, a small window looking out on an inner courtyard. A desk took up practically the whole room, from one wall to the other—there was just space for a narrow divan and a stool. On the two walls that were free of books hung one or two icons, a profile of Eleni Samios,[22] a watercolor by Takis Kalmouchos—and, in the center of the ceiling, the head of an austere Madonna, copied by Photis Kondoglou from the monastery of St. John the Theologian.

Kazantzakis raised his eyes from the papers spread on the table and at once leaped from his seat, a backless stool. His head almost touched the ceiling, and his lithe body was outlined against the wall of books behind him. He was about forty years old, at what the ancients called the "acme," the peak age, when all man's capacities are at their best. His appearance was like that of a Saracen, and his face also was exotic, something like an African mask. Impulsively he held out his hand, ornamented with a ring of a broad stone set in gold.

That cell, to which I was to return so often, is even now before me. But now, as then, it is its occupant who draws my gaze. Kazantzakis is sitting at his desk, with the light from the little window falling on his right cheek. The sunburned face looks as if it were hewn from wood.

[ 21 ]

His raven hair, thrown back, curls slightly at the sunken temples. The broad, high forehead falls abruptly and overhangs the deep eye sockets, shadowed by bushy eyebrows. He has small shapely ears and small eyes, black and round, almost invisible except for their brightness. When Kazantzakis looks you in the eye—which is rarely—you are abashed by the host of things his glance contains: his anguish, his purity, the visions abandoned for a moment in order to look at you. The nose is strong and clear-cut, with bold nostrils. A thick, trimmed mustache covers the upper lip and partially hides the bitterness of the mouth. The chin is small for such a massive forehead.

Kazantzakis' dress was remarkably simple. In the house, he wore next to his skin a cotton jacket closed up to the neck like a military tunic, but without pockets. Outside, his dress, though plain, had a certain affectation. He wore a tieless shirt, on which the top button was replaced by an upright pin with a gold coin of Alexander the Great upon it. His coat had four buttons and narrow lapels in the military style; its neatness had something homely about it; it did not suggest the work of a good tailor. The baggy trousers were fastened tightly at his narrow waist by a silver Caucasian belt. Strangely enough, Kazantzakis always went out with his gloves in his hand, or at least with a book: it seemed that in this way he gained assurance. In spite of his upright figure, his erect, bare head and striding gait, Kazantzakis did, indeed, give one an impression of timidity, of inexperience, like a well-brought-up youth not yet touched by life's cynical ways.

He was at that time quite alone. His only support in his daily needs was his sister Eleni, with whom he boarded. He had shortly before divorced Mme. Galatea after fifteen years of marriage, more than ten of which they had lived apart because of Kazantzakis' unceasing travels.[23] This separation from his wife resulted in his estrangement from her brother, Lefteris Alexiou, who for many years had been his follower and friend. Another childhood friend and comrade, Yannis Stavridakis, had died seven years earlier at Tiflis during the repatriation of the Greeks from the Caucasus.[24] Ion Dragoumis had been unjustly killed in 1920.[25] Of his old companions only Anghelos Sikelianos was left. But he too had grown estranged and, submerged in preparations for the Delphic Festival, behaved as if he did not know his brother poet. This living separation without doubt wounded Kazantzakis most of all. For many years he and Sikelianos had shared enthusiasms and dreams: how could he now forget the God-beloved, the inspired and magnanimous, the superb and tender one? The poet of *Alaphroiskiotos* (The Visionary) was always for Kazantzakis the first among his fellow artists, even if he had been temporarily drawn into work foreign to his destiny: "The poet is a light thing, winged and sacred!"[26] But their fates had sundered them conclusively.

Kazantzakis' isolation and his falling out with Sikelianos—who at that time was setting himself up as a god at Delphi, like a second Wagner—at once made me think of the fate of Nietzsche and see how it corresponded with the life of Kazantzakis, as that mask which I had noticed over his door seemed to indicate. The welcome he reserved for me made me later think of the young Heinrich von Stein's meeting with Nietzsche in 1884. The philosopher was then forty years old, his visitor twenty-six. When the latter wrote announcing his first visit, Nietzsche welcomed him with a letter signed: "The hermit of Sils-Maria." But he received him with all the warmth of his heart and hailed their meeting as an event "which could not be without far-reaching consequences"; the hermit longed for a break in his tower, the herald of total despair awaited, unavoidably, the refutation of his theory.

Nietzsche had entered Kazantzakis' life in a curious way. "In Paris, at the Sainte-Geneviève Library, an unknown girl came up to me, holding an open book with a photograph. She hid the name beneath the photograph with one hand and said to me, 'Look, here is a photograph of you! Is it you?' I was amazed. It was quite true: forehead, eyes, look, were identical.... It was Nietzsche. From that day, I studied him greatly, admired him greatly, and wrote a monograph entitled, 'Frederick Nietzsche and the Philosophy of Right.' I traveled on purpose to follow his trail, from the little village of Roecken in Germany where he was born, to Naumburg to the ancestral house where he lived, then to Basel where he was a professor, to the Engadine, the Riviera, Turin and Nice . . ."[27] Kazantzakis' pilgrimage signifies in fact nothing less than a progressive identification with his hero. At the beginning of the century a host of young men all over Europe, even in Greece, were inspired by Nietzsche's philosophy. Kazantzakis absorbed his very soul. Alexander the Great believed that he had the soul of Achilles within him, Julius Caesar that of Alexander. Such illusions at least made possible the writing of the *Parallel Lives*. A parallelism between Nietzsche and Kazantzakis is in a certain way maintained from now on, not only through the external events of their lives, but also through their fundamental experiences—the loneliness, the tension, the struggle and the creation—and most of all through the relationship between, not to say identity of, their ideas.

From his long association with Nietzsche, Kazantzakis had been strengthened in his belief that the mission of the superior man is to formulate a world view containing his personal vision of the origin and destiny of both the world and man. To this end the poet of *Zarathustra* had fought all his life, and he had gone out of his mind in that struggle. But before the final holocaust, the great martyr had been found worthy of some triumphant moments, some lucid intervals, which he had celebrated in mad exultation. In his struggle he had often reached the heights of Dionysiac certainty. When I first met Kazantzakis, he too lived in temporary certainty. His loneliness did not trouble him, it was the climate he needed: for he was the master of his own soul and had a great poetic creation before him.

Kazantzakis' messianic drive had for the time being been set aside. Travel had excited his imagination and had enriched it with an inexhaustible treasury of images and symbols. In the winter of 1925 he had begun the writing of an epic: the *Odyssey*. From now on, he was able to conceive this superhuman work as a master mason in the Middle Ages must have seen his cathedral from the moment he planned it on paper. His face radiated serenity and power. It is the creator's lot to sense his greatness from the very beginning of his work and even to increase it with the fame he acquires after death. He may lose this exalting illusion while he is working or after; but he may also bequeath it to the centuries as the image of an unrivaled personality.

The subject of our first talks was not his recent journey to Spain, as might have been expected; still less was it the *Odyssey*. Kazantzakis, like a true "fisher of souls," wanted first of all to find out who I was. Many times later I heard him put exactly the same questions to the unknown visitor: what was the purpose of his life, with what sacrifice was he prepared to defend it? He gave himself only to those who possessed some noble passion. Their ideas did not concern him so much. The criterion of virtue was the intensity, the daring to undertake something beyond one's powers. He himself, he let you understand, had, in Stendhal's phrase, "his passion as a calling." He taught independence from every attachment, the sacrifice of all human happiness. Life ought to be a complete dedication. "Happiness would be to give your soul to a huge beast to eat!"[28] It is unnecessary to add that such a theory was more than appealing to a young man. From the first, Kazantzakis seemed to me the one living person in a world of shadows. His presence sounded like armor to me.

By 1926 his dedication to poetic creation had almost entirely determined Kazantzakis' personality. But his spirit was still drawn toward the world which he had renounced. Beneath the poet, the mystagogue was buried. From time to time suppressed ambition would make itself felt in his talk and his longing for total deliverance would break forth. He dreamed then of cutting himself off from the world, of leaving the works of mankind behind him, of hiding himself in the desert. The denier of life, the destroyer of desire, the prophet of nonexistence still spoke through his lips. The state of mind which had nurtured his tragedy *Buddha* had not yet been exhausted. Buddhist renunciation filtered through Kazantzakis like an unfulfilled presentiment, a way of living which he had planned but had never carried out. But its cold light often shone in his eyes.[29]

Kazantzakis' mental luggage is not to be labeled only with the names of Nietzsche and Buddha. Without depreciating the originality of his own personality, we must remember the sources of his education. One of his instructors—as we said earlier—was Bergson. What we may call Kazantzakis' "anti-rationalism" was principally derived from Bergson's teaching. In one of his old studies, in which he summarized his teacher's thought up to 1912, Kazantzakis appears as the herald of the philosophy which "combated intellectualism and limited its competence, and consequently that of science, to material phenomena alone; which showed to what errors mankind was led by the confusion between *durée réelle* and uniform space; which made clear the strength and weakness of intuition, and called for the collaboration of intuition and intellect in philosophical inquiries."[30] Bergsonian thought did in fact free Kazantzakis from the mechanistic conception of the world, revealed to him the true nature of time and made him capable of "seeing the things themselves behind the signs which represent them." But this is not all. Bergsonism threw light for him on the problem of free will and armed him with the theory of the *élan vital* which was to be the yeast of his thought.[31]

Each age gives birth to similar children. The theories which Kazantzakis took from Nietzsche, Bergson, William James—heroic pessimism, anti-rationalism, vitalism—are founded in the works of his leading contemporaries: D'Annunzio, Barrès, Claudel and Péguy. But the currents of Western thought encountered in Kazantzakis a being who lived in a different historical time and in a country with a low level of civilization. It was natural for his reactions to be original. For instance, Kazantzakis as a poet was content to use the modern Greek language, a language which is not abstract like the more developed European languages. Each word is still an image, the treasury of an experience, the raft of a living thing. The modern Greek language itself is a foretaste of poetry. There is no need to "thaw out" the language, as Claudel did with French. It is enough to reject the "purist tongue" and to plunge into the sea of the "demotic." All the same, Kazantzakis' inherited rationalism and inborn love of learning made it hard for him to renounce well-tried methods, the wisdom of books, and to give himself entirely to life. Everyone, according to the vitalistic theory, must fulfill himself in his entirety, must reach his limits; personal experience and individual truth are more valid than rational knowledge. Leaders of Western literature, from André Gide to G. K. Chesterton, from Miguel de Unamuno to Giovanni Papini, repeated this counsel. Kazantzakis heard it and did not doubt its truth. But an unconquerable prudence paralyzed his limbs.

This raises the following question: Apart from the conditions prevailing in his own country, to what point did Kazantzakis' own attitude match the spirit of his time? This lover of mystery had so many rational elements in him, such imperturbable balance and will power, that one is forced to believe that if he had been brought up in the positivism of the nineteenth century, the powers he now rejected would have overwhelmed him. On the other hand, the vitalistic theory received no real response from Kazantzakis' ascetic nature. His poetry might release others, compelling them toward an elementary reality. But he himself had to seek a third means of deliverance, beyond the condemnation of reason and his innate timidity before the unbridled forces of life. His means of deliverance was to lie in poetic creation.

According to Kazantzakis, something of the nature of the divinity is expressed in poetic creation. Amid the general corruption, certain privileged beings are endowed with the capacity to carry on the work of "God."[32] Generally speaking, the action of all rational creatures participates in this mystery.[33] But poetic creation is the God-bearing activity par excellence. The poet's longing for immortality is not only a desire to triumph over the common lot of man. It is the manifestation of a supernatural reality, of the primordial impulse "penetrating plants, beasts and men."[34] But "God," if He is ever present, is not almighty. Man's dedication to creative activity alone "saves God" (*The Saviors of God*). Beneath this pretense of submission to the spirit of creation smoldered a tyrannical ambition and a haughty faith in the power of man such as had not been seen since the Renaissance.

To these remarks must be added an observation which will throw further light on Kazantzakis' relationship with poetic creation. His final casting off of illusion made him elevate himself to the rank of the Prince imagined by Richard Wagner in his brief essay on social metaphysics "Concerning the State and Religion," which he wrote for Ludwig II of Bavaria. According to Wagner, the common man is supported by the twin illusions of patriotism and religion, and thus his life may be stable and happy. The life of the Prince, who distributes and hence controls the illusions, is, on the contrary, one of tragedy. The Prince, like every enlightened person, sees life in all its nakedness, and consequently "he finds himself almost daily in that very condition in which a common man despairs of life and resorts to suicide." For the Prince and for the elect there is need for some soothing illusion which they themselves must devise. This is art: "If it is unable to raise us fully and actually above life, at least it raises us to the highest regions in life itself. It gives life the appearance of a game, and, converting its most terrifying aspects into unreal images, it detaches us from common need, charms us and consoles us. . . ." One must recognize in this conclusion one of Kazantzakis' habitual themes—in spite of the fact that it weakens the theory of divinely inspired creation.[35]

"The Saviors of God," the God-bearing heroes of thought and action, formed the company which Kazantzakis took as his examples. As the ascetic has the saints, the martyrs, the athletes of faith, so Kazantzakis had Homer, Dante, Shakespeare, Nietzsche. And he had also Moses and

Mohammed, Genghis Khan and Lenin, Theresa of Jesus and Cervantes, Leonardo and El Greco. The list of the cantos he dedicated to them is the index to his hagiology. In times of despair, of abandonment and want, these titanic wills heartened him in the struggle and preserved his creative fever. Their presence filled the atmosphere of his cell; they were the unseen spirits ever near at hand. He himself had made pilgrimages to each in his own home: to Florence, Stratford, Alcalá de Henares, Roecken, Avila and Toledo. If it is true that the souls of the redeemed are able after death to assist in just struggles, Kazantzakis was helped by his heroes and was not mistaken in calling them "bodyguards of the *Odyssey*." It was they who held his spirit high while he composed, as the Jewish priests held up the hands of Moses while he prayed.

This hero worship which I have indicated had a more tangible object in works of art. I do not mean works of literature: everyone turns to these. I mean masterpieces of art in space. Kazantzakis regarded these with true love and honored them as sacred relics. In the achievements of the great artists he beheld the "evident miracle," "the worm creating immortality." He knew well enough that artistic forms are significant in themselves. But his visionary and mystic nature saw in them his own ideas made visible; he recognized in them his own dreams. When he was writing the *Odyssey* in Aegina during the summer of 1927, he had a colored print of Rembrandt's "Warrior with a Golden Helmet" tacked over the window opposite him. When in 1929 he came to the mountains of Gottesgab he hung El Greco's "Knight with His Hand on His Breast" above his bed. "I cannot have enough of Titian's 'Charles V,' " he wrote to me from Madrid (November 1, 1932). "As he emerges from the dark wood, pale, tired, unyielding, he reminds me greatly of Rembrandt's 'Warrior.' . . . These two are my mystic portraits. Whenever I look at them, I shiver as if I were looking at my own true face in deep secret water."

On another occasion he recognized his desire to write an Eastern poem, a legendary poem, out of time or place, in the Persian miniatures of the British Museum.[36] Some years earlier he had come to understand the teaching of ancient Greek sculpture. "The other day at the Museum [with the plaster casts] I had a strong, life-saving sensation. I saw at the entrance the statues from Pergamos, *criards,* tumultuous, baroque; then the 'Charioteer of Delphi.' At once I felt most bitterly the unworthiness of my own art: I must leave Pergamos for Delphi. For the first time in my life I felt what that Charioteer brings us in his victorious chariot. Perhaps for the first time I feel myself capable of victory."[37]

Alas, "choice of a style" is also one of the distinguishing marks of an age of decadence. No one can change the spirit of the civilization which surrounds him. Still less can he change his own soul. Kazantzakis' eclectic education—itself a symptom of the last phase of a civilization— incited him sometimes to violate the laws of the time and sometimes to curb his own nature and to create a style of his own choosing. He had long since completed the first and second draft of the *Odyssey*, of an epic —that is, of a type of work condemned to narration—when he decided to adopt the musical, fluid lyricism of pure poetry.[38] But he could not avail himself of the teaching applied by poets like Poe or Mallarmé and developed by theoreticians like Henri Bremond. He continued to serve an outmoded style with a reason-subjected sensitivity. "But to teach, to narrate, to portray, to induce shudders or tears—for all that prose is more than adequate."[39]

It would be useful here to devote a paragraph or two to Kazantzakis' eclecticism and to see him in a new light. From a recent study on Maurice Barrès by E. R. Curtius[40] we will borrow the term "creative critic"—an instrument of study—which is introduced into comparative literature with a renewed content. The "creative critic"—whom the German philologist presents as an artistic type with its own distinguishing marks —"carries out a task which touches upon all aspects of the spiritual life of his age, betraying a soul hungry for all the aliments of culture. . . . He grasps of these what his powers of assimilation and the intensity of his spiritual life permit. His art is all reflection. . . . His production corresponds to the need to master, by means of a purely personal system of control, the waves of lived experience which break on all sides . . . The bringing into use and setting in order of his intellectual experience is effected by means of an analytical dissection which leads finally to synthetic formulations capable of being developed into critical essays, into historical interpretations, into dramatic or epic works. Sainte-Beuve, Taine, Renan and Stendhal, plowing the field of creative criticism in various ways, reveal to us the great number of possible solutions." The thought of Barrès, which gave rise to this analysis, is "nothing but a stylization of his personality": the search for the sources of vital energy, the invocation of the heroes of the past, of places and masterpieces, are not due only to an elective affinity but also to the *horror vacui,* to a failure of internal tension, to the lack of spiritual force. "I struggle to increase my power and to grow.... The only fruit of victory we seek is to acquire more soul." (Maurice Barrès)[41]

According to Curtius, the "creative critic" is a type that could have been fully realized only in France—this is because France, more than any other country, has weighty and rich traditions. But, strangely enough, the term "creative critic" can be applied to Kazantzakis. The reason must be sought first of all in personal psychophysiology and then in the conditions of his upbringing and the intellectual state of his country. Kazantzakis escaped at an early age from the rusticity of his native island and fell like a thirsty wayfarer on the spring of French literature, particularly that of the nineteenth century, which sought to present a total understanding of the world.[42] The education which he received from the French monks in Naxos was based entirely on texts—on the endless book learning which a whole lifetime cannot exhaust. If Kazantzakis was not to die of undernourishment, he had to continue feeding on the great tradition which had first satisfied his appetite. This would have as a consequence a progressive separation from the interests of his fellow artists in Greece, from their possibilities and customs. Kazantzakis would develop through contact with foreign literatures, particularly French, under the auspices of eclecticism. His education could not remain one-sided, as happens in the case of authors who belong to nations with an undisturbed tradition. The inadequate sustenance offered him by modern Greece was to be supplemented by both fresh and conserved food, of European, Asiatic and even African provenance. The different levels of the civilization of these sources and their lack of homogeneity were to make a "monster" out of Kazantzakis' primitive nature. The head in which their nourishment was to ferment would crack in the process. Such a fate is, indeed, not foreign to the Greeks, either when they set out to civilize Asia or when they emigrate to try their luck in the West. Theotocopoulos (El Greco) is an example of the truth of this.

"Every now and then I am seized with a childish aversion for the printed page; I feel as if I were looking at dirty paper." So Nietzsche wrote to Malwida von Meysenbug in 1873. This aversion is a habitual

[30]

theme in Kazantzakis' confessions and is indeed the main subject of one of his novels. But it requires elucidation. Nietzsche has no need of other people's blood to keep him alive. Possessed by the daemonic originality of his vision, he rages in fury at the thought of the Philistines. He is himself an element, a whole world, a burning sphere. Kazantzakis suffered from a superfluous weight. He envied the primitive nature of Zorba (a man of the people, whom he knew during his mission to the Caucasus before he made him the hero of a novel), who ate directly from the flesh of things and was impertinent before the murderous wonder of life. Kazantzakis chewed inky paper "like a goat."[43] It was both food and opiate to him. If poetic creation attracted him so deeply, it was because only then did he succeed in listening to his inner voice. His independence, even though it was illusory, intoxicated him.

Again, according to Curtius, the "creative critic" feels the need to arm himself "with a mental discipline which would enable him to dominate and command the heterogeneous and explosive mass of material he is handling. He would be the victim of complete anarchy, of the torment of disintegration, of a formless fluidity, if he did not create for his own use some order with clear-cut categories." The *Odyssey* is Kazantzakis' superhuman attempt to use and set in order his vast intellectual experience. This explains its size, the nightmare flood of incidents, the accumulation of so many myths, customs and beliefs, the abundance of images, the endless procession of motives, even the destructive force which courses through it from end to end, to the final union of Odysseus with Death. The polymorphic nature of such a work could only be embodied in the baroque style. The archaic or classical style, or the fluid lyricism for which he sought, would have been incapable of embracing Kazantzakis' "Hellenistic" spirit. Besides, the tension which characterized his whole intellectual life did not permit him to remain within the limits of his capacities, as the classical artist is able to do.

The unproductive circumstances and inward difficulties which Kazantzakis had to overcome were well enough known to him. This gave him a certain humility. I do not mean humility toward the public: he was neither hypocritical nor stupid not to recognize his superiority. He was humble in the face of the merciless, the tyrannical spirit of perfection, he was tortured by doubts and self-judgment. But at the time of creation his titanic nature swept aside all hesitation. His hand could not

[31]

keep pace with his vision, and the mental word seethed within him like a waterfall. Like all mystics—but also like a true pupil of Bergson—he complained of the inadequacy of human language, and in the intervals between the creative act he would gather words, meanings, ways of expression; his ultimate purpose was to express an inexpressible experience. On the threshold of complete dedication he threw every kind of material into the mill of his mind, from glossaries and folklore texts to works of natural history and factual information.[44] His thirst for knowledge then had an insatiable, burning violence, like that of Michelangelo's Prophets turning the pages of their enormous ledgers.

His "animal" health allowed him to concentrate on his purpose without wavering and to stretch his thought to the limit. Isolation preserved and stimulated his mental excitement. The following passage from Nietzsche might have been written with Kazantzakis in mind: "In order to understand this type [that of the superman], one must first be enlightened about his physiological predisposition: it is that which I call *great health* . . . a health stronger, more spiritual, tougher, bolder and more joyful than all health hitherto." Kazantzakis' ascetic retreat was usually on the mountain or the seashore. He needed the sight of the elements and of broad horizons to liberate his internal riches. He wanted, like Nietzsche, to live six thousand feet above mankind and time.

He had in fact cut himself off from mankind. The affairs of common men did not at the time I met him nourish his art. He was indifferent, not to say hostile, to institutions. In Kazantzakis' view, marriage, the family, an ordered life stifle the metaphysical significance of the world. He would often call marriage paradoxically the "betrothal of divorce," and he did not conceal his amusement at the sight of a large family out on its Sunday walk, with the paterfamilias degraded by the destructive wills surrounding him. An undisturbed and settled career, comfort, respectability were in his eyes indications of a sluggish metaphysical life. His contempt for such a living death had in it something of the wrath of a Hebrew prophet.

Herodotus narrates somewhere that Xerxes, looking at his countless host, burst into tears at the thought that the earth would one day devour it all. Kazantzakis did not lament for the fate of mortals, unless it was for that of those who struggled to become immortal. The divine struggle —that was the mark of recognition, the bond of a new brotherhood! His own dedication had eliminated worldly cares, had even blunted the instinct of self-preservation. *"La obra!"* (Work!)—he loved to proclaim like a reveille this call which he had once heard on the lips of Juan Ramón Jiménez. One felt then that his taut will power would destroy him altogether rather than allow him to slacken for one moment. This was made evident later when, severely ill and in danger of his life (December 1953), he dictated the most impassioned part of *The Poor Man of God.*

His attitude towards his fellow artists was uncompromising. He was profoundly conscious that history in the end preserves very few names. Thousands of voices are silenced, never to be heard by future generations. A false acclaim may deceive people for a while; but time, like another Leviathan, will devour the guilty and the victims. Many who pass for living are shown to be dead, and only for very few does death announce the beginning of eternal life. Kazantzakis was always ready to say a good word to every blotter of paper, either out of sympathy or indifference. But he considered that his companions in the struggle, among the living or among the dead, were very few. I do not think he was often mistaken in his appreciations; his great intellectual experience made him capable of discerning the true from the false. An *Anthology of World Poetry,* which he had gathered together from his early years, may, if it is ever published, give a false impression of his judgment: this anthology was a small Pantheon where he enshrined those who had not achieved a separate memorial of their own.

He was always fair and without envy. In contrast to Dante, for whom the two peaks of Parnassus were too few, he used to say that the sacred mountain ends in a plateau on which there is room for all the elect. Moreover, countless paths lead up to it. By this he meant of course that there are various types of art. His aesthetic judgment was always demanding, as was proper to his lofty idea of perfection. His opinion was unaffected by the fashions of the market: he was well aware that a reputation destined to survive is not determined by the mob, but is gradually built up by sober minds. This wisdom did not desert him even when he himself gained the admiration of the crowd, and it seems to me that he showed the same dispassion toward the "conspiracy of noise" as he had toward that of silence.

In his moral judgments he was more tolerant. His insistence on ac-

[ 33 ]

cepting both "yes" and "no" as an answer to social questions shocked many people. Some indeed took him for a moral agnostic. I think that good and evil had for him more a metaphysical than a moral significance. In this he followed the ancient Zarathustra (the Persian initiate of Agni, not the creation of Nietzsche), who first saw "the mainspring of the movement of things" in the contest between good and evil. This contest is a primordial antithesis. Evil too is given from above, it exists in order to reveal the good, and it works together with the good. In its historical manifestation, this contest permits a moral judgment: The harder the fight, the more honorable it is, and the more worthy is the victory. He who is enlightened keeps aloof from the fray, he understands its many-sided beauty. "I have found that the eye which sees the whole circle expresses our soul simply and perfectly," Kazantzakis once concluded in a letter.[45]

His moral independence and the freedom of his mind led him inevitably to ridicule the Philistine. For him the typical Philistine was the pseudo-learned scholar. Kazantzakis himself had studied and had worked extremely hard at law, taking a first-class degree. Now, however, his youthful service to "learning"—and in particular his blind devotion to his teacher at the University, Neocles Kazazis—reduced him to laughter whenever he thought of it. At a fairly early period, the value of the art of law as it is understood in Greece, and the sorry plight in general of the "educated Philistine," had become clear to him. Did the first of Nietzsche's *Thoughts Out of Season* contribute to his awakening? Be this as it may, among Kazantzakis' articles of faith and even among his instinctive reactions was included a contempt for the unpoetic and barren, the petty and narrow-minded "scholar." He did not of course discriminate between supporters of the "purist" tongue and the "demotic." He could find in both camps what Nietzsche calls "the labyrinth," "the bog," "the poisonous fog," and the "sands of the desert."

It must not be imagined for a moment that his will-tensed nature was at all arrogant. If he was a fugitive from the world, it was because he was feared by the forces of mediocrity. He guarded himself from such mediocrity as one guards oneself from contamination during an epidemic. He had drawn aside, into the calm of voluntary exile, free from human vanity and persistently seeking to fill his art, and indeed his whole life, with daemonic power. For beauty, virtue, noble passion, he was ready to sacrifice the wealth and honors of the world. "First of all, you must be a great man and a saint to yourself!" These are words of Baudelaire, adopted by—whom else?—Barrès.

He had no desire whatever to make a show of his originality. His rule of life was retirement rather than display. He lived in a cell—in Athens, Aegina, Paris, Gottesgab—with few objects about him, except for the many and varied books, and content with but one proper meal a day and a rusk and tea for breakfast and supper. His only luxury, the only wealth he required, was free and unbroken time. In this too he followed the rule of life laid down by Nietzsche when he retired to Genoa in 1880: "An independence which hurts nobody; a gentle and concealed pride, a pride which does not annoy others because it is not jealous of their honors, their satisfactions, and because it abstains from mockery. . . ."[46] Yes, Kazantzakis annoyed no one with his way of life except the envious and the Philistine. Even his superhuman health was never provocative. He knew how to suppress his vitality in front of others, like some treasure that courtesy prevented him from flaunting.

His discretion and virtue did, moreover, attract considerable sympathy. He returned friendship warmly and sometimes with effusion, but in the end he judged people by their actions.[47] He was always on the watch for deeds of heroism, even among his enemies. At first glance there was something artificial and forced about him, due to his great devotion to his austere rule of life. But often, during conversation, his spontaneous, warm-hearted and playful nature would break out. If his company gave him the attention he deserved, he did not refuse to charm it with his own particular eloquence—strong, impetuous and sometimes ringing with studied assonance. Such occasions were of course interludes and no more. I myself never saw him lost in such moods for more than a few moments.[48] He suffered from the speed of time, and he followed the rhythm of his mind with the same persistence as a wounded person touches the edges of his wounds. His behavior, both social and private, had also to be without fault. I remember once telling him that St. Francis of Sales would not permit himself to sit comfortably even when he was quite alone, a fact ascertained by the other monks through the keyhole of his cell. Kazantzakis went one better than this with the story of how Bossuet had traveled in a post chaise from Paris to Calais without once leaning back on the seat. He told of another prince of the

Church, who would not condescend to quicken his pace in his garden even though it was pouring with rain. Kazantzakis, whom—in order to convey his image of himself—we might describe as a pirate, envied the ways of a Benedictine!

Kazantzakis' asceticism was, however, of an Oriental type. The setting which I like to imagine for him is the Brook Kerith, where the Prophet Elijah waited for the raven to bring him his daily bread.[49] In truth, Kazantzakis did not know how, would not consent, to embellish his hermitage. He had never kept domestic animals; he did not work the strip of earth outside his door. The horizons absorbed him. His renunciation could not but include woman also. The surpassing of the erotic instinct is another of the themes of his art, one most apt to feed, and indeed to deceive, psychoanalysis. Man slaughters woman—in the literal and metaphorical sense—in order to dedicate himself completely to his Rule. The hero of *Serpent and Lily* had started the hecatomb when he induced the woman he loved to commit suicide: he had been driven mad by the incapacity of their souls to commune totally (as Giorgio Aurispa, one of D'Annunzio's characters from the *Triumph of Death,* had also been when he failed to penetrate the subconscious mind of his beloved Hippolyta). After that comes the *Master Mason:* he builds his beloved into the foundations of the Bridge. Tsimiskes sends Theophano into a nunnery.[50] Christ ignores the charms of the Magdalene.[51] Odysseus denies Penelope and later Helen of Sparta and Diktena, the Cretan Princess, and he burns the ascetic's daughter, the creation of his own mind, on a pyre.[52] Woman, according to Kazantzakis, is the agent of the Evil One. Evil is whatever obstructs the creative urge, whatever puts out the flame of noble passion. But, as may well be imagined, the sacrifice of woman is in spite of this no easy matter. It is the most tragic condition of the higher human destiny, it is the endless repentance of Jesus upon the Cross—until this "Last Temptation" is also overcome.[53]

Woman's sacrifice by man has its counterpart in something else—in the destruction of the sensible world by the poet. "As you know and first discerned," Kazantzakis wrote to me in 1928, "this harsh pleasure of great violence and sudden obliteration has characterized all my writing up till now."[54] Is this to be interpreted as an extension of ascetical renunciation? Is it an unsatisfied desire for communion, changed

[ 36 ]

into vengeful nihilism? Whatever it is, the creation and obliteration of the world were from the beginning customary themes in Kazantzakis' poetry. In his tragedy *Christ,* for example, all the action takes place in the imagination of the faithful:

The roof of heaven opens and there descends
in a white sheet the mystic Apparition.

The tragedy develops, reaches its climax, and is destroyed:

Ah! All have sunk to earth, both gods and men!
It seems the head has opened and engulfed them!

The phantasmagoria of the world vanishes in a similar way in the *Odyssey*: the actor is sometimes Odysseus himself (XVII, 1166 *ff*. and 1246–47) and sometimes Prince Motherth-Buddha (XXIV, 830 *ff*.). Even the poet, concluding his narrative, leaves us in doubt as to whether all he has related was true or not. These observations on Kazantzakis' preoccupation with creation and obliteration are confirmed by the development of his tragedy *Buddha,* and even more by the Prologue and Epilogue of *Japan-China*: in the Prologue, the author proclaims Epaphos, the god of Touch (and not Buddha), to be his god, and in the Epilogue he calls Nirvana "the highest prey." They are further confirmed by the conclusion of the revised 1945 edition of *The Saviors of God:* "THAT EVEN THIS ONE DOES NOT EXIST!"

It is not surprising that this man concentrated on his myth, this high-minded and stoical character, recognized solitude as the primal condition of his life. "Solitude is the fundamental passion of my being," Nietzsche had also declared. Kazantzakis was driven to solitude both by his indwelling daemon and by his "vulnerability." Solitude means, in this context, a retreat into nature. Created nature, *natura naturata,* was a loving refuge to Kazantzakis, a treasury of all the experiences which could help him to make his ideas visible. Creative nature, *natura naturans,* was, on the contrary, the dreadful melting pot, the devourer of everything, the inexorable power which sweeps away mankind like "withered leaves." In *The Master Mason* it is the river which destroys the bridge, in *Sodom and Gomorrah* it is the light of heaven, in *Buddha* it is the flood, in the *Odyssey* (Book XVI) it is the volcano and the earthquake. The God who rules nature—a God made in the image of

Kazantzakis' father, the psychoanalysts would say—is hostile to man. But man is indomitable, he builds in chaos; his dignity and moral autonomy make him invincible.

Kazantzakis took refuge in nature in order to find himself, in order to possess his own soul.[55] At the same time he turned to nature in order to gather images and sensations, the tissue and blood of his poetry. None of our contemporary Greek poets, with the possible exception of Anghelos Sikelianos, has lived so close to nature. Kazantzakis' stays in cities were always temporary. Most of the years during the time I knew him were spent on Aegina, at Gottesgab and at Antibes. And his eyes were not closed. He worked immersed in his papers, but he had windows opening to the four winds through which he could gaze at the clouds and the waves. And—to alter the tense of Solomos' lines—"Often at the dawn or in the noontide/ and when the waters cloud and the stars grow thick," he used to watch from some vantage point or to walk with bowed head studying the "poor starlight of the earth." The work of no other modern Greek poet is so full of images of the numberless aspects of the world. At the same time, his descriptive powers were enriched by inexhaustible reading—on stars, birds, fish, flowers, on the life of the peasant, the shepherd, the sailor—and by that association with country people which he always sought in order to quench his thirst both for the living Greek language and for the thing itself.

The earth supplied him with images; the heavens declared their magnitude and gave him fresh sensations. The vertiginous vision of the stars was increased by his study of modern cosmology and astronomy. "The Earth is one of the smallest planets depending on the Sun, which itself is merely one member of a cloud of stars occupying an unoriginal position in the Galaxy, while the Galaxy itself is one of hundreds of millions of similar starry agglomerations."[56] A passage like this would feed Kazantzakis' imagination for days.[57] He cultivated what Freud calls the "oceanic feeling"—he possessed it by nature—this consciousness of the infinity of the universe which alarmed Pascal. He was delighted to conclude that though man is a speck of dust in the cosmic whirlwind, he yet faces up to his fate.

Heroic pessimism is the basis of Kazantzakis' view of the world. All his works without exception could furnish material for the development of this theme. It is expressed most forcibly in *Buddha:* "Mercy! Mercy!

men cry: they are afraid, hungry, cold. . . . But you, my heart, from now on will despise mercy, for you have ascended far aloft and have mastered the whole cycle of vanity! . . . You play without purpose, because you are strong; you play alone, because you have no hope.

"You build castles on the borders of time; you mold gods, children, grandchildren with sand and water. You open your eyes, and they become alive; you close them and they disappear.

"You are dancing, my heart, you are dancing in the desert. You love no one, you hate no one, you hope for nothing: you are free."[58]

The moral is formulated by the "Old Man" at the moment of total disaster when the terrifying, cataclysmic river Yang-Tse has overflowed its banks: "Mei-Ling, my child, man has only one thing of worth—have you not felt it yet? Only one: to see the Yang-Tse come down—to see it and not to cry out!"

"Cursed be hope!" the Old Man exclaims later on, and he concludes, "I cross oars, hands, mind. I surrender to the torrent. I cry: Hey, torrent, where you go, I go also. It is good that you came. I ride on you as on a horse. Let us set out!"[59]

Kazantzakis took refuge in nature in order to find himself. Let us pursue this thought further. I head what now follows with three quotations. One is from Goethe, another from Nietzsche, and the third from one of our contemporaries. On a high mountain, with the ample view of half of Thuringia spread out beneath him, the German poet, after a good breakfast, exclaims: "Here you feel yourself great and free, like the mighty Nature you have beneath your eyes, and as you ought always to be in fact."[60] And Nietzsche says: "If we do not give our souls firm and serene horizons like those of mountains and forests, then our inner life will lose its peace. It will be dispersed and insatiate, like that of man in cities, which knows no happiness and cannot confer it." An Irish commentator on Kazantzakis, W. B. Stanford, writes: "The Lonely One: here is the nemesis of the absolute freedom. Kazantzakis does not flinch from its terrors. . . . Absolute freedom means absolute separation from one's fellow men; and each degree of freedom must be achieved by giving up some element in social life. The hermitage, the ivory tower, the mountain top, are familiar emblems of the effort to find freedom by rejecting society."[61]

In mountain solitude Goethe found greatness and freedom, Nietzsche

[39]

sought peace, and Kazantzakis absolute freedom. Each age, each individuality, has its own particular need. But whatever it is, "great Nature" is always a benefactress. Kazantzakis understood this fairly early in life, almost from the time of his first renunciation of society, of his first sporadic sojourns in the mountains of Crete, on Athos and Taygetos, in the Engadine. Once having understood it, he always sought out the climate he knew to be healthy for his soul. Nietzsche's example was to dictate one form of his quest.

On July 14, 1870, the day on which he learned of the Franco-Prussian War, Nietzsche wrote agitatedly to Erwin Rohde: "Friend, dear friend, we have met once more in the twilight of peace. What sense have all our longings now? We are perhaps at the beginning of the end. What a wilderness! Monasteries will soon be indispensable. And we will be the first brothers." "Here is assuredly the most paradoxical idea engendered by this time of war and victory: *a modern eremiticism,*" he wrote six months later in his notebook. Nietzsche did indeed imagine a seminary where young philosophers, all friends of one another, would form a coenobium, free from all temporal occupation, and would study eternal problems. He dreamed of a new Platonic Academy, of a Pythagorean brotherhood, the Port-Royal des Champs, or Emerson's hermitage. Both his classical education and his stay when a youth at the monastic college of Pforta directed his imagination. "Let us try to find a little island where we shall not have to stop our ears with wax!" he wrote again later to Rohde. "Then we shall teach each other. . . . Let each live, work and rejoice for the other!" And he signed himself *Frater Fridericus.* The plan still occupied Nietzsche twelve years later: "I have a project for this summer," he wrote to Peter Gast in 1882. "It is to find in some forest a castle arranged by Benedictines at one time for their meditations and to fill it with companions, with chosen men. . . ."[62]

Kazantzakis adopted Nietzsche's unrealized scheme. Was his instinct directed also by memories of his stay in the monastic college of Naxos? Did his habit of calling his closest companions "Brothers" originate there? Be that as it may, he too dreamed of a "phalanstery," of a "modern monastery," an "ideal colony," a "free university," to use Nietzsche's expressions. The first people with whom he discussed the idea—before 1922—must have been Anghelos Sikelianos and Costas Sphakianakis, the musician.[63] He introduced me to the idea a short while after we met.

[ 40 ]

His desire had been revived by the promise of Alexander Papanastasiou[64] to expropriate the abandoned monastery of St. John the Hunter on Hymettus and give it to the community. The same concern is evident in Kazantzakis' letters from Aegina written after August 1927. It was not a passing fancy. He wrote telling his friends to exert pressure on Papanastasiou, and he himself came to Athens, burning with the hope of realizing Nietzsche's scheme as if he himself had dreamed of it in another life.

Kazantzakis' isolation was not destined to be sweetened by the presence of friends and companions. The foundation of such a coenobium seems today to be a purely utopian idea. But this need not prevent us from devoting a few words to the very real meaning which friendship had for Kazantzakis. We have mentioned above how he had loved Stavridakis and Dragoumis and lamented for their deaths. The death of Anghelos Sikelianos (June 19, 1951) also moved him deeply. We have his written testimony to show how strong his love was for his fellow fighters: "Anghelos has never been so close to me, so much within me, as he has been these last days. For some people death cannot be admitted: it never entered my head that he could die, and what I felt when the frightful blow fell was indignation and astonishment . . . I wanted to open the black door and to escape. My mind, like Job, stands over the dunghill of this world and cries, 'It is unjust, unjust, I do not accept it!' "[65]

This needs no comment. But further testimony of what friendship meant to him will be given when the time comes to publish the four-hundred-odd letters which he sent me from 1926 up to his death. This correspondence is a monument to friendship. Its pages will constitute a new and unique work by Kazantzakis and will enrich Greek letters with a form which it lacks: literary correspondence. At the same time they will reveal his wild and tender soul, unsociable yet ardent, self-sufficient yet loyal.

The discussion on the subject of nature will remain incomplete if I do not say something of the people. The archaic sanctity we attach to the idea of the "people" is due no doubt to the fact that in Greece we are not yet very conscious of class differences. But at the same time it is due to the sacrifices and achievements of the Greek people, sung by Greek poets. From Solomos' admiration and reverence for the holocaust of the

Greeks in the War of Independence in 1821 sprang the ideal figure of the Fighter, the most purely Greek figure in our new culture.[66] Palamas had deep sympathy for the people, "tortured, humble, redeemed and equal!" and celebrated its mythical and historical heroes like a true national poet. Finally, Sikelianos thought the people worthy of a mystic adoration: the people is the possessor of an incorruptible wisdom, bearer of the divine, representative of all humanity. For Sikelianos, "people" meant the peasant. For him, the peasant does not represent a social class, as he does for Balzac or Zola, for example. He is the unhurried and venerable humanity we meet in Giotto's frescoes. "The peasant is he who beholds God," according to Ramuz. "When Justice left the earth, she planted her last steps in the peasant's cottage."[67]

Solomos, Palamas and Sikelianos are national poets. The mythical figures of their poetry enshrine the soul of their race; they are heroes, not rebels.[68] Kazantzakis, at least up till the time he became a novelist, gave expression to "ideas of spirit" and not "ideas of blood" in his poetry. He did not suffer because of his roots. He never aspired to become a national poet; it was enough for him to be a poet. Poetry, without qualification, is the noblest contribution to the national heritage. Kazantzakis' relation to the people had, therefore, its own character, neither idealistic nor mystic. The people are a continuation of nature, they live indeed "according to nature," their works and days follow the course of the seasons. As a poet turns to nature for the images in which to clothe his ideas, so also will he turn to the people. The people, in their workaday life, will supply him with another treasury of archetypal images and at the same time will teach him to discern the objects of common experience. It will teach him to name sensible things. "Name and thing," words loaded with life, are the raw material of poetry.

We are describing conscious mental processes. But before pursuing our subject, we must consider the moral significance which Kazantzakis attributes to his life among the people, with Cretan shepherds and the fishermen of Aegina. His contact with them was neither close nor continuous; he did not go to church in order to meet them during the Liturgy or on feast days; he did not haunt the public square. But by their example they taught him simplicity, meekness, frugality, thus permitting him to remain faithful to ancestral custom: to be industrious, temperate and persistent. Living close to the people also protected him from the feeling of homelessness which torments the uprooted inhabitants of great cities. In the midst of nature and close to unsophisiticated people, life has a solidity. The soul is rooted; bough and branch can grow.

Kazantzakis was intoxicated by the language of the people. Language and poetry appeared to him as a two-headed Janus. The modern Greek language does indeed excite and charm the imagination with its descriptive power. Words speak with images, thought is translated at once into pictures. Even abstract concepts end as an image, the word links the intelligible with the sensible. "Knowledge and action," the people tell you, learning and skill. The modern Greek language—"the custom of customs" as the Greek writer Tertsetes calls it—manifests the undivided nature of the Greek, reveals the soul of the people's civilization in Greece. The superlative use of such a language in itself gives birth to poetry. "The time has come to call bread a breadlet," I heard an old woman complain during the last war. In Greek, even the diminutive of an ordinary word can give the sensation of poetry. "Bread, salt, blood, sun, earth, water, light, darkness, as well as all the names of metals— these nouns are neither the brothers nor sons but the fathers of sensible things!" (O. V. de L. Milosz).[69]

In an old French reader graced with old-fashioned type, I came across a simple woodcut representing little Pierrot beside the Tree of Knowledge. Each branch of the tree supported a word encircled by leaves, and above the word was depicted the object it indicated: cottage, church, cow, and so on. The child raised a hatchet in both hands and cut out each word together with its object. I saw a herb-gatherer whom I met one spring on the Acropolis root from the soil more herbs than there were names on the branches on the Tree of Knowledge. I approached her and spoke to her, as I had seen Kazantzakis do on so many similar occasions. Without moving more than two or three paces, she bent down and named, as she pulled them up from the ground, more than forty plants.[70] Such is the treasury of the modern Greek language. And such is the sea of wine which intoxicated Kazantzakis.

"First submit to the language of the people and then, if you are capable, master it," commands Solomos.[71] The popular writer, with his unsophisticated soul, has already submitted to it. He says what he feels; the inner meaning goes straight onto the paper. An example of such a writer is General Makrygiannis, that Patriarch (even though he remained a

[ 43 ]

layman). Other examples are Panayis Skouzes and those among the people who wrote their memoirs of the War of Independence. Fortunate is he who has learned their lesson! George Tertsetes, for instance—weak as a poet but strong as a patriot—conformed his speech to that of the people. You can see how genuine his language is: "One dawn, showing me the olive grove, you see, he says to me, that tree by itself, the big hollow one? There Erotocritos came, hung up his arms and spent day and night watching the army of Arethusa." I am not remarking on the mythical quality of these words; but what is admirable is their rhythm and flow.

An educated person finds it hard to submit in this way to the speech of the people; he has become sophisticated and the spirit of that speech is strange to him. His language becomes abstract, loses its contact with sensible things. Abstract speech sometimes becomes not only un-Greek, but inhuman.[72]

Kazantzakis sought to gather all the riches of the popular tongue, he sought to submit to its spirit. His many-sided learning impelled him toward the first but hindered him in the latter, even though his poetry required such a submission. Kazantzakis' style shows once more how correct is the saying, "Style is the man."

Something must now be said on the subject of solitude—a subject which has already crossed that of nature and of poetic creation. As yet I have said nothing of the "harsh time" which drives the poet into solitude as sinful Babylon drives the ascetic into the desert. Goethe once said to Eckermann: "A production like Shakespeare's, undisturbed, innocent, somnambulatory, by which alone anything great can thrive, is no longer possible. Our talents at present lie before the public. The daily criticisms which appear in fifty different places, and the gossip that is caused by them among the public, prevent the appearance of any sound production. In the present day, he who does not keep aloof from all this and isolate himself by main force is lost. Through the bad, chiefly negative, aesthetical and critical tone of the journals, a sort of half culture finds its way to the masses; but to productive talent it is a noxious mist, a dropping poison, which destroys the tree of creative power, from the ornamental green leaves, to the deepest pith and the most hidden fibers."[73]

Goethe complained also of the subjective (romantic) tendencies of his contemporaries, which were in opposition to his own objective nature.[74] What irritated him was a harmless joke compared with the debauchery in which the romantic adventure was destined to end. With the decline of reason went the dissolution of the venerable rules of art. Everyone now had the right to live his own truth and to express it in forms of his own invention. What chiefly characterizes the history of literature in the first thirty years of the twentieth century is the lack of solidarity among writers. Each of them sought to exploit his sudden emancipation to the limit. The demons of the imagination and of the subconscious had taken the place of the mild spirit of reason and measure. The old, tried Greco-Latin humanism, which for centuries had been the inner regulator and rule of the educated man, had yielded to an un-oriented eclecticism, ready to be influenced by the civilizations of all lands outside Europe. This modernistic mania, this wilful experimentation, had reached the point of hysteria. *Enfants terribles* and excited elders quarreled as to who would produce the strangest monstrosities. Eschatological prophecies and eudaemonical utopias, reform teachings and religious conversions, caricatures and contentions of reality, hermeticism and travel mania, Freudism and the idealization of action, hedonism, amoralism, aestheticism, pessimism—all tendencies and all affectations had the right to enter the ancient sacred enclosure.[75] "God is dead!" The terrible phrase of Nietzsche was the password of the new Walpurgisnacht. He who with sober mind desired to work creatively amid this pandemonium had to "stop his ears with wax" or seek refuge in solitude in order to master the tumult of the age. Kazantzakis did the latter, laying down for himself a discipline according to which he could live.

Nature calls the poet to her embrace. The "harsh age" and the requirements of poetic creation drive him from the city. In Kazantzakis' case, another force contributes to this centrifugal movement: his own eremitical nature, his inherited destiny. The Cretan is a lone fighter, more readily the shepherd of shadows than the companion of man. Centuries of revolt against the ruling power have made him solitary and unsociable. There is a spark in the Cretan song of Pipos which could have fired the *Odyssey*. The Turks are about to enter Pipos' village. The villagers shoulder their belongings and vanish in a body. Pipos is a man of the nobility: his riches are greater than those of all the others together. Hence his pride and loneliness are also greater. The humbler people panic, try to take

[ 45 ]

away whatever they can of their few possessions. "One takes his goat, another takes his donkey. Pipos the unfortunate only takes himself!" His sense of his superiority has condemned him. Once a person of lofty spirit denies his equality with other men, solitude is his lot.

Solitude is a complex experience. It includes both greatness and servitude. Even during the happy periods of creation and inner peace, the longing for intercourse with the rejected world still works in the soul. To obtain its approbation would be to experience an intoxicating sense of deliverance, of the most desired freedom. One form of liberty is to look in the same direction as others, to act in such a way that one's actions are at once swallowed up in the river of common activity. Kazantzakis had the strength to rise above the adversities of life, and even to regard them from the viewpoint of an inquiring spectator. He was never faint-hearted, he never surrendered, he did not curse his fate. But a sense of moral isolation often depressed him. Up to his sixtieth year, the public had noticed only his travel books. Greek critics ignored his message; strange as it may seem, certain of his works remained without comment in Greece. Even now his reputation is based more on articles in newspapers than on responsible criticism. But Kazantzakis experienced not only the bitterness of a thinker whose message was without effect; he was deserted on the other side as well: he never met a living master. He often gave me the impression of someone cutting a path through a jungle.

"In time of peace," Nietzsche wrote, "every man with warlike instincts turns against himself." Kazantzakis' persistent struggle always seemed to me a testing out of his world view upon himself. This world view, which we have already called "heroic pessimism," became fully explicit in 1927 when he published his *The Saviors of God* in the Athenian monthly *Anagennisi,* edited by D. Glynos.[76] A lively discussion had already appeared in the columns of this periodical on the subject of historical materialism, and Kazantzakis presented his text as "the first call of the post-Communist credo." He wished to indicate that it was an attack on "the narrow, out-of-date, materialistic conception of communism." These circumstances must not mislead us. Kazantzakis' text is indeed a condemnation of materialism and of intellectualism, the first—if I am not mistaken—anti-rationalist proclamation in Greece. It was a challenge to the Greek intelligentsia which, with the exception of

Sikelianos and one or two others, had remained uninfluenced by the crisis of rationalism in Western Europe. But the text is chiefly a classification, a *mise en oeuvre* of Kazantzakis' philosophical studies. It is at the same time an essay in self-knowledge and a program of creative life, something similar to Ion Dragoumis' *My Wisdom* and the *Consciences* of Sikelianos. Kazantzakis himself regarded *The Saviors of God* as "a mystical book describing how the soul can ascend from sphere to sphere until it reaches the highest sphere. There are five spheres: Ego, Mankind, Earth, Universe, God." Kazantzakis' philosophical activity may be said to have ended with this book. With the exception of the last chapter of *The Saviors of God,* added a year later (which consisted of material combined from the previous chapters), Kazantzakis from now on was concerned only with giving poetic form to the ideas he had already developed. In this he differs from his "parallel": Nietzsche, during his whole life, was continually struck by new revelations, and his struggle gave birth to a host of contradictions.

Kazantzakis had written *The Saviors of God* between 1922 and 1923 when he was living in Berlin. The distress of Germany on the one hand and on the other the faith with which he himself had inspired a circle of intellectuals—most of them enthusiastic girls—[77] had determined the exalted and mystic character of the work. A violent lyricism runs through it; it is stirred by a convulsive rhythm. Both manner and content remind us of the writings of the Hebrew prophets, of the Ionian philosophers, of Lucretius and Nietzsche. Kazantzakis appears to have followed the advice on style which the latter noted in 1887: "The form. The style. *An ideal monologue.* Whatever has the appearance of learning must be absorbed to the depths. All the accents of deep passion, disquiet, and at the same time of weakness . . . Go beyond demonstrations; be completely personal, without using the first person. . . . Say the most abstract things in the most concrete and full-blooded manner. . . . As far as possible, visible, precise things, examples . . . No description; every problem transposed to the level of sense, to the point of passion. Expressive terms. Superiority of military terms . . ." This Mediterranean style, which Nietzsche went to Venice to find, was in Kazantzakis' blood and in the language of his own people.

*The Saviors of God* is about the ascension of the soul. Man "prepares himself" for the ascent by recognizing the limited power of the human mind in the face of the world's mystery, by thirsting after God and by triumphing over hope.[78] Man then "proceeds" from the ego to the race, from the race to humanity, from humanity to the earth. What is meant by "proceeds"? He sees an Invisible One turn man's ego into a bridge, transcend race and humanity. "Through all this human material he ascends with hands and feet, drowned in tears and blood, and he struggles to be saved. Saved from what? From the body which encircles him, from the people that support him, from the flesh, the heart and the brain of man . . . I am afraid! The dark ascent has no ending," cries the Invisible One. "My head is like a flame eternally consuming the body. But the night wind blows to extinguish me. I am threatened in my struggle every moment. In my struggle every solid body is a danger. I walk, stumble among flesh like a benighted wayfarer, and I cry: 'Help!' "[79] The struggle of the Invisible One does not involve mankind only: it involves the whole earth, the whole universe. In the wild flower and in the star the same breath courses, storms, generates. Man "has visions" of the Invisible One that "treads on what is visible and ascends." Struggle is the essence of the Invisible Power. "What is the object of this struggle?" man asks, forgetting that the Great Breath does not work within human time, place, or causality.

"The last and most sacred form of the theory is *Action*. . . . Our deep human duty is not to divine the rhythm of God's course, but, as far as we can, to conform the rhythm of our tiny ephemeral life to it." To achieve this, "we must strive to shape a new face of our God with our own flesh and blood." Our God is not an abstract thought, he is not a pure figment of our mind. He is man and woman, mortal and immortal, dung and spirit. God dances beyond the bounds of logic. He is not almighty, not all-holy, not all-wise. God is like an erotic wind shattering corporeal forms in order to pass through them. God battles without any certitude. "God, within the sphere of our ephemeral flesh, is in peril. He cannot be saved unless we save him with our struggle. We cannot be saved, unless he is saved. We are one. From the blind worm in the ocean's depth to the infinite arena of the Galaxy, there is one alone who is struggling and in peril: ourself. And within our small earthy breast there is one alone who is struggling and in peril: the Universe."

This conception of God has as a consequence a new morality. "What is our duty? To ascend this bloodstained path with God. Whatever presses upward and hastens to God's aid is good; whatever leads downward and impedes God's ascent is bad. All virtues and vices assume a new value, are freed from time and place, exist absolutely within man, before and after man, eternally. For the essence of our morality is not the salvation of man who changes with time and place, but that of God, who through countless fugitive human forms and adventures is always the same, the indestructible rhythm struggling for freedom." In every critical period, another social class embodies the upward impetus. "Formerly kings, priests, noblemen and burghers created civilizations, liberated the divinity. Today, God is a worker, made savage by toil, wrath and hunger. . . . Fire! That is our great duty today. . . . The wind of destruction is blowing: that is now the breath of our God."

*Silence* is the last stage of the ascent to deliverance. "He who has passed through every contest attains at last the highest peak—that of respite—beyond all contest, all content, beyond all purpose and certitude. He questions no longer, he does not struggle, is not separated; he ripens in silence, indestructible, eternal with the Universe. He is reconciled at last, has come to rest in the Abyss, as the seed of man in the womb of woman." How to reach the womb of the Abyss cannot be disclosed. "In deep silence, let this confession of faith alone sink your mind in ecstasy and your warm heart in works:

"I believe in one God, the Borderman, the Twin-born, militant, suffering, magnipotent, not almighty, a fighter on the frontiers, a general, emperor of all luminous forces, visible and invisible.

"I believe in the countless masks which God has assumed throughout the ages and hear of their indestructible unity with awe.

"I believe in his vigilant struggle, taming and fertilizing matter—the life-giving source of plants, beasts and men.

"I believe in the heart of man, the earthen threshing floor where the Borderman wrestles day and night with Death.

"Help! you cry, Lord, and I hear.

"Blessed are they who hear, for they shall be saved, fighting.

"Blessed are they who are saved, for they liberate God, creating.

"Blessed are they who bear Supreme Responsibility on their shoulders!"[80]

*The Saviors of God* is without doubt an indispensable text both for the understanding of the mythical figures to which Kazantzakis gave form and for a knowledge of his character. Such works are always the product of some psychophysiological reality. In *The Saviors of God,* all the introvert frenzy, the enterprise, messianism and willfulness of Kazantzakis break out. This book alone, with no other testimony, would tell us how Kazantzakis sensed the universe and take us to the core of his personality. His very misfortunes in his relations with the world could be foreseen from these pages, even if the reception they met with in Greece were unknown. As our poet's insistence on the traditional poetic (despite his longing for a flowing lyricism) deprived him of the support of modern writers, so here the anti-rationalist and apocalyptic nature of his text (notwithstanding his concessions to the times) made it suspect for those who were politically progressive and caused it to be without effect on the masses. Except for the understanding shown by the late Photos Polites[81] *et unus alius,*[82] criticism, both written and verbal, was generally unfavorable and sometimes derisive. At best, *The Saviors of God* was judged as a philosophical text and the sources of the writer's thought were investigated.[83] The unique personality here revealed was not noticed.

3

> But I hold my thought alone and by others unbeguiled.
> —*Agamemnon* by Aeschylus, translated by Gilbert Murray

*The Saviors of God* came out in *Anagennisi,* and as a reprint, at the beginning of September 1927. For three and a half months before, Kazantzakis had been living on Aegina. He loved this island, where he was to live for some twenty years, from the first moment he saw it. Its scant earth, its enclosed sea stirred by the west wind, its fruit and fish suited him. Aegina is a part of Attica, and it has the same dry, clear sky. There is no better climate for intellectual work. It proved so for Kazantzakis: he wrote eighteen books of the *Odyssey* (VII–XXIV) there between May 20 and September 22, 1927. (As has already been mentioned, the first six were written in Crete during the winter of 1925.)

Kazantzakis' dwelling was a two-storied cottage in Paul Hanos' garden, situated inland and about three hundred yards from the prison. The main room was on the upper floor and had windows on three sides. From the table where he worked Kazantzakis could see the gardens with the pistachio trees, the dome of the church of the Virgin, and the sea. His room was as barely furnished as that of a third-class hotel, and his personal belongings would have gone into a soldier's knapsack. He led a monastic existence; he did not even spare himself time to bathe in the sea. From dawn till nightfall, Kazantzakis, pencil in hand, an oblong notebook in front of him, wrote down his seventeen-syllable lines. An old woman called Kyra-Zoe brought him his food once a day. Now and again, at twilight, he used to call the landlady's children—Stavros, Eftychia and little Costa—and give them sweets. On Sundays he liked to entertain a friend from Athens.

Kazantzakis' pace of work was incredible. A month after he had begun to work he had already finished Book X. By July 7 he had finished Book XIV, and by the 30th of the same month he had embarked on Book XVII. It took him only four months to reach Book XXIV. He wrote some two hundred lines a day. "I am beginning to be worried," he wrote to me on August 1, "about this violent deluge which is lasting so long and which not only does not tire me but makes me feel stronger." "It is not easy to have a precise idea of the vehemence of such creations!" Nietzsche once wrote to his sister. And in *Ecce Homo,* in certain pages which sound like fireworks, he describes the frenzy which gave birth to *Zarathustra:* "Has anyone," he asks, "at the end of this nineteenth century a clear idea of what the poets of the great periods called 'inspiration'? If not, I am willing to explain it here...." Further on, he describes the mood of inspiration as revelation, enchantment, exaltation, beatitude, illumination, freedom....

It must not be concluded that Kazantzakis hurried over his work. Time indeed is indifferent to works to which it has not contributed. The poet was aware of this. Kazantzakis only needed a few months for the first draft of the *Odyssey.* But to finish the work—writing and rewriting it up to the seventh and last time—he needed thirteen years.[84] Is it not said that Plato rewrote the Introduction to his *Republic* seven times? Kazantzakis spared no pains to improve his first version: the sense of the absolute and at the same time of something unfulfilled compelled him to do so. "I am working. Book XX will soon be finished. I am quite untired and terribly worried. Without any reason. The fearful metaphysical gale that has parched my body is passing over me. I welcome it."[85]

"I am working." These are the accented words. Temporarily setting aside all other activity, Kazantzakis worked. His work consumed all his capacities. "One too many!" he once wrote over his door in Aegina. "A single virtue is more of a virtue than two, because it has more knots for fate to catch on to—" thus, with romantic excitement, Zarathustra also proclaimed. Kazantzakis gave himself totally to what he wrote, as if he would leave nothing for next time. All the experiences he could recollect, all the knowledge he had gathered with piratical avidity flowed like violent torrents into the river of the *Odyssey*. Words were too few for him, expressions inadequate, the sequence of ideas sluggish. The work required the animation of all the poet's faculties, the undivided concentration of his mind. A consequence of this volition is a style tremendously taut, overloaded, unsatisfied with its own vitality. Spontaneous sensitivity has been suffocated by the dictatorship of the mind: even where it breaks through, one feels that the poet has dragged it to the surface like a shipwrecked thing.

From Kazantzakis' point of view, poetic creation was a sortie: a sortie from time and place in the natural and metaphysical sense, an escape from the corrupting environment of mediocrity, lethargy and compromise. But a sortie, in its very vehemence, leaves much behind it. "The heart is not being released: this means that a host of visions and emotions have remained within me unspoken, unliberated, weighing me down."[86] Another reason for the poet's tormenting dissatisfaction came not so much this time from omission as from overbidding: an imposing mass of material had been introduced into the poem purely by will. The fact that it was so introduced gives this material a sick appearance, even reduces it to inertia. The reader of experience can recognize it; the poet was aware of it, even though he would have liked to forget it. This awareness exercised a disheartening sorcery on his conscience, a kind of mockery of and a longing for inspiration.

The grandeur and the servitude of the poet are inexhaustible subjects. But mention should be made of the silent support which Kazantzakis received from the living tradition of his birthplace. The epic, both as a spiritual climate and as a poetic form, is still alive in Crete. The *Erotokritos,* a poem of several thousand lines, is still known by heart on the island. Shepherds on the mountains console themselves in their solitude by reciting hundreds of its verses. The same is true of lesser-known poems like the *Rimada* of Sachlikis, Daskaloyiannis' little epic and the song of Alidakis, the *Cretan Girl* of Hadjimichalis Yannaris, the former warrior who recounted his own exploits in song. I myself remember a coffeehouse keeper in Rethymnon, called Klados, who used to gather his fellow soldiers together each evening and relate in endless couplets their common sufferings after the Smyrna disaster.

The epic is the heroic form—it is not surprising that Kazantzakis chose it. But it cannot express the tragedy of contemporary man. The epic corresponds to a view of the world perceived through the senses. This is its beauty and its limitation. Tragedy is needed to express the cosmic feeling and agony of man before his fate. Kazantzakis served the epic abundantly and tirelessly with his inexhaustible store of sensory experience, almost entirely visual. The particular characteristics of tragedy also appear here and there in the *Odyssey,* once (in Book XVII) as a pure dramatic dialogue. But the tragic spirit runs through the whole warp of the poem. It lies in the very temperament of the poet—the lover of life who at the same time regarded life as an insubstantial illusion—and also in the puzzling character of the hero ("absurd, contrary longings leapt within his breast" I, 408). The *Odyssey* reminds me of another narrative text in which—*mutatis mutandis!*—a tragic soul breaks forth: St. John's Gospel.

What sacred beast attends the new evangelist? Lion, eagle, archangel or bull? "I feel that these months are the best of my life," Kazantzakis wrote to me on August 1, 1927, himself astonished at his own creative fever. "Perhaps because while I have seen many things I have been liberated almost entirely from what is human and have succeeded in concentrating the substance of my soul—which is certainly without human form, being both beast and god. More and more I free myself from human nature and struggle, like an Egyptian god, to find an organic synthesis of beast and god—of a beast of prey (falcon, tiger or what you will) and of a restless, ephemeral god who does not love the ephemeral, transient form of man." This is the state of mind of a hermit on a tower built with his own hands, a hermit made savage by solitude. It is also the breaking of a long *silence.* (I happened to see Kazantzakis in his retreat after many days of complete silence: his jaws were benumbed, and his lips could not form words.)

Once more the subject of loneliness. "German author equals German martyr," exclaimed Goethe, in 1830, at the height of his glory. What could Kazantzakis say when at the age of forty-four he had no other follower than an inexperienced youth? "In waste, in desolate waste, even a worm's shade is good!" we read later in the *Odyssey* (III, 100). "I do not regard it as coincidence," he wrote to me in August 1927, "that in this critical moment of my life you should appear on my horizon and stand beside me and help me. For both of us this fact ought to have a great value. . . ." (Note, on page 23, Nietzsche's words to Heinrich von Stein!) Twenty centuries ago, a Roman poet withdrew from the world and wrote what became a great national poem. The poet was Virgil, and his work the *Aeneid*. Before he had finished it, the Romans recognized the magnitude of the undertaking. Propertius, announcing the work which was in progress, foretold that it would be more beautiful than the *Iliad*. The Emperor Augustus himself several times asked to see something of it, but the poet refused, consumed by a passion for perfection which made him give as his last order instructions for the manuscript to be destroyed. Kazantzakis, too, lived like an anchorite in order to work, but without the feeling that anyone paid him any attention—he struggled "behind the sun."

Are there certain similarities between the struggle of Virgil and that of Kazantzakis? In the creation of a long poem there are always features common to all such creative activity. But each work must develop in its own way.[87] Virgil aspired to be a *national* poet: he took a national legend, enriched it with national beliefs and characteristics and raised it to the level of poetry as a harmonious whole of symbols in which the nation was summoned to recognize its own soul and the meaning of its historical life. Every people seeks to preserve an idealized memory of its past and to have the feats of its ancestors recorded for comparison with its own. A people with no memory tends to revert from history to nature. The mission of the national poet is to keep the consciousness of history vivid through a living educational myth. The higher a people is raised by its national education, the more familiar and beloved become the symbols given it by its poets. By its preference for certain symbols, each people manifests its particular soul. E. P. Papanoutsos,[88] for instance, has very rightly observed that the sortie from Missolonghi is closer to us as Greeks than the taking of Tripolitsa: the Greek people tend to recognize their historic destiny in a holocaust rather than in a triumph.

In a national literature one generally encounters a dominating idea which expresses some fundamental longing, some unshakable orientation of the national spirit within the framework of a given period. Ancient Greek literature was dominated by the idea of liberty; the classic Spanish drama by that of honor; the Russian novels—before the Revolution—by the ideas of justice and predetermination. Certain "national" types also occur in national literatures: Homer's Odysseus, the Prometheus of Aeschylus, Cervantes' Don Quixote, Goethe's Faust, Pushkin's Aleco (the first of so many vagabonds in Russian literature) in *The Gipsies,* Solomos' Fighter. . . . These types are incarnations of a dominating racial tendency which persists through the years. World-wandering, crafty and homesick Odysseus makes visible the soul of a seafaring race that sailed in protohistoric times a sea closed between the Nile Delta and the Pillars of Hercules. Don Quixote represents Spain's grandiose urge to Christianize the universe. Faust is the symbol of the modern European soul, thirsting after the infinite—a soul which has rightly been called "Faustian" in order to distinguish it from the Euclidean soul of the ancient world. Solomos' Fighter is an idealized personification of the struggle of the Greek people for rebirth.

The types in a nation's literature belong to the people which gave them birth, even when they "ridicule" rather than praise the spirit of this people, as in the case of Don Quixote, or of Stavrogin in *The Possessed.* The literary type who does not represent national legend and character but is, rather, an arbitrary personal creation cannot be described as national. Yet he is valid, since he too expresses a state of the national soul, that which arises when its harmonious integration is disrupted. At the critical phases of civilizations are to be found curious literary types who deliberately break away from their environment in order to judge it as "strangers": an example is the Persian of Montesquieu's *Persian Letters,* or Voltaire's Candide. In contemporary Western literature, such flowers of decadence have run riot: Thomas the Impostor in Jean Cocteau's novel of that name, Lafcadio in Gide's *Caves du Vatican,* Kafka's heroes, Meursault in Camus' *The Stranger,* Roquentin in Sartre's *Nausée,* and others. These types are not "heroes" in the old meaning of the word; they are rebels or maladjusted people. The environment provokes them, enrages them, disquiets them, or remains a riddle to them.[89]

When Kazantzakis withdrew to Aegina to write his *Odyssey*, very few people in Greece were aware of the direction of his mind. In the tragedy *Odysseus*—a work deeply influenced by Gerhart Hauptmann's *Bow of Odysseus* (1914)—he had unquestionably shown an inclination for the Homeric hero, but he neither renewed nor elaborated the theme: no one could then suspect the extent of the poet's identification with the legendary figure or the nature of his new symbolism. From a fragment of the new epic published in the review *Anagennisi*, the reader could affirm nothing except that the subject did not altogether belie the title of the poem and that the meter adopted by the poet was the iambic seventeen-syllable line. But Kazantzakis' friends—even if they did not possess that knowledge of him which I have tried to outline in these pages—knew very well that the new Odysseus would not be a national hero: he would be a rebel, uprooted, even a desperado. The arena of his action would be the whole world. Instead of the friendly setting of his native land, there would be threatening horizons. Instead of well-known faces, there would be magic masks. Instead of the fruit of honest toil, there would be desperate piracy. The climate of his soul? Solitude and revolt! Cosmic terrors, a feeling of homelessness, excitement of the ego. Inhumanity. Despair. Nihilism.

## 4

The Irish professor W. B. Stanford, a student of comparative literature, has in a very important study traced the development of "The Ulysses Theme" in European literature, from Homer to Kazantzakis.[90] There are two interpretations of Odysseus by which poets have been inspired: the nostalgic Odysseus on the one hand and the incurable wanderer on the other. The first, the creation of Homer, is also to be found in Ovid, Joachim du Bellay, and others. The second, the man intoxicated with broad horizons, also appears in ancient times. Later he was to inspire Dante, Tennyson, Pascoli, D'Annunzio. "This is the essentially romantic conception of the Odyssean hero, owing something to Byron and Nietzsche, as well as to Faust and Columbus" (Stanford).

Of the incarnations of the non-Homeric Odysseus with which Professor Stanford presents us, the only ones which could have excited Kazantzakis' imagination are those of Dante (in the twenty-sixth canto of the *Inferno*) and Tennyson (in his "Ulysses," written in 1833). It should at once be noted that Dante does not devote more than thirty triplets to Odysseus and that Tennyson's poem does not exceed seventy lines. The *Odyssey* of Kazantzakis contains 33,333 lines.

Dante's Odysseus did not return to Ithaca. After escaping from Circe, his longing to know the world drives him past the Pillars of Hercules— the *limit* of human daring—in order to venture with very few companions into the ocean. He sails southward for five moons, is privileged to see "the stars of the other pole." Dante's Odysseus relates the story of his own wreck when a whirlwind strikes the ship, in the following words (Henry Francis Cary's translation):

> Thrice it whirled her round
> With all the waves, the fourth time lifted up
> The poop, and sank the prow: so fate decreed:
> And over us the booming billow clos'd.[91]

There is no need to underline what significance this mythical germ had for Kazantzakis' huge work.[92] As Dante himself says: *Poca favilla gran fiamma seconda!*[93]

The Ulysses described in Tennyson's seventy lines possesses many of the characteristics of Kazantzakis' hero. He too chafes on his island and scorns its race "that hoard, and sleep, and feed, and know not him." He also has "enjoyed greatly, suffered greatly," he seeks "to drink life to the lees," his heart is hungry. He has known cities of men, but not less has he known himself, whom he regards as "a part of all that he has met." He craves for new experiences, wishes to "shine in use," to save as many hours as he can from the "eternal silence." His spirit yearns "to follow knowledge, like a sinking star, beyond the utmost bound of human thought"; he longs for "something ere the end," "some work of noble note," "a newer world." Finally, both Odysseus and his companions have "free hearts, free foreheads" and the heroic resolve "to strive, to seek, to find, and not to yield."[94]

All these characteristics and desires belong to romantic psychology; but they were not unknown in antiquity. The ancient himself was often daring and a lover of danger. The ancient ancestor of the second type of Odysseus, the unrepentant wanderer, demonstrates this. Pelops tells us in his prayer to Poseidon:

The great danger never descends upon a man without strength;
but if we are destined to die, why should one sit
to no purpose in darkness and find a nameless old age
without any part of glory his own?
          —(The *Odes* of Pindar, translated by R. Lattimore)

Thus, together with the characteristics of the homesick Odysseus of the Homeric poem, Kazantzakis could have found many of the distinguishing features of the eternal seafarer in ancient tradition. But this is not in question. An epic hero is not put together from reading: he is rooted in the being and fed on the experiences of the poet himself. We must seek for the origins of the modern Odysseus less in his ancient incarnations than in the "character" we have tried to portray and in the conditions of our times. There are indeed certain features in this modern Odysseus which belong exclusively to our own times. Our study will be concerned mainly with a consideration of these features.

"Have we really asked ourselves what is the worth of this age which recognizes its art in that of Wagner?" Nietzsche inquired, only to give the answer himself in a revealing manner: "[This age] is radically anarchic, exhausted, insatiable, formless, unsure of its foundations, ready to despair, without candor, conscious to the marrow, without nobility, violent, cowardly." The artist's attempt to affirm and to control himself in so inartistic an age is, according to Nietzsche, monstrous—poison for poison. The results of this extreme consciousness are known. Nietzsche struggled without hope, visited by terrifying illuminations, cut off from his age. To characterize this strange condition, Stefan Zweig likens Nietzsche to the desperadoes, those piratical figures of the sixteenth century who descended like vultures on the Spanish Empire. "Nietzsche, like them, did not conquer anything for himself or for anyone after him, or for God, or for the king, or for faith. He struggled for the sake of the struggle, for he did not desire to possess anything, gain anything, acquire anything."[95]

The desperado shortly became part of the modern vocabulary. He has been recognized as the new "child of the age." This danger-loving pirate, "who has no nation, no king and no flag," does indeed represent, if not the whole, at least some aspects of the modern mind. He is the product of an age of dissolution, a child of unbelief, fruit of anxiety in the face of the absurd world. His shadow haunts the works of contemporary writers: of Malraux, Sartre, Hermann Hesse, Ernst Jünger, T. S. Eliot. The desperado has something of Don Quixote, but lacks his credulity. He is an open-eyed lover of chimeras, a megalomaniac without any consecrated material for his mania, a hero with contempt for the rewards. Through the disinterestedness of his actions he mocks the edifying virtue of a hero in the ancient sense of the word. His own heroism is nihilistic: he lays no foundations, he does not build, he contributes nothing to the common fund. He represents an excitation of the ego, an inflammation of man's substance, a revolt against institutions, a challenge to conformists. Without the desperado as a model, we should find it difficult to describe the modern Odysseus.

To understand how such a type grew in Kazantzakis' imagination, we must go back to the history of his thought. We have already spoken of his identification with Nietzsche, of his sojourn in Germany in 1923. For Greeks, that year was the one after the disaster in Asia Minor: in the flames of that disaster the national myth which had sustained Hellenism for some four and a half centuries was consumed. For the Germans it was the morrow of a total defeat. Until that time the nihilistic idea was merely a conception or presentiment of certain daring thinkers like Nietzsche. But when a catastrophe has occurred which "has discredited society with all its myths, institutions, and traditions"—a contemporary German philosopher affirms—"the idea of nothingness can penetrate the consciousness of everybody. The history of the twentieth century, disjointed and barbaric, has produced consequences which may be interpreted as a confirmation of the gloomiest prophecies of Nietzsche, Burckhardt or De Tocqueville. Many countries, but none more pronouncedly than Germany, have confronted situations in which 'nothingness' seemed to become almost tangible, because the conflagration of war and the public frenzy had consumed the social structure."[96]

Kazantzakis had been to a unique degree prepared by Nietzsche's philosophy to regard 1923 in Germany as a Day of Judgment.[97] The lines in *"The Saviors of God"*: "Fire! That is our great duty today . . ."; "War against the infidels! The infidels are those who are satisfied, sated, sterile!"; "We hate, we do not compromise, we are unjust, cruel . . ."; "Fire, to cleanse the earth . . ."; "A world has been destroyed, another is not yet born . . ."; "The wind of destruction is blowing . . ."—all these terrible lines had been dictated by the presentiment of the end of Western civilization.[98] But, strangely, Nietzsche's eschatological prophecy was being confirmed, in a nonsensical Germany, by prophets of another kind, vindictive toward the possessors, giving hope to those who had nothing. These prophets were called Marxists, and their prophecies were founded on the theory of class war. It may seem even stranger (it certainly would have seemed so to Nietzsche) that the void left in Kazantzakis' consciousness by the overthrow of the idols should have been filled—albeit temporarily—by the edifying (and rationalist!) theory of Marx.[99]

As has already been stated earlier, Kazantzakis flirted with Marxism for some years, though he never became its servant. When his connection with the revolutionary movement proved a disappointment, he fully accepted the idea of Dionysiac nihilism which had attracted him from his early days.[100] The circumstances of this definitive orientation will be told later. For the period we are here describing we must investigate another important aspect of Kazantzakis' thought. This is Oswald Spengler's theory of "historical comparative morphology."[101]

Historical comparative morphology centers around the idea that cultures are living organisms passing through youth, old age and death. The gigantic history of Chinese culture, for instance, corresponds for the morphologist to the tiny history of a single man, plant, or animal. According to Spengler, the waves of history, starting from what is formless, mold a "logical organism" which, once it has produced its flowers and fruits, returns to formlessness in order to yield its place to another wave, to a new culture, which itself must develop in accordance with the laws of organic necessity. "A culture is born the moment a great soul awakes, detaches itself from the primeval psychic state of ever-childish humanity —a form risen from the formless, determination and mortality risen from the infinite and the permanent. It grows up in the soil of a place which can be defined with precision and to which it remains as faithful as a plant. A culture perishes when the soul has realized all its possibilities, molding peoples, languages, religious systems, arts, states, sciences; it returns then to its primordial psychic state."[102]

The idea of the mortality of civilizations was the most important intellectual experience in the time between the two World Wars. Western civilization is perhaps the first in history to be conscious of its own death. Many of the philosophers and poets of our age have devoted thought to this fearful subject. Kazantzakis felt it for the first time in Germany, during the tragic years of inflation and hunger, and he accepted it intellectually with the aid of Spengler. *The Decline of the West* (in the German edition of 1923) was one of the books he brought back on his return home. When French thought, in its turn, took up the subject, Kazantzakis—who always kept abreast of new ideas in French literature—was able to perceive it even more clearly, in, for instance, such illuminating works as Paul Valéry's *Prologue to the Persian Letters* (1926), *Glances at the World of Today* (1931), and his other *essais quasi politiques*.[103] In Greece, also, Kazantzakis saw now and then that the gloomy prognostic of the end of Western civilization was having an effect on the sensibility and thought of his contemporaries—in a good many of Cavafis' poems,[104] in certain writings of Petros Vlastos[105] and, later on, in the tragedies of Sikelianos and other younger writers.

To the descriptive imagination the death of civilizations means overturned thrones and smoking ruins. To the nonpictorial mind it means something less startling but much more terrible: it means the *void*. The gods have died, myths and institutions have become ineffectual, man finds himself disconnected from the world: there is no faith to explain it to him, there is no morality to direct his actions. Suddenly everything seems "strange," "absurd"[106] and—what is more terrible—"everything is permissible."[107] From this "limit situation," which puts man face to face with ultimate realities, there is only one release: the creation of a new God. "True anarchy," according to Novalis, "is the birthstone of religion." "It is God's nature to make something out of nothing. Therefore, he who is not yet nothing, of him God cannot make something," writes Luther in his commentary on the Epistle to the Romans.[108] But if God is not revealed, man will remain an orphan—a desperado!

Kazantzakis' messianism was not then only a psychic tendency: it was a necessity dictated to him from outside. In order to fill the void, Kazantzakis wished first for a resurrection of the Christ of the Gospels, untouched by the dogmas of the church. Later, he sought for an acceptable metaphysic and ethic in Buddhism. Finally, disheartened by the impossibility of achieving the rebirth for which he aspired, he flirted with Marxism and planned to enlist in the revolutionary movement. This last failure was to bring him—or, I should say, to bring him back —to poetic creation. But all that went into his previous spiritual struggles was to make of the *Odyssey* a "theology." Kazantzakis' Odysseus goes in search of God as Homer's Odysseus goes in search of his fatherland. Nostalgia consumed both of them. But the difference between them is that the one finds Ithaca, the other, seeking but never meeting with the true God, becomes a killer of the gods, and knows a transcendent experience only in the embrace of death. The death of the modern Odysseus is his only Transfiguration.

# PART II

# THE POEM

My *Odyssey* continues the enormous epic of the white race—the epic of Homer. It closes a circle left open for so many centuries. And it closes it when the state of the world is astonishingly like it was in the twelfth century B.C., shortly before the descent of the Dorians and the creation—after a middle age—of a new civilization.

*—From a letter written by Kazantzakis from
Siberia, February 22, 1929*

W e have now come to the point at which I must say something of the *Odyssey* itself—that is, give an account of it and then comment on it. In this way I will be able to give evidence for and complete the "character" I have been sketching. But to give a full account of such a vast work is like opening a dam before a cataract—it would sweep these pages away. To avoid this, I shall publish separately the synopsis of the *Odyssey* which I have drawn up for my own guidance and give here a "synopsis of the synopsis."[109] In what follows, I shall try to take certain figures as symbols and to indicate the poet's intentions in this way.

## 1

PROLOGUE. The poet beseeches the Sun, which beholds all things, not to lose sight of Odysseus: to recount to the poet his feats and all that happens to him in the world. And the poet will pass these things through his secret inner workshop and give them an intelligible form.

BOOK I. *Odysseus subdues a revolt in Ithaca.*[110] The great wanderer has come back to Ithaca and has slain the suitors. The new *Odyssey* starts with a bath of purification, presaging a new life. The poem will disclose what the new life is to be. Odysseus has shown himself to be a competent king, for he has quelled the rising of the maimed and the widows of the victims of the ten years' war. He has shown himself to be a good householder, governing his life on land as he did his ship at sea. But on his island he is restless. The Fates who blessed him in his cradle—Tantalus, Prometheus and Heracles—

have set a "bottomless heart" in his breast and a "great seed of light" in his head; in his hand they have placed a "knife of iron." Odysseus is not destined to waste away in Ithaca.

BOOK II. *Odysseus leaves Ithaca forever.* The world-wanderer relates his achievements and his sufferings to his family—to Penelope, Telemachus and Laertes. He escaped from the embrace of the goddess (Calypso), from that of the beast (Circe), renounced human happiness (Nausicaä). This last renunciation cost him dearly; but he will enjoy the happiness of which he was deprived through his son, Telemachus, whom he will marry to the beautiful girl.[111] As for himself, after such triumphs he certainly cannot adapt himself to "grandmother virtue" and to the "respectable hearth." Odysseus decides on a new departure. He chooses his companions: *Captain Clam,* an old sea wolf; *Hardihood,* a fair-haired barbarian; the palace bronzesmith, *Kentaur,* a fat, good-natured fellow; *Orpheus,* a lightheaded flute-player; *Granite,* an outlaw. All of these, and each of them separately, represent qualities attacked by society. Odysseus buries his father, marries Telemachus to Nausicaä, builds his ship. One night he and his companions gather supplies from his own storerooms. At dawn they set sail.

BOOK III. *Odysseus goes to Sparta.* They escape from Ithaca—that suffices. They do not know where they are going. At the time of their sailing, Helen of Sparta, in the palace of Menelaus, is also restless. Her complaint is borne on the wind to Odysseus: he sets his helm for the Peloponnesos. Landing, he goes to fill his water flasks at a spring; on the way he meets a girl going to water her calf. He makes love to the girl and carries off the calf. Next day he steals a chariot with two horses and sets out for Sparta. In the plain he meets for the first time the blond barbarians who are descending from the North. The Bronze Age is dying, the Iron Age is about to be born. It is a time of war. An internal enemy also threatens Menelaus' kingdom: the hungry people demand food. Odysseus hesitates over whom to support: the people or the king? He chooses the king. But he pours his venom into him also, foretelling tempestuous times.

BOOK IV. *The second abduction of Helen.* Menelaus takes his guest to see his lands and sheepfolds. Up at the sheepfolds, Odysseus enlists a new companion, *Rocky* the goatherd. The two kings return to the palace; they dine. Menelaus presents his old comrade in arms with an idol of Zeus, god of hospitality. The next day, Odysseus carries off Helen. To pass the castle gate, they kill the guard.

BOOK V. *Arrival in Crete.* The pirate ship is again at sea. A storm drives it down to Crete. Odysseus' first act is to sell the golden idol of Zeus. On the mythical island, an exhausted civilization is in its death throes. The king, Idomeneus, has ascended the sacred mountain where he will go to the cave of the Bull-God to replenish himself with fresh power. On his return, in a public orgy in the palace halls, he will copulate with a woman-calf: the divine power will be poured out among the people. Odysseus sets Helen on the throne of Idomeneus, like a new Wooden Horse: the "wily enchantress" will become the instrument of the castle-shaker, she will be the calf, will copulate with the Bull-King, and will drag him to his ruin.

BOOK VI. *The bull rituals at Knossos.* Both the nobility and the common people take part in the Bull Ritual. There is sport with the bulls. Krino, the king's daughter, is slain by the bull. Then the common people are driven out and the nobles abandon themselves to the orgy. Diktena, another of the king's daughters, makes love with Odysseus. A third princess, Phida, moon-struck, screeches like a bird of prey: she has plotted with a blond barbarian, the palace ironsmith, to rouse the slaves, to tear the king from the throne. The orgy ends. In the meantime, another barbarian has made love to Helen. The crafty Odysseus involves the conspirators in his own schemes. He is possessed by a longing for destruction: that, for the moment, is the command of "God."

BOOK VII. *The conspiracy to destroy Knossos.* Odysseus has made up his mind to burn the palace of Knossos. "God" can dwell no longer with the doomed king and his barren lords. A new civilization will be born from the downtrodden people and the fair-haired barbarians. Odysseus divides the work of destruction among his companions. He includes Helen in the secret. Summer passes, winter also passes. The palace is gaily decorated for the Festival of Spring: it is like a sacrificial beast.

BOOK VIII. *The destruction of Knossos.* The king and the nobility cele-brate spring in the halls of the palace. Night falls. The conspirators put out the lights, kindle the fires. The tread of the barbarians arriving from the direction of the sea is heard. The palace slaves rise in revolt. Idomeneus is slain by the hand of his daughter Phida. A Negro bodyguard transfixes her with his lance. Day breaks. The ruins smoke. Odysseus summons his com-panions to depart. He puts Hardihood, his barbarian comrade, on the throne, as he had promised. He buries Phida and Captain Clam, who had been killed in the skirmish at the harbor. He bids farewell to Helen, who is with

LIBRARY
STATE TEACHERS COLLEGE
WAYNE, NEBRASKA

child by the barbarian. With his remaining companions (Kentaur, Orpheus, Granite and Rocky) he sets sail for Egypt, taking the Princess Diktena with him. They land. What is their aim? To reach the source of the Nile! This is the sudden inspiration of their leader. But Diktena is useless in their new enterprise. Odysseus is soon to abandon her on the shore.

BOOK IX. *The decadent empire of the Egyptians.* From a blind man's song they learn of the suffering of the workers. They sail up the Nile, pass a necropolis, and arrive at Heliopolis. Odysseus sees in his sleep a dead Pharaoh (Amenophes IV), who seems to command him to free him from the tomb: a grave robbery follows. Next day, while sailing, he throws their booty into the river, lest their souls be seduced by wealth. Orpheus makes them think of Helen: at that moment she is giving birth to the blond barbarian's son, symbol of the crossing of the two civilizations. Odysseus cries: "Hunger is a mighty goddess too!" Till now, Beauty (Helen) has stimulated their imagination. From now on, they will be guided by Hunger—that is, by the longing for social justice. They reach the "holy city," capital of the kingdom. The young Pharaoh is wasting away in his palace. The people of the crowded city take no notice of Odysseus and his crew: hunger devours them. Their leader leaves his companions for a few days in order to seek out a solution by himself.

BOOK X. *Rebellion in Egypt.* The workers revolt in Egypt. Their leaders are "the savage phantom of hunger" and a Jewess called Rala (Rachel). Odysseus is involved in the rising. He is wounded, thrown into jail. There his companions are Rala, Hawkeye the worker, Scarab the peasant, and Nile the revolutionary. Odysseus had helped the revolutionaries, not because he believed in their cause but because he was prompted by an inner voice. The young Pharaoh is sunk in dejection. He brings Rala and Odysseus from the prison, hoping that they will cheer him up. He sets them free. The captain returns to his ship. In the meantime, Rocky and Granite have fled. The fair-haired barbarians from the north have now reached Egypt. Pharaoh sets out with his army to attack them. Odysseus sails downstream to be present at the war.

BOOK XI. *Revolution and defeat in Egypt.* Pharaonic civilization is also in its death throes. The fresh-blooded barbarians must build up a new civilization. Odysseus becomes a "herald of God" and sides with the barbarians. Pharaoh's forces attack. Rala allows herself to be trampled to death. The invaders are overwhelmed. Odysseus and his companions (among them

Granite, who has rejoined them) are taken prisoners. Prison. They await death. From a piece of wood Odysseus carves the mask of his god, "The Fighter." Pharaoh again summons him. Odysseus puts on the mask of the god and dances a frightful miming dance. The king is terrified: he had seen in a dream the same horrible head as that carved by Odysseus. He allows Odysseus to leave Egypt and to take whoever he wishes with him. Odysseus feels reborn, as if he had come back from Hades. A new purpose is revealed to him: to take his companions far south and to found an ideal City-State.

BOOK XII. *The flight out of Egypt.* On his exodus from the land of slavery, Odysseus takes with him only those who have transgressed the great commandments. Their first act is to eat the raw meat of two buffaloes. With both hands, Odysseus raises the mask of his god and proclaims his vision of a city which they will all build together. Hunger and thirst in the desert. The company mutinies. Later, they fight with a Negro tribe and take their village. The black king, who is, like the Pharaoh, also in his decline, makes Kentaur his son-in-law. Odysseus' companions, young and old, give themselves up to eating and drinking, and the Negro king plans to put them to the sword. The wily Odysseus senses this, gathers his band and leaves with all those who hear his call. That night, round the fire, he describes his god to his chief warriors.

BOOK XIII. *Through dark Africa to the source of the Nile.* Rocky escapes from cannibals by performing a vigorous dance. He comes to a large village, where he is made king. Meanwhile, Odysseus' band, having passed through desert and jungle, also comes to a village. Odysseus sends Orpheus to "sell God" to the Negroes and to ask for victuals. The lightheaded piper falls a victim to his own game: he begins worshiping the wood which he himself has carved as a god. Odysseus fails to bring him to his senses and abandons him. A young leopard cub, given Odysseus by Granite, endears herself to him with her play. The band reaches Rocky's kingdom. Odysseus greets Rocky in his palace and tries to get the king to rejoin him. But Rocky does not follow: he stays where fate has placed him, to bring "freedom and light to the blacks." The band reaches the source of the Nile. Odysseus retires for seven days and nights on the mountain in order to meditate on the City-State he is to found and on its laws.

BOOK XIV. *Odysseus communes with God.* Odysseus ascends to a mountain top, accompanied only by the leopard cub. Stage by stage his consciousness rises from the ego to the race, to mankind, to the earth itself. He is granted a vision of God as a flame penetrating the universe. He is now ready to build the city to guard the flame. But a lean serpent, Temptation, rises in his mind and mocks him for not yet having set to work. The city must be built with stone and wood! Odysseus makes a first model in mud and pebbles.

BOOK XV. *They build the ideal city*. Odysseus comes down from his retreat. In the meantime his two chief warriors, Kentaur and Granite, have quarreled. They have split the people into two parties. But Odysseus is to save them all, even against their will. He lays the foundations of the city. He sacrifices six cocks and six hens—the twelve gods of Olympus—and buries them there forever. Every evening, after the day's work, the leader instructs his people about his God. Slowly he formulates his decrees in his mind. A terrible God, inhuman decrees. The ideal of the City-State is that the son should surpass his father. At the same time, Odysseus ordains communal festivals, continues the initiation of the people into his ascetic—that is, into Kazantzakis's own (*The Saviors of God*)—and carves his Ten Commandments on the city walls. The city is completed, the laws are laid down. Inauguration is to be at the full moon. But there are bad signs. Nature is preparing some terrible event. Rocky arrives. He has sensed the calamity and has hastened to be at his leader's side.

BOOK XVI. *Odysseus becomes a renowned ascetic*. The volcano which rises above the city erupts. There is fiery rain, an earthquake. So that the walls will not crush Odysseus, Kentaur props up the lintel with his shoulders and is himself crushed. The next day, Odysseus searches among the ruins for his other companion, Rocky, whom he had set at the city gate to tell people what path to take in their flight. He finds only a charred lump. He is overwhelmed by despair. He sends Granite off with the band, and he himself enters on his second retreat, entirely alone. His asceticism purifies him from matter, the odor of sanctity which he gives out draws throngs of pilgrims to him. But his words terrify them: there is neither God, virtue, nor justice! There is neither Heaven nor Hell! Odysseus reaches the height of his hopeless autonomy.

BOOK XVII. *Divertissement: The drama of life*. Odysseus has attained "total freedom": all things are dreams, the mind gives birth to them for a moment, then "it blows and all vanishes." Now Odysseus can "play." His mind creates figures of every sort. He retains five of them and involves them in a dramatic action, beyond good and evil. He blows, his creations vanish.

Odysseus salutes his mind, "the Great Master of Ceremonies," which has freed him from unconfessed desires. His pain is lightened by the play of his mind. A new day dawns. Cleansed, he starts to descend. He feels that his mind is purified, that the world is the creation of his own eyes. Thought and action are reconciled within him.

BOOK XVIII. *The prince and the prostitute.* Odysseus travels southward. Death appears before him like a great fly, a "black night-moth."[112] Odysseus beholds Greece in a dream. Temptation urges him to commit suicide, but he resists. A caravan arrives one day at dawn. It bears the Prince Motherth (a prefiguration of Buddha), who expects to hear the word of salvation from the lips of the "great ascetic" (Odysseus). Motherth is incurably tormented by the knowledge of death: why are we born to feed the worms? Odysseus does not resign from life because he must die. Death is the salt of life. Prince and ascetic enter a city. A famous courtesan, Margaro, entertains them in her gardens. Odysseus' world-view is compared with that of Motherth-Buddha. Margaro is fascinated by Odysseus' words. Even though life is a shade, she will enjoy it until her eyes are closed. Odysseus continues his journey alone.

BOOK XIX. *The hermit's avid hand.* In the center of Odysseus' forehead a "third eye" grows. Death reappears, but the great wanderer asks to be given time to reach the sea, to build his last ship, his "coffin." On the way he meets a hermit, who also questions him about the way of deliverance: his virtue has not given him rest, and if he were to live again he would take the path of life from the start. The hermit dies in Odysseus' arms; he stiffens, but his hand remains open. It closes only when Odysseus fills it with a lump of earth. The much-tormented wayfarer comes to a populous city. A black singer squats in the shade, singing about "Captain Elias": a king's son, Prince Elias, chose song as his crown, but his lyre would not play until he had dipped it in the blood of his seven sons. The black singer had seen Prince Elias redeemed, singing or keeping silence on the mountain. Odysseus approaches: "He whom you saw was I. But my spindle did not spin what you sang."—"And what does your life matter to me, ascetic? I could have sung my own suffering!" Odysseus makes as if to embrace the proud singer (who is none other than Kazantzakis himself).

BOOK XX. *The impractical idealist, the hedonist, and the primitive man.* Farther on, Odysseus encounters Captain Sole (the double of Don Quixote), and rescues him from some Negroes who are about to roast him. Odysseus

[ 71 ]

salutes in his person a "madness equal to his own"; but he rejects his view of life. Later, he finds himself in the tower of a nobleman who embodies a hedonistic theory of decadence: to sip like a bee at everything but not to commit the soul. Odysseus confronts him with his burning love of life. Below, night falls in a thickly wooded ravine. He has a nightmare: he sees an old man being slain and eaten by his sons, who want to possess his wives. Odysseus shakes the frightful vision from his head and cleanses himself in a pool of water. The phantoms of night vanish in the light of day.

BOOK XXI. *The gentle Negro fisher-lad.* Odysseus at last reaches the sea. In a port tavern he hears for the first time of the aurora borealis from an old sea-wolf. He desires to die standing beneath this splendor of the heavens. A procession is passing outside the tavern: the blacks are honoring a new god, brought to them by some Cretans: it is Odysseus himself, who has coursed like a divine fire through their island. Odysseus is seized with hunger; he starts to beg. Old Dame Goody, a prostitute, gives him two pomegranates. It is autumn. He decides to cut timbers in the forest for his ship. He builds his hull. One day some fishermen nearby are drawing in their nets. A virgin fisher-lad (prefiguring Christ) speaks to them of a Heavenly Father and teaches them of love and meekness. Odysseus approaches, opposing his own world-view to that of the new prophet. They part. A little later, he launches his boat. Just as he is setting off, Dame Goody brings him all the pomegranates of her garden.

BOOK XXII. *Odysseus sails toward the South Pole.* He is in absolute solitude: "Mighty, free happiness!" The sun gradually vanishes in mist, the day shortens, the currents grow stronger. The aurora borealis. Exaltation! The same night, his boat is smashed on the rocks. Odysseus lands and reaches a village glittering in the night. He spends the winter with its inhabitants. Ice, hunger, cosmic terror. "Do not kill me, my God!" is their prayer. Spring comes. Odysseus launches a new boat, made of sealskin. The people of the village joyfully set out on sleighs for their summer quarters. From the sea, Odysseus watches them strung out across the snow. Suddenly the white plain splits in two, villagers and sleighs are swallowed. God has killed them. Odysseus by now knows that man sails on the waters of despair, with Death as captain.

BOOK XXIII. *Odysseus blesses life and bids it farewell.* The poet begs the Sun to take Odysseus into its embrace. The Sun laments for him, Death seats himself on the prow of the boat, opposite the captain. Memories crowd the

mind of Odysseus: sieges, shipwrecks, cities built and destroyed, women.
. . . A full life: he could not have wished a better! A dream lightens his
mind: birds, beasts, stars, great thoughts, spirits come, wave upon wave, to
bid him farewell. Death vanishes from the prow. Odysseus folds his arms
and lets the current take him. Till now his body has held the elements reconciled within itself: it is time now for them to separate from each other. He
takes leave of them and praises them: earth, water, fire, air, and finally, Mind,
the great Master Mason who has mingled them all. An iceberg passes before
Odysseus: "This is the white elephant which shall bear me to Hades!" He
jumps from his skiff and clambers up the crystal wall. He is unarmed and
naked. The sun laments for him, the sea sings his dirge. The "great athlete,"
like a dying lamp, sends out a final ray of light: "O faithful and beloved,
O dead and living comrades, come!"

BOOK XXIV. *The death of Odysseus.* His comrades, living and dead, hear
the call. Kentaur, Orpheus (still alive), Captain Sole (on the point of death
himself), Hardihood (killed on the throne of Crete), Dame Goody and
Margaro, Rocky (mounted on a white elephant), Granite (mighty king in
Africa), Helen of Sparta (who has assumed the appearance of a twelve-year-
old girl), the old ascetic who had wasted his life, Diktena, Krino (mounted
on the bull which slew her), Captain Clam and Phida. As Odysseus uttered
his last cry, Motherth-Buddha was also in the throes of death, among his
disciples in a monastery. An eagle seizes him in its claws and sweeps southward. Rala takes the road which the bird has shown her. With her goes a
shadow, the young fisher-lad who preached of love. The "caravan of shades"
is seated on the iceberg. All the things Odysseus had loved come, borne on
clouds: fruits, plants, lyres. Rocky's elephant, Krino's bull, Odysseus' dog
and leopard cub all assemble on the iceberg. Then the three mythical ancestors—Tantalus, Prometheus and Heracles—settle themselves in the center
of the "vaporous deck" like masts. Finally, Odysseus summons Temptation,
who also appears. The iceberg moves like a mist. The "song of all return"
is heard. Dematerialization. Odysseus' mind makes a leap and frees itself
from "its last cage, that of its freedom."

EPILOGUE. The poet invokes the Sun once more. The Sun weeps, seeing
his beloved vanishing "like a dwindling thought."

The *Odyssey* is both direct and indirect evidence for Kazantzakis' personality. The way in which the poet regards the world is the direct evidence; the figure of Odysseus is the indirect. Kazantzakis has indeed filled the poem with the most important events of his life, he has allowed his instinctive reactions to reveal themselves. He has tried to set in order his intellectual experience and at the same time to express his convictions about the great themes of human thought. The *Odyssey* is a *summmum*.[113] It is also a self-curing of inhibitions, a journey toward complete liberty. On the other hand, the figure of Odysseus, although indeed it cannot be identified with that of the poet, is a "parallel" of the character we have described. To show that this is in fact the case, it is enough to remark that Odysseus' whole world-view is contained in Kazantzakis' *The Saviors of God*.

Proof of these assertions should perhaps be given. Before commenting on the character of Odysseus, I will enumerate certain traits common to the poet and his creation. Both Kazantzakis and Odysseus are molded more by the movement of their own thought than by outside events. They do not like to be conscripted, and they very rarely are; they sacrifice human happiness to their higher destiny; they are continuously conscious of the presence of "God" and they identify him with the primordial force which drives man to surpass himself; they burn with the desire for action and suffer from the irony of things; both have a mania for far places and wish to taste all earth's fruits; they are inspired by the heroes of the past and are jealous of their exploits; they live at times like hermits, persistently searching for a satisfactory view of the world and man; they look on poetic creation as one of the principal means of deliverance; they undertake things beyond their powers; they know that the mystery of the universe is not to be resolved by logic and yet they worship Mind, the Master Mason; they seek total fulfillment—to reach their limits, and to leave only the lees to death; they absorb the ideas of their time and master them with a personal intellectual discipline; they are detached from human concerns and resolutely, even cruelly, sacrifice beings and objects to the struggle; they apply rigid standards even to their friends; they affirm opposites and despise the coward and the conformist; they spurn social conventions, which weaken creativeness and originality, and they stimulate their sensibility in the cosmic vortex; they transcend the erotic instinct and dissolve sensible reality itself with their thought; they attribute mystic significance to the dreams of sleep and to waking premonitions; they train themselves in solitude—this is the "fundamental passion of their being." They keep their eyes open before the dazzling sights of the world, but consider nature to be indifferent, if not hostile, to man. They are heartened rather than discouraged by the pessimistic understanding of the universe, and they oppose an insatiable appetite for life to the absurdity of death. They grasp sensible and abstract things as a unity, like primitive men; they are impelled forward by their own nature and by their devotion to the One to ever greater isolation. They act disinterestedly, for the sake of the struggle and not for finite ends; they profess a fire-worshiping theory, which reconciles extreme pessimism with indomitable heroism; they measure themselves against the great spiritual leaders, with the aim of realizing, if not a new religion, at least the sense of absolute freedom. They live an intense and resolute life, are restless, and have the mentality of the besieged. They struggle without God, and gaze haughtily at the ultimate Nothing, but often they behave like desperadoes.

Some of these themes I shall now develop, not only as proofs of the parallelism of Kazantzakis and Odysseus, but more as pointers to the specific psychology of the hero. I shall begin with a preliminary remark. The *Odyssey* covers a considerable period of time, crowded with important events: from Odysseus' return to Ithaca up to his death. To this period must be added the ten years at least of recollections which Odysseus relates to his family. In such a long period, the mythical hero changes: it would be a mistake to describe him as though there were no development. On the contrary, the protean vitality of his nature must be stressed. But for reasons of method, and so that the reader may grasp the significance of the hero's mental development, I shall define its principal phases.

In the first rhapsodies, Odysseus experiences the world through the senses and is driven to action by the sight of phenomena: his attitude is *aesthetic* and its symbol is Helen of Sparta. Even when he performs deeds of world-wide significance, such as the burning of the palace at Knossos, our hero is not committed—his soul is still detached. His acts have the disinterestedness (and the irresponsibility) peculiar to youth. But from the moment he sets foot on the soil of Egypt, human suffering touches his heart. He still remains uncommitted, but he lets the will of history direct him. The demon of hunger becomes his guide. He takes part in a workers' revolt and in an invasion of barbarians, both aimed at the destruction of a decadent dynasty. His "aesthetic" attitude is at an end: ". . . but now man's soul has soared above your beauty, Helen!" (III, 1203). The *ethical* phase is traced: Odysseus concerns himself with the relationships of phenomena. Indeed, from the time when he beholds Death, in Pharaoh's prison, he is completely reborn. He is drawn toward constructive work: to build a city-state, to decree new laws, to put forth roots. But earth swallows up his state. Heaven's fury kills two of his companions. Odysseus is thrown into despair, turns entirely toward himself, cutting himself off from the world. His attitude may now be called *metaphysical*: only the essences of things now interest him. These three successive phases—which, according to Kierkegaard, are the only ones possible for man—finally bring Odysseus to *absolute freedom*.[114] Odysseus, freed, devotes himself temporarily to art. But the last rhapsodies of the poem are equivalent to a *study of death.*

The world-view which directs and inspires the action of the "reborn" Odysseus is continued by and large, as I have stated, in *The Saviors of God.* The whole of Book XIV (Odysseus' retreat) transposes into action and images—into poetic diction, that is to say—the philosophical content of the *The Saviors of God* up to the chapter entitled "Action." The remainder of the text—from "Action" to the concluding "Credo" —is itself transposed into Books XV and XVI (The Action of Odysseus). At the same time, fragments of the *The Saviors of God* are to be found in all the books of the *Odyssey.* Here are a few examples. The world is a deceptive dream: Prologue, 68, VI, 1271–92; man "saves" God: VII, 233 *ff.*, XIII, 476–84; man must not enter the struggle until he hears God cry out to him for help: VII, 233 *ff.*, X, 212; God is without beginning, the mind does not know him: III, 477–79; God ascends from the mire to the light: V, 588–634; God calls for liberation in every particle of matter, and man in liberating God from his prison at the same time sets his own soul free: VII, 819–35; the social class which frees God is different in every period: VII, 977–85; Good and Evil are primeval powers, equal in the sight of God: VIII, 771–72; God is not an abstract thought but the product of our bowels: VIII, 847-48; God and the beast fight in every man: IX, 387-94; to cleanse the world with fire is our great duty today: XI, 238; in our own times, God is an outraged worker: XI, 892.... The sole difference between the world-view of Odysseus and that of the *The Saviors of God* in its first form (1927) lies in the concluding Credo of the latter: the hero of the *Odyssey* (1938) finally reaches a position of total nihilism. This difference, as we shall see below, is due to the development of Kazantzakis' thought.[115]

Odysseus lives between a civilization that is dying and one that is about to be born. Both the poet and his creation are well aware of this. In the very first rhapsody, the world-wanderer conveys this somber knowledge to the sedentary Telemachus:[116]

My son, on shores and islands far away still smoke
luxurious palaces, still groan their slaughtered kings;
our people have grown haughty, wars have smudged their hearts,
they rage to cut down man's most venerated peaks;
I see the scales of fate now tottering in the balance.

(I, 167–71)

This theme (popular revolt) recurs several times in the course of the first rhapsody. Another theme is interwoven with it: man has discovered "black bronze" (iron) and has forged arms of the hard metal. Later, a third theme is introduced: the fair-haired barbarians press down from the north. The poetic elaboration of these three themes is colored by two different philosophies of history: Marx's dialectic of history and Spengler's theory of historic comparative morphology. The rising of the people in Ithaca, and later in Sparta and Egypt, has the form—even if it is not clearly defined—of a class struggle. The themes "fall of the nobility," "discovery of iron," "descent of the barbarians" are treated as signs of a *fated* organic necessity.[117] The myth of the *Odyssey* is developed in the light of these two theories. The causal conception of historic events is evidently the weaker of the two: to live history as an immediate inner certainty is indeed more in accordance with the conditions of poetic creation. An old devotee of Bergsonism would not be in doubt about that.

The kingdoms of Sparta, Crete and Egypt all have common features of decay: the rulers live in dissipation, the people starve, one king is worn out, another prematurely aged. The three kingdoms are invaded

[ 77 ]

by the barbarians and are shaken by internal revolt. Odysseus passes through them, perceiving clearly by what fate they are visited:

"Blessed be that hour that gave me birth between two eras!

----------------------------------------------------------------------------------------

I see deep cliffs before us and dark streams behind;
we'll leap in darkness soon, and who knows where we'll land?"

(III, 742–45)

Odysseus' reactions to the spectacle of dying civilizations supply, in the final analysis, most of the psychological material of Rhapsodies I-IX. In Ithaca (Rhapsody I), Odysseus quells the rising of the people and hands over the rule to Telemachus, after telling him of the difficulties in store for him. At Sparta (Rhapsodies III-IV), he does not know whether to side with the king or with the people, and he finally chooses the king. In Crete (Rhapsodies V-VIII), he burns the palace of Knossos, but in his action is a certain indifference. In Egypt (Rhapsodies IX-XI), Odysseus, although his soul is not committed, does take part in the rising of the slaves and in the invasion of the barbarians. "God's will" has been revealed to him for the first time in the palace of Knossos: the time has come for "the contented, the satisfied, the sterile" to die. The barbarians and the outcasts "will liberate God." They will progress "all phallus and belly," they will reach the peak, "they'll eat, they'll drink, with heavy minds,"

"and then, my God, another Archer will spring on earth!
Our stock is strong! Don't be distressed, God, we shall free you!
'How long will this game last?' you ask. To the world's end!"

(VII, 983–85)

To Granite, who had spoken with contempt of the barbarians, Odysseus had replied:

"That's true, but the world's rotted and bears no other sprout;
I think all hope on earth now, brother, has gathered around
these barbarous loins and shaggy chests that swirl about us,
and thus God often wills, that broncobuster of men."

(XI, 274–77)

And when he had to choose a successor to the dead king of Crete, he did not hesitate to give the crown to a barbarian, his companion Hardi-

[78]

hood. Later, another of his men, Rocky, was to succeed to the throne of the effete king of an African kingdom, who was killed by his own magicians (XIII, 97–252).

A civilization perishes when the myth which holds it together dissolves. With savage delight, Odysseus sees the gods tottering on their pedestals, and himself gives them an extra push when the earthquake overthrows them. *God-slayer*: this is the epithet which the poet attaches to the hero's name throughout the poem. Menelaus had given Odysseus a golden idol of Zeus, patron-god of friendship. When the crafty man decides to abduct his friend's wife, the god descends terrifyingly while he sleeps, to dissuade him from the crime:

He foamed with fury at the lips, his thunderbolts
twisted and turned like scorpions in his monstrous hands.

(IV, 1258–59)

But Odysseus remains unmoved:

    "Unhappy creature of our hearts,
I pity your sad doom and harmless thunderbolts.
Should I but bend or move a little, or open my eyes,
poor orphaned child born of your fear, you'd fade in air!"

(IV, 1260–63)

No sooner has he landed in Crete than Odysseus sells the god to a peddler.
The open-eyed Cretans do not hold gods in greater esteem:

In their plush homes, the gods, demeaned to bric-a-brac,
cooped up like parrots in their cages of gold bars,
were hung in windows where with human voice they squawked
and cackled back those words which they were taught to say.

(V, 311–14)

The gods have died! Odysseus mocks their death. When he digs the foundations of his city—which is to guard Flame, the symbol of the new God—he sacrifices over the pit six cocks and six hens (the twelve gods of Olympus) and he buries them in the cornerstones forever.

Lest there should be any doubt about the origin of the gods, the poet devises the episode of the Flute-player in Rhapsody XIII. The Flute-player, Orpheus, the moonstruck member of the crew, carves a god in wood, but forgets to give it a head. It does not matter—that it has a fat belly is enough! The Flute-player shoulders the piece of wood and sets off to "sell God" to the Negroes. But the god starts working miracles. The blind see again, the lame dance. The Flute-player himself falls a victim to his own invention, kneels down and worships the idol. This incident gives Odysseus the chance to revile human credulity:

"Piper, wake up, an evil dream has poisoned your brain!
What shame to worship wood! Open your cross-eyes, see,
this is that same doomed belly you hacked but yesterday.

----------------------------------------------------------------------

Orpheus, think well on man's nobility, his freedom!"

(XIII, 723–25, 734)

In the same frenzy, Odysseus rails at every kind of taboo. The men he takes with him on his new wanderings are the dregs of society: a barbarian, a sea-wolf, a glutton, a half-wit, a fugitive from justice. Their first exploits in Ithaca are such that the sorceresses cast spells to keep their leader in check (II, 939-88). No sooner do they make a second landing than they steal, seduce and kill. Odysseus himself tramples on honor and hospitality and later becomes a mocker of the gods, a pimp, an incendiary and a grave-robber. When he gathers his forces for the exodus in the desert (Rhapsody XII), he enlists men from the stake and the gallows: murderers, robbers, perjurers, pregnant harlots and bastards. He traces a line on the sand with his sword:

He who has never killed or stolen or not betrayed
or murdered in his mind, let him now rise and leave.

(XII, 73–74)

Odysseus rejects every form of social life and domestic morality. He demands that his companions cut themselves radically from the dead myth: *Tabula rasa!* They will have to start from zero if they are to attain to the new myth which their leader affirms. All they have hitherto worshiped are idols.

Rhapsody XII (the exodus) is terrifying. The band that Odysseus leads into the desert is a herd of desperadoes—exactly as Stefan Zweig has described them. The pitiless choice is made: the hungry wolves are gathered. Before setting out, they bathe in the river to wash away "slavery's mire": "Our God now seeks to pierce new flesh, and lie en-sheathed." An uncontrollable feast on raw meat follows, frenzy masters both herd and shepherd. "Hold me, my lads, don't let me fall! God stalks and groans!" cries Odysseus in the midst of a daemonic seizure: "He felt God's spirit pour within him like thick flesh." But for God to be wholly revealed, there has to be a second choice. The desert itself makes it, with its hunger, exhaustion and tormenting mirages. Odysseus be-comes savage during these trials. For his people who leave their bones in the desert he feels no pity, only disgust:

"I want your stench no more, for I hear clamoring wings,
and in my brains my brothers rise, the famished crows!"

(XII, 460–61)

Tender-hearted Kentaur dares answer his master. He calls him "dragon," "uncompassionate" and "slayer":

"Slayer, you've swallowed mankind whole in your cruel chest
till in your entrails' root only a wild beast moves."

(XII, 474–75)

Odysseus has indeed reached a point of complete inhumanity in the double sense of the word: he is cruel to men and cut off from men:

and his mind moved and took untrodden hidden paths
and pushed his secret thoughts toward steep man-eating cliffs.

(XII, 640–41)

At last, as a result of his trials in the desert, Odysseus achieves a new ethic:

"May he be cursed for whom both sorrow or joy suffice,
may he be cursed who smothers not in mankind's virtues;"

(XII, 1232–33)

"Only great hunger feeds my god, and great thirst slakes him."

(XII, 1237)

The canons that have been revealed to him, "the commandments of the terrible god," Odysseus will one day carve on "skull and stone" and will brand them on bodies with "a flaming iron." He has visions indeed of building a city-state and of ruling it with these inhuman laws.

The desperadoes pass through desert and jungle and reach the sources of the Nile. Odysseus ascends the mountain to seek out the new god and then, like another Moses, to bring the tables of his law to his people. As we said, his religion had been formulated in *The Saviors of God*. Rhapsodies XIV, XV and XVI are the confirmation of this latter, both in a theoretical and a practical sense. After the retreat on the mountain, action follows: Odysseus builds the city he has visualized. But the earthquake shatters it and it is consumed by fiery rain. Odysseus then despairs utterly. He abandons his companions forever and dedicates himself to his second retreat. The fruit he reaps this time is a lump of smoldering ash:

"When you have purified your heart of gods and demons,
of virtues great and small, of sorrows and of joys,
and only Death's great lighthouse stays, the glowing mind,
then rise, my heir, and sternly cleave your mind in two:
below will lie your last great foe, rotten-thighed Hope,
above, the savage Flame, no light, no air, no fire,
scornful and superhuman in man's hopeless skull."

(XVI, 1176–82)

Odysseus again becomes a desperado. The void left in his soul by the fall of the idols is filled temporarily by the Fighting God. The destruction of the city leaves him empty once more. This time the void, instead of being filled, is *deified*.

The fall of the idols had to take place before the new god could be drawn from the void. At the same time, it cures Odysseus (and the poet) of all inhibitions and frees him from the disgust he felt for the "satisfied and barren." The spirit of Odysseus belongs to the humble, to the hungry, and particularly to the outcast. He blesses the courtesan Margaro, whom he meets after his second retreat, and justifies her erotic struggle (XVIII, 1165–84). Further on, when he bids farewell to the world, he himself, a king who had embraced goddesses, takes to begging. He passes through the respectable neighborhoods and knocks at the doors of the brothels. His "painted sisters" mock his white hair, but an old whore takes pity on him and offers him two pomegranates. This same woman, Dame Goody, hastens down to the beach from where Odysseus sets out on his last voyage, and brings him all the pomegranates in her garden:

"Ah, dear Dame Goody, I never hoped for such good treasure!"

---

He gently touched the thin knees of the much-kissed whore:
"Dame Goody, if a god exists to pay a man's good deeds,
he'll sit you throned on high beside his greatest warriors . . ."

(XXI, 1385, 1392–94)

Human virtue is embodied in this "limping, white-haired, one-toothed"
whore. A despised woman calls out the last farewell from land as
Odysseus sets out on his journey to death: she too symbolizes the contempt for established morality, the scorn for respectability.

Irresponsibility and lack of self-interest characterize the acts of the
desperado: neither morality nor usefulness guides him:

but as the wasp clings to the grape and sucks it dry,
so did the comrades seize and glean each fleeting hour.
Where they were going or toward what goal or what they wished
and what sword hung above them ready to cut them down
they scorned to ask themselves a moment even in thought.

(III, 560–64)

A dream (III, 273 *ff.*) makes Odysseus set course for Sparta: the beauty
of the world beckons him. What, later, makes him support Menelaus in
quelling the insurrection of his people? Perhaps a residual feeling for
royal solidarity, perhaps a subconscious desire to compensate for the
injury which he is shortly to do him. But one such action is not habit-
forming:

"and if I were here—then, who knows?—I might not raise
my hand to save you from the serpent's mouth, dear friend,
for my soul forges forward, spurning loves and virtues."

(III, 1241–43)

The time has come for Odysseus to carry off Helen:

He climbed the staircase softly to the women's rooms
and smiled with cunning pride at his own shifting will,
for he was free, he knew, to change fast fortune's wheel
at the last moment even, or stop at any stair . . .

(IV, 1287–90)

[ 83 ]

But where is he shortly to sail with Helen?

As the world-wanderer held the tiller, he recalled
far-distant shores, and wondered where to set his course.

(V, 101–2)

A storm drives them to Crete. Well and good. But why should Odysseus burn the palace there?

"Nor enmity nor friendship pulls me toward the castle;
my vacillating spirit is armed to right and left
for a sweet friendly feast or the red sword of war."

(V, 685–87)

One night, Odysseus hears a "murmuring voice" calling him: "Odysseus!" It is the voice of "God." Odysseus makes a vow to him: "I shall save you!" This means: "I shall burn the palace of those who are grown effete!" The Savior of God does not even wait for the fire to go out before he sets off for Egypt. There he risks his life in a social revolution. One would have thought that this time he would really have committed himself. But no:

"Whatever it is, I like the voice, it wakes my blood,
and I don't ask if it's true or just, and I don't care,
I hear my heart alone and do what it commands."

(X, 557–59)

Odysseus' comrades follow in his tracks. If their blood boils, they will bleed themselves for relief (XI, 246–47). Once Granite separates from the others and takes the road toward the north: "nor knew toward where I went nor did my mind once ask" (XI, 226). When the band stays for a time in the kingdom of Rocky—the other comrade who broke away without knowing that Fate had decreed that he should become a king—Odysseus in his cups confesses the perpetual non-attachment of his soul:

"When I was born, they say, it was not day or night
but that the black and the white hours both gaped wide,
and that's why I've a wind-chart in my breast for heart,
why each new step I take is a new road each moment,

[ 84 ]

and why my every thought is a splendid star that pours
and flashes with green-azure flames in the vast dark."

(XIII, 1216–21)

At another critical moment, Odysseus says:

"Ah, all things merge in kinship in our final hour;
the down of a small wing is balanced in the mind
and weighs as much as the most glorious realm on earth.
What joy! No man is paid for life's fatiguing trek."

(XXIII, 407–10)

Lack of self-interest, lack of morality, non-attachment, the transmuta-
tion of all values!

It is not surprising that solitude is one of Odysseus' chief experiences.
Odysseus is born to be alone: he does not care for company. He has given
up his family, has once and forever forgotten them; he uses his companions as instruments for the carrying out of tasks which he is not
able—or does not wish—to undertake; he has denied woman: most of
his caresses during the years we have followed his course are reserved
for a leopard cub. He is the Lone Man. He turns away from every form
of regulated life—family, society, the church. He hates contentment,
peace and comfort. During his last days, when he bids farewell to the
elements, he confesses to Fire: "I don't love man, I only love the flame
that eats him!" (XXIII, 884). With such a nature and such a world-
view, Odysseus could not avoid experiencing loneliness in all its forms.
At sea, he experienced the loneliness of the shipwrecked sailor (I, 1052–
58) and among the crowds on land, the loneliness of a king (I, 1212).
He sought refuge in solitude, sometimes to still his heart's storm and to
put his thoughts in order, sometimes to rouse his being and to commune
with God. He plucked all the fruits of loneliness, from the releasing
tears of unspoken suffering and unspoken joy (XIV, 897) to the final
contemplation of Nothing. His struggles, on land and at sea, are accompanied by an endless consideration of the subjects of solitude and
freedom; and they lead him finally to a state of nakedness in both
the literal and metaphorical sense of the word: Odysseus on the iceberg,
in the "white breathless silence," has neither clothing, weapons, nor
hope. He is completely alone and quite naked. He even seizes the down
which falls on his nakedness from some passing bird and flings it upon

[ 85 ]

the waves (XXII, 51–52) : the image of total solitude must be complete. But, as sometimes happens in the *Odyssey*, this final image is suddenly reversed and its other side is revealed: a strange company of shades gathers on the iceberg, the largest and most friendly company the Lone Man has ever known. One cannot help but wonder whether the cause of this voluntary isolation was not perhaps a disappointed longing for the perfect fusion of souls, for total love.

Odysseus, in the final rhapsodies of the *Odyssey*—or, more exactly, after the destruction of his city-state—is called by the poet the "Ascetic." He is an ascetic because he struggles like a yogi and at the same time because he has retired from worldly things. It may be worth while to say a few words about his renunciation of sexual love. The Homeric Odysseus—who passes like a recollection through the tale told to his family by the world-wanderer (Rhapsody II)—had made many sacrifices to Aphrodite. His relations with Calypso and Circe were well known— relations which, according to his own story, he himself ended out of fear in the one case of becoming a god and in the other of becoming a beast. His meeting with Nausicaä, who personifies human happiness, never led to a closer tie, for Odysseus became alarmed at the power of this siren, the sweetest of them all. But his heart "had never gleaned such rooted Victory" (II, 428). Returning to Ithaca, Odysseus marries Nausicaä to Telemachus and thus, we may say, cures "by proxy" his repressed desire. His wife, Penelope, does not stir him even to a fleeting caress. But we must not think he is without desire because of this. While he is building his new ship, he invites the ship's carpenters to carouse with him a little each evening: "Kisses and wine belong by right to the hard worker" (II, 935). The company need no further encouragement: starting with a young girl, they soon turn to unprotected widows (II, 939–53). Odysseus does not appear to abstain from the revelry.

When later he confronts Helen of Sparta, his first reaction is to regard her as a spur to his ambition:

for this seductress drew him far from carnal wars
to the high valor of the mind, the peaks of passion.

(III, 671–72)

But when at night he lies in Menelaus' palace and smells the fruiting apple trees,

Then the man-slayer's mind was wounded and unhinged:
"So must her coffers smell of apples now," he thought,
"her clothes, her hair, her breasts kissed by so many men."

(III, 1291–93)

Later, when he has her at his mercy on the ship, his mind clouds and he is seized with the desire to cast his companions into the sea,

and he would lie on vine leaves, fondle her with pride,
and in her womb entrust a son that one day would surpass him.

(V, 163–64)

Odysseus is not to relinquish the Beauty of the World without struggle. He is to suffer deeply when he sees her in the arms of King Idomeneus or the fair-haired barbarian. He abandons her in Crete so that "she may fulfill her mission—to nourish, to transubstantiate in her womb the barbarian seed and to give birth to her son, Hellene. But Odysseus, of course, does not separate from Helen so easily: he leaves with the incurable bitterness a man always feels when he sees a beautiful woman in the arms of another, even though he has never sought to possess her. Helen was a warm body, not a fleshless idea," as Kazantzakis himself puts it.[118]

While he is in Crete, Odysseus takes part in the Bull Ritual—that is, in a Dionysiac orgy. He caresses the Princess Diktena, of the "thousand husbands," and finally copulates with her, while hundreds of couples lie around them in the moonlit open-air theater. His companion Hardihood cannot bear to see him in so abandoned a state:

"For shame! Your bright eyes, great sea-eagle, have grown glazed!"
The headstrong man's gall rose as he rebuked the smith:
"I may now taste unfearing the most deadly joys,
the most seductive sweets, for these can't conquer now."

(VI, 486–89)

Hardihood's rebuke seems to be approved by the poet (if not by Odysseus himself). Heaven regards the palace orgy with a stern eye:

the court dames sighed like nightbirds still on cooling stones,
and stars, unsullied and disdainful, passed above the earth.

(VI, 846–47)

[ 87 ]

The palace of Knossos is cleansed by "wind-nourished fire." The castle wrecker "like a lion climbed a salient rock, stretched out." (VIII, 469) Two young men see him up there alone and still boiling like a caldron.

"Brother, how can the wildfire in his roused heart die
since after so much blood he's not yet kissed a woman?"
They spoke, then rounded up five crisp young girls, and drove
toward their great leader that the male in him might cool,
but he frowned wrathfully ...

how many times he'd shamed his mind with suchlike fruit.
His mind now barked beyond such women and such joys.

(VIII, 506–10, 514–15)

Odysseus' change of heart will appear from now on in his behavior. True, he takes Diktena with him when he sails off to Egypt, and he does in fact lie with her again at night on the deck (VIII, 1126–31). But he soon leaves her, somewhere in the Nile delta, among the reeds, like Theseus leaving his Ariadne (VIII, 1330–35). Yet he does not cast her off without a pang:

Odysseus looked, and seeing not a soul in sight,
freely allowed his tears to trickle down his cheeks.

(IX, 18–19)

With this lament, Odysseus bids a final farewell to woman, as the new contests which he sets himself demand. At this point, his "aesthetic" life ends. During the "ethical" and "metaphysical" stage of his life, he remains chaste. The only female he is to touch—and that with his finger tips—is a Negro girl: he has at last crossed the Dark Continent and has reached the sea which is to bear him to his final ordeal; there, in a seaside tavern, he lightly caresses the black breasts of a whore seated on the knees of an old sailor:

"Let this be my last fondling of a woman's flesh!"[119]

(XXI, 380)

The poet does not leave us in any doubt of his opinion on the subject under discussion: woman kills the creative impulse, "and a home's honeyed bliss destroys a man's intent" (IX, 620). All the "leaders of souls" we meet in the poem—Buddha, Jesus, Don Quixote, the Lord of the Tower and even Prince Elias—are personifications of some great dedication or final knowledge, and, consequently, of a renunciation. Even Odysseus' companions—those who are conscious of responsibility —voluntarily renounce woman, like Hardihood, or seize and abandon her, like Granite:

—women are cooling water to drink and cast away—[120]

(XII, 1079)

The rest of the band abandon themselves to the flesh. But it will be a pitfall for them, in the second choice in the desert: all who do not answer the leader's summons remain ensnared in "the sweetness of the kiss"—that is, in the trap set for them by the black king (XII, 1050–1102).

The same rule applies to women: the woman who gives herself a lofty aim in life will renounce man. Krino and Phida, the Cretan princesses, respectively embody an ideal of virginity and a passion for vengeance: both die undefiled. The third woman possessed of a soul with lofty ideals is the revolutionary Rala. She allows herself to be trodden beneath the hoofs of Pharaoh's cavalry because she feels herself wavering between duty and love. It is worth noting that these three women repent the path of abnegation which they have taken. When Odysseus at the point of death cries, "O faithful and beloved, O dead and living comrades, come!" the three shades hasten as fast as they can to be present at his death, as the Twelve Apostles flew on clouds from the ends of the earth to be present at the dormition of the Virgin. On the way, they utter their lament to whomever they meet: should they ever return to earth, they would take another path and enjoy their youth (XXIV, 617–22, 721–22, 1136–40).

The overcoming of the sexual instinct is not dictated by any moral prohibition: the "poetics" of great enterprises demands it. It must moreover be observed that whereas the poem gives many examples of ascetic conduct, it is at the same time pervaded by an erotic atmosphere which here and there is positively lascivious. The reason is that the poet and his creation both burn with a violent love of life. No expression could convey adequately the direct sense of the titanic vitality of the characters in the *Odyssey*. The ascetic morality of some of them seems only to

[ 89 ]

emphasize the terrible struggle of god with the beast, of the spirit with the flesh. Kazantzakis himself writes: "For higher men, this struggle is inexorable, long, unceasing: God is a bird of prey with but one desire: to devour the flesh and to turn it into spirit. The flesh must be rich and powerful if god's victory is to be magnificent and perfect; for by this alone is the bird nourished."[121]

The long lament and the praise of woman in Rhapsody XXIII bears witness among other things to the richness and strength of Odysseus' flesh and to the erotic desire which he overcame. Odysseus lies in the little craft made for him from a seal's skin and allows the ocean current to bear him to his death. The whole "of his life's bloodstained campaign" passes through his memory: shipwrecks, sieges, earthquakes. He is suddenly seized with regret that there is no one to wish him good luck, no one to bid him farewell:

As he was speaking, mourners from his memory rose,
groups of lamenting women whose entranced eyes shone
like black, green, sea-blue stars within the ruined air,
each one with an entreaty on her firm-locked lips.
His heart remembered and rejoiced, took back its words,

-------------------------------------------------------------

All good, all progress which his mind had known on earth
he owed to maids alone, for they tore down all flesh!

-------------------------------------------------------------

Splendid are the mind's blazing lamps and the soul's flames,
wondrous the heart that battles with all azure shades
and pours out all its blood on earth to rise in spirit,
but all—gods, demons, laughter, tears and giddy thoughts—
swirl swiftly like a whirlwind, merge in one, then sink
and drown in the curved womb that lies supine and beckons;
it only is real, all else on earth are gaudy wings.

(XXIII, 420–55)

One may speak of contradictions in the soul of Odysseus. But these contradictions are consumed in the unity created by his burning love of life and by his passion to surpass human nature. Odysseus is undoubtedly inspired by the vitalistic theory adopted by the poet, in harmony with the spirit of his own age: "He absorbs the earth and the sky like the plane tree," as Claudel puts it;[122] he does not leave a single "earthly food" untasted.[123]

He's harvested the sea and all the joys of earth,
he's plucked their flower whose honeyed poisons choke the heart
and hung it on his ear, then sung and strolled toward Death.

(XXII, 15–17)

This is of course poetic exaggeration: man cannot exhaust the treasures of land and sea in his brief life. But he can spend himself to the last drop, so that when Death comes he finds only "the body's dregs":

The archer has fooled you, Death, he's squandered all your goods,
melted down all the rusts and rots of his foul flesh
till they escaped you in pure spirit . . .

(XXIII, 34–36)

A man wholly fulfilled has no complaints against life:

"All's well! I gaze with cheerful calm on all my roads
through earth and sea, on all my roads through every heart,
and if the fire and water that first shaped me merged
once more on earth, a second, third, or a tenth time,
I'd take the same roads once again, the same sharp arrow
would twang unsatisfied from my right breast forever!

-------------------------------------------------------------------

for the soul has no ending, nor can thirst be quenched."[124]

(XXIII, 481–90)

Odysseus' furious, gluttonous hunger could not be satisfied with one life. He had within him the insatiable heart of Tantalus (I, 1184–87). His chief characteristic (in the poet's view, his chief virtue) is *dissatisfaction* (IX, 688–91). No human action was ever enough to still his longing. There is no better illustration of this than his words after the burning of the Cretan palace: Odysseus overthrows a kingdom and, at that very moment, "sends a letter to Death":

"Death, castles do not fool me nor does plunder shake me,

-------------------------------------------------------------------

I've thrown the castle behind me now, and drive straight on!"

(VIII, 624–26)

To his companions, who have given themselves up to lust and greed, Odysseus says:

"Dear friends, you've had your fill of food and kisses now;
great is that joy which treads upon a crumbled castle
and roasts it like a partridge on the hearth of freedom,
but it's a greater and more difficult good to plunge
to the near shore once more and hear the oars of flight
beat foaming in your mind like two enormous wings.
Rise up, man's heart, that the whole world may rise with you!"

(VIII, 718–24)

On his last journey, when he has drunk the sea, Odysseus remembers Tantalus and greets him:

"O Tantalus, O great Forefather, blessèd curse,
O bottomless mouth, O hoping yet despairing heart,
O hunger by strewn tables, thirst by cooling streams."

(XXIII, 282–84)

But if one life does not satisfy Odysseus, he will increase the number with the lives of his companions, living thus six other lives "by proxy." Odysseus, according to the poet, is

like a huge octopus whose tentacles were all
his friends that now played, lashed, and spread on waves, on sand,
as he through many souls and bodies sucked at life.[125]

(XXI, 96–98)

He casts Captain Clam to certain death: through him he realizes extreme heroism (VII, 650–55). He crowns Hardihood, the fair-haired barbarian, king among the smoking ruins of Knossos, and gives him his political precepts (VIII, 851–80). Through Orpheus he lives the final subjection of the spirit to its own creation (XIII, 510 ff.), the supreme self-sacrifice through Kentaur (XVI, 243–64). Rocky, after he had ruled over the Negroes, is, like another sentinel of Pompeii, burned alive at the post where Odysseus has placed him (XVI, 199 ff. and 358 ff.).[126] Through this holocaust, Odysseus will once more appease his unconfessable remorse at his perpetual non-attachment. Finally, Granite replaces Odysseus in the leadership of the people he has abandoned (XVI, 408–11). Each companion is a branch. When Odysseus comes "to walk and bid the world farewell," the shadow cast by his body is like "a windmill's wings,"

and in his heart he carried all his precious friends.

(XXI, 24)

And when, after the final summons, he sees them gathered together on the iceberg, he welcomes them with the words:

"Forward, belovèd forms, small branches of my soul,
O mind's starved tentacles . . ."

(XXIV, 1269–70)

But the "many-faced" one has not been delivered through his companions alone. Molding the fates of Helen, Diktena, Rala and Margaro, he inspires new lives with his own soul. But he himself remains always "insatiable." When he has attained "complete freedom" and can form men and caravans out of air, he chooses five of his creations and launches them into a drama which he himself directs with his funereal flute:

The many-faced man spread his hands most tenderly
and felt his five dream-mortals formed on the firm ground
as though he'd brought five plowmen to plow up the earth,
five dappled oxen yoked to pull his daring dream.

(XVII, 285–88)

The great vitality of the poem derives, as we have seen, mainly from the energy of the titanic natures of Odysseus and his companions. There is no need to add that it is the poet who has given them their blood. But there is in the poem another source of vitality, and this is the *African spirit* which emerges here and there, either in the myth or in the elaboration of the themes. In the very first rhapsody (lines 595–710), the poet reveals a spirit foreign to the "sweet southern mood," to use Polylas' phrase.[127] A prehistoric breath, an equatorial temperature, suddenly scorches the Ionian island, rousing the poem's hero to a daemonic fever. This recurs with greater force further on, when Orpheus aboard the ship sings the song of the Worm (III, 86–181). This "insertion," probably taken from the anonymous treasure of African mythology, leaves one in no doubt of Kazantzakis' sympathy for the primitive world. Lastly, Odysseus' entry into the Dark Continent enables the poet to introduce directly into the work an imposing body of African legends, beliefs, rites and scenes: large and important parts of Rhapsodies XII, XIII, XIX and XX are derived from the African myths and songs collected by Leo Frobenius.

The vogue for Negro art in Western Europe before and after the First World War is well known. Primitive art brought the tired European into contact with an absolute. It revealed to him "subterranean" powers which Western art either could not or dared not express, in spite of the teachings of Freud. Kazantzakis, as we have seen, had a hereditary leaning toward the primitive—a leaning which he acknowledged on several occasions. The fashion of his time was propitious to such a leaning. Moreover, the theory of historic comparative morphology which he applied in the creation of the myth of the *Odyssey* allowed him to introduce those barbarous forms that, according to an organic necessity, succeed refined forms. Finally, Freudism—which, with the idea of the mortality of civilizations, was the chief intellectual experience of the epoch between the two World Wars—offered dark and convulsive material, hitherto either ignored or rejected, to the poet.

What this signifies can be better understood in the light of the "rhapsody of Rocky," with the murder of the old king and the enthronement of the new; of the "rhapsody of Prince Elias," with its terrible symbolism; and, lastly, of Rhapsody XX, with its phallic mythology and the frightful account of the father being eaten by his sons (lines 749–1295): so "dark and convulsive" is this incident that even Odysseus covers his eyes in order not to see it (XX, 1063). Unwillingly he becomes the spectator of things which do not even reach the threshold of waking consciousness: only a nightmare may draw them up from the darkness. The mind will master them at last, but not before they have filled it with terrors known for the first time:

and as the sun at daybreak sucks mists from the grass,
thus did the lone man's blazing eyes gulp down the huge
dark ghosts that rose from the damp earth to haunt his soul.
Then the earth cleared and the mind calmed, once more the pitch-
black portals of the bowels closed, and the dread demons

crouched howling in the sunless cellars of the mind
till the glad archer wiped his sweating chest in sweet relief.

(XX, 1289–95)

The African material assimilated by the poet allowed him to pour black blood into his verses and to handle themes which—though familiar in modern literature—could not have been included in the traditional form of the epic.

At this stage of our acquaintance with Odysseus, it will not be out of place to define his "God" more precisely. Odysseus, as we have seen above, set out in search of a new god when he had finished with the gods of the dead civilization. The god he met is that of Kazantzakis. Odysseus himself names God the "inconceivable, invincible Breath" which draws upward men and peoples, plants and beasts, gods and demons. Each time he is in a productive mood—has the desire for dangerous deeds or the urge to create—he believes that he either sees or hears God: God's essence is the unceasing struggle. God, however, is not almighty: God's comrade and fellow fighter is man. Whatever a man undertakes, as long as he undertakes it with heart and soul, "liberates" God. God is imprisoned in every particle of matter, is in peril in every doubtful battle. A countless host, from the humble potter molding a jug upon his wheel to Hercules slaying the lion, is struggling to "save God." According to the work that every man undertakes, the God who co-operates with him will be a laborer, a seaman, a warrior, or a builder. The forms of God cannot be numbered. Whatever springs from nothingness to life, whatever is whirled upward, is inhabited by God.[128]

The God who was to dwell in Odysseus' city-state was the Fighting God we have described. But after the destruction of the city, the god-slaying frenzy once more seizes Odysseus. He recalls the ultimate realities he has worshiped, considers the ruin he has suffered, and prods and threatens God (XVI, 1082–1104). As he speaks, so he acts. He strips the feathers from God's idol and treads it into the earth. At the height of his new freedom, the eternal god-fighter conceives God as a pure flame, and finally as total despair (XVI, 1108–94):

"No master-god exists, no virtue, no just law,
no punishment in Hades and no reward in Heaven!"

(XVI, 1241–42)

[ 95 ]

The wilderness. Inconsolable solitude. Exaltation of the individual. Man will not be redeemed by gods, but by the kindling of his own being:

"I've no more children, comrades, dogs, or gods on earth.
May they speed well and prosper, may winds fill their sails!
Enough! I want their breaths and their sweet swoons no more,
for I'm all ships, all seas, all storms, all foreign strands,
I'm both the brain-begotten god and the anti-god,
I'm the warm womb that gives me birth, the grave that eats me!
The circle is now complete, the snake has bit its tail."

(XVI, 1364–70)

Though he is "without desire, regret or hope," Odysseus later succeeds in defeating Temptation, who urges him to commit suicide because life has no further peak or flower to offer. He does not consider that he has actually reached the end: he enjoys the wilderness as a condition of absolute freedom. He mocks at those who seek or think they have found God and boasts that he knows the great secret:

by God is meant to hunt God through the empty air![129]

(XVIII, 1017)

At the same time, he has the presentiment that his thought will raise him to "an even higher peak." This is to be the contemplation of nothing. Even the union of the ransomed man with God is unreal: "Even this One is empty air!" (XVIII, 1208) Voyaging finally toward death, Odysseus concludes:

"What is this life, what secret yearning governs it?
There was a time I called its lavish longing God,
and talked and laughed and wept and battled by his side
and thought that he, too, laughed and wept and strove beside me,
but now I suddenly feel I've talked to my own shadow!"

(XXII, 409–13)

Fortified by the consciousness of Nothing, Odysseus is taken by the poet to meet the great leaders of souls, "Buddha," "Jesus" and "Lenin": the destruction of idols must not only purge the past; it must be extended into the future, until it embraces the "gods" which Kazantzakis himself has worshiped and renounced.[130] Odysseus' nihilism is compared with

[96]

Buddhism, Christianity and communism, and is shown to be a dogmatic as any other theology. During this comparison, not only the glacial aspect of this nihilism is revealed, but also what we may call its living aspect, its "Dionysiac pessimism." It may be observed, however, that Odysseus does not meet Kazantzakis' gods in the order in which the latter worshipped and rejected them. In the poet's spiritual history there was a coherence which led him to a personal comprehension of the world. Odysseus embodies this final comprehension, and consequently his successive meetings do not reflect his own evolution but serve to measure his wisdom against that of the others: they amount to a defense of a world-view.[131]

Odysseus first meets "Lenin" in the person of Nile (almost an anagram of Lenin), the Egyptian revolutionary also imprisoned by Pharaoh: his appearance and his revolutionary theory and practice leave us in no doubt of his identity.[132] A quarrel soon breaks out between Odysseus and Nile. The Egyptian is the herald of equality, a materialist, sure of his aims and methods, hostile to idealism and mysticism, one-sided and fanatical. Odysseus embodies Kazantzakis' "post-Communist" theory: God is not limited to justice and virtue; he is "an inhuman flame which burns in our black bowels." The avenging god of today is the "dreadful worker." "God spreads the enormous wing of good from his right side, the wing of evil from his left, then springs and soars" (XI, 737–38, 835–43, 892, 999–1015). Nile, naturally, jeers at such a theology and morality:

"The world, with brains like yours, grows wild, unpruned, unclipped,
but we don't spoil the earth with fondling, for we fight her,
and water all good things she bears, and kill all evil."

(XI, 1005–7)

Odysseus' meeting with Prince Motherth (Buddha) is more vivid and prolonged (XVIII, 840–1438). The two pessimistic world-views keep pace with each other until they reach their moral conclusions. Motherth preaches the renunciation of all things. Odysseus hurls himself headlong into life. The theory of heroic pessimism is presented as the antidote to death: "But I hold death like a black banner and march on!" (XVIII, 904) Odysseus finally sums up the relationship and divergence of the two theories in an apologue:

[ 97 ]

"I've heard it said that in old times two bosom friends
were cast in a dark slave-ship to be killed at dusk;
the first lost heart at once and his eyes sank in pits,
but his friend's sturdy spirit stood erect and gazed
on the blue sea and mountains, smelled the briny air,
tasted a cup of wine, possessed a lovely lass,
and moments passed like sated years as he caressed
the earth and life with his deep palm and said farewell.
Aye, king's son, both were souls, but who is worth your love?
Who can we say is a free soul, and who a slave?
Come, cast your judgment, prince! We're both in a slave-ship!"
                                                    (XVIII, 1355–65)

   "Jesus" appears last of all in the form of "a slender virgin lad with
flaming, fawn-like eyes." (XXI, 1130)[133] He teaches love, gratitude to
the Heavenly Father, and long-suffering. Odysseus draws near and hears
the prophet teaching his disciples: If someone strikes you on one cheek,
turn to him the other also. He immediately strikes "the unsuspecting lad
hard on his tingling cheek." And he replies: "O white-haired brother,
strike again to ease your heart!" Odysseus is not disarmed by the harmony between the prophet's conduct and his preaching. He arrays the
godless, hopeless, heroic view of the world against the youth's angelic
wisdom. No heaven awaits man, there is no God to comfort him:

"Good are your words of love, but my mind walks the earth
with a bold stride, alone, and has no need of balms."

--------------------------------------------------------------------

Then the boy's gentle voice was heard with a sweet sadness:
"I pity souls that live and die far from their God."
"And I, too, pity both the soul and flesh of man,

--------------------------------------------------------------------

and [the wind] left but one fruit in my hands as my life's loot—"

--------------------------------------------------------------------

"That man is free who strives on earth with not one hope!"
                                                    (XXI, 1333–51)

   The reckoning with the leaders of souls is now at an end. Odysseus,
even if he is dogmatic, feels no enmity for any of them. Motherth's pessi-

mism is familiar to him; the loving-kindness of the fisherboy has brought him relief ("Your song is good, my friend, and it's refreshed my mind"); he fought side by side with Nile against the tyrant. Motherth and the fisherboy both hasten to Odysseus' side in answer to his summons at his death: "O faithful and beloved, O dead and living comrades, come!" They too have him in their hearts. Other shades, each of whom embodied a theory about the world and man, are also enthroned on the iceberg. There is Captain Sole (Don Quixote), the old Hermit (the unredeemed anchorite), Rala the Jewess (a figure who recalls Rosa Luxembourg in her tenderness and self-sacrifice). Throughout the poem other figures, representing some metaphysic or ethic, appear from time to time: the peace-loving Pharaoh (X, 755 *ff.*), representative of a political policy in favor about 1927 and scorned by Kazantzakis; the "Lord of the Tower" (XX, 361 *ff.*), a rotten product of decadence; and finally the two Greeks (XXIV, 868 *ff.*), representatives of a race which triumphed over cosmic terror by setting manly virtue on "the brink of the abyss": all the beliefs and illusions which misled the poet till the moment when he fixed his gaze on the face of the Medusa.

We shall not exhaust the subject of Odysseus' theology unless we say something about his "pyrolatry." We have already recalled his often-repeated phrase: "I don't love man, I love only the flame that eats him." The flame is the emblem of Odysseus' God, and the leopard cub corresponds to the flame in the animal kingdom (XXIV, 1202). Three times at least Odysseus declares that fire is the ultimate criterion of life. The first time is when on the shore of Crete he buys that strange idol with seven superimposed heads which symbolize a favorite idea of the poet: that God's purpose is to make flesh spirit. The lowest head, "a brutal base of flesh," "with large boar-tusks," belonged to the original beast. Each head above it corresponds to a stage in the upward path to final dematerialization. The last head is like "unmoving flame":

as if it were a crimson thread that strung the heads
like amber beads in rows and hung them high in air.

(V, 625–26)

Odysseus proclaims the same theory for a second time, standing before the wall of a tomb which an Egyptian painter was decorating. On the lowest zone of the fresco he had seen a broad river flowing between reeds. In the second zone cultivated ground was depicted. In the third zone the masters were sitting in the shade, enjoying the spectacle of slave-girls dancing and of the blind singing. In the fourth, the Immortals were receiving man's soul for the last judgment. The artist had covered the highest zone with his colors:

... the archer shook to see tall flames, wild famished tongues,
clutching and streaming swiftly from mountain peak to peak.
Gone were the waters, wheat and gods; pure flame remained,
virgin and uninhabited, man's ultimate heir.

(XI, 1128–31)

This eschatological prophecy is once again recorded, with still greater emphasis—and, it might be said, with the intention of inspiring moral terror—when the dying Odysseus bids farewell and praises fire, among the other elements:

Fire will surely come one day to cleanse the earth,
fire will surely come one day to make mind ash,
fate is a fiery tongue that eats up earth and sky!
The womb of life is fire, and fire the last tomb,
and there between two lofty flames we dance and weep.

(XXIII, 932–36)

One does not indeed expect an edifying political theory from a nihilist, even though he affirms life and action. But Odysseus only faced the final Nothing after the volcano had destroyed his city. Until then, he some-times acted as a politician. The commentator has therefore to determine the motive and the moral of his activity. What must first be examined is his political behavior on his return to his island: the need to consolidate the insecure throne there did indeed bring into play his political capacities.

Odysseus has hardly cleared the suitors from the palace when he is faced with a popular insurrection. His instinctive reaction is to finger the dagger in his belt. One may suppose that this is due to habit. But Telem-achus is not deceived:

"Father, your eyes are brimmed with blood, your fists are smoking!"

(I, 158)

Odysseus, in fact, does not regard his people as if he were a shepherd: it is as if the theory of class war had taken hold of him. The people are not the beloved flock so much as the enemy. Odysseus derides Telemachus' old-fashioned ideas about being able to rule the people by justly distributing both freedom and bread:

"Ah, you were born too late, for grim times crush, and soon
your peaceful plane tree shall be hung with gruesome fruit—
either with our slaves' heads, my son, or with our own heads."

(I, 215–17)

Odysseus' initial aggressiveness, far from abating, returns more strongly:

and in his wrathful heart a lightning longing seized him
to fall on his isle ruthlessly and to put to the sword
men, women and gods, and on the flaming shores of dawn
scatter to the wide winds the ashes of his own homeland.

(I, 283–86)

It is not surprising that Telemachus regards him as a stranger. He is really an *Étranger*, cut off, that is, from the whole, from its customs and communal ways. He is someone uprooted from his own country and from its myth. If at this moment he does not unleash "his lion mind that men and demi-gods disdains," it is not because he pities the people; it is because he finds "pity to his advantage" (I, 322). When a cry of revolt bursts from the crowd, Odysseus, instead of being disconcerted as a ruler, feels "an unexpected joy blaze through his heart," as if he too were a rebel. In order to quell the people, he does not invoke his kingly authority: this had died within him. For him the *Führerprinzip* lies in a man's own worth. He does not hold his scepter through any right of succession or cession by the people. He has won it and goes on winning it daily through his own superiority (I, 380–82).

Later, Odysseus inspects his property and receives his tenants: nowhere does he act like a politician who believes in social life and who reconciles antagonism between classes within him with a view to the final welfare of the State. Nor does he behave like a feudal lord, forming one body with his own men. Odysseus does not commit himself. How independent he is of common interests he himself discloses to the basketmaker (who represents submission) when he meets him in the olive grove: he is familiar with a man who

. . . scorned the comfortable virtues, nor made friends
with wealthy shepherds or with lambs or honest dogs
but outside his own sheepfold howled like a wild wolf.[134]

(I, 820–22)

It is true that Odysseus sends forth heralds to summon his people to a feast. This may give a false impression, for in fact he invited them in order to shock them: he does not pour libations to the gods and he drinks to "the health of man's mind." The people find their king impious, and the king replies:

"This is my people, a mess of bellies and stinking breath!"

(I, 1069)

This last experience does nothing to strengthen his bonds with his homeland. Instead of finding peace on the throne of Ithaca, Odysseus thinks he is haunted by a nightmare (I, 1223). He only recovers his calm when he is standing alone before the sea, with his mind like "a virgin boy" and with the presentiment of his departure.

When Odysseus is telling his family the story of his last ten years, he does not present his exploits as actions *pro bono publico*. They are all trials and exaltations of the individual. Even the stratagem of the Wooden Horse, which opened the gates of Troy to the Achaeans, he regards as a trap in which he caught the lawless gods: an opposition to the immortals, the opening of a personal account not yet closed (II, 42–70). The ruses he employs later to quell the peasant uprising at Menelaus' castle (III, 964 *ff.*) certainly presuppose the experience of a politician (who has read Machiavelli's *Prince*!),[135] but they do not have the mark of real political action, a real commitment to a cause. They are gratuitous acts of a deposed, homeless, or—better still—noncommitted person. He who could part from Telemachus without leaving him a political testament (II, 1403–4) could indeed derive nothing from his amoralism and from the continual ambivalence of his will (III, 969) except irresponsible actions born of a momentary caprice (III, 1241–43).

In Crete, Odysseus burns a palace and brings to an end a civilization. This might appear to be a political act of historic significance. But Odysseus himself did not regard it as such: he still felt himself a "foreigner." When after the disaster the inhabitants send a deputation to him with the keys of the city to ask him for peace, Odysseus has nothing to say to the people that he has released from tyranny except these aggressive words:

"Eh, ancient archon, stop your crying, don't lick my feet!
Peace is the daily food with which our holds brim over,
the stench of home, of honor, life, of farms and vineyards . . .
Oho! You make me sick! Pounce on them, leopard soul!"

(VIII, 562–65)

It is hardly surprising that the messengers, stepping back in terror, regard Odysseus as Death himself. Whatever he did was dictated not by any political thought but by the fullness of his blood: "Who holds a sword is tempted, who has youth must play!" (VIII, 560) At the time he parts from Hardihood, the barbarian whom he raised to the throne of Crete, the only political warning he gives him amounts to advice to ignore the ancient gods entirely. The new god demands, as we have said, a *tabula rasa:*

"Hew out broad virgin roads, my brother, that deeds may march.
The stubble of earth's been scorched, the land's been plowed with knives
and now awaits new seed to burst with flower and fruit!"

(VIII, 738–40)

This teaching—which will be shown to be the only one consistent with the new myth and the new political theory born in Odysseus' soul—is not understood by the uncouth Hardihood, who later pays for the blindness of his spirit with his life. Nonetheless, this barbarian has the capacity to understand the Cretan Odysseus:

"Great spirit, the earth can't hold you, and all houses fear you,
you've done all you've set out to do, you've quenched your fires."

(VIII, 751–52)

In Egypt, Odysseus again acts in an irresponsible manner. He rejects the revolutionary theory, proclaims the independence of his spirit (X, 541–96), and yet sides with the rebellious natives and the invading barbarians: he is driven by the spirit of God, who hates what is rotten and sterile. This, it is true, is not politics but "quenching of his own fires." The exodus from the land of slavery (Rhapsody XII) makes Odysseus the leader of a people, or rather, of a band, which is neither of the same

[ 103 ]

racial stock nor from the same soil, and is only united by a longing to escape from Pharaoh's tyranny. This heterogeneous band of desperadoes, after being purified in the furnace of the desert, range themselves mentally round Odysseus when he brings the new "God" down from his mountain retreat and all set to work to build the city-state where he will dwell. During this period of his life, the many-faced Odysseus reveals himself at last as a statesman. He takes the responsibility of the whole community on his shoulders, organizes social life, pursues a purpose. His daily action permits him to envisage his utopia and to frame day by day the laws of the new life. All the values of the vanished myth are to be replaced by untested regulations which will give a new flavor to everything. Odysseus has to conceive the new myth in his own mind—its metaphysics, ethics, aesthetics, and even its ritual—and then to proclaim it to his comrades. This indeed is the mission of a statesman.

The "Republic" or the political theory of Odysseus—in which one may recognize elements from Plato, Nietzsche, Marx and even Thomas More[136]—does not come within the scope of this study except in a synoptic form. The theory is of course based on that youthful disquisition by Kazantzakis, "Concerning the State," contained in the treatise *Frederick Nietzsche and the Philosophy of Right* (1909), and even in *The Saviors of God,* which is, as we have noted, the summing-up of the poet's thought. God is He who struggles eternally; men are destined to become the *"saviors of God"* (XV, 515–27, 812–23, 899–924, 1117–37). The ultimate aim of the state and the hierarchy of its citizens are determined by these two "theses." The aim of the state is inexhaustible creation, vigilance, the impulsion of the citizen to surpass himself.[137] Whatever obstructs or does not contribute to this is condemned by inhuman laws (XV, 622–26). At the base of the state are the manual workers, above them the warriors, and at the top the sages (XV, 540–44). Joint possession (XV, 1096–98); coenobitic life (XV, 550); free love (XV, 555); group education of youths (XV, 561–64); men's quarters; women's quarters; hospices for the old; festival of Spring for the youth: three days and nights dedicated to mass sexual intercourse (XV, 692–701); festivals for men during the summer, for the old people during the autumn, for the dead in winter (XV, 707–8, 867 *ff.*, 1077 *ff.*); rejoicing at the death of an old man (XV, 1010–13), lament at the warrior's death (XV, 1014–16). . . . When the new myth had

[104]

been ordered in his mind, Odysseus takes the chisel and carves his "ten commandments" on stone:[138]

"God groans, he writhes within my heart and cries for help."
"God chokes within the ground and leaps from every grave."
"God stifles in all living things, kicks them, and soars."
"All living things to right or left are his cofighters."
"Love wretched man at length, for he is you, my son!"
"Love plants and beasts at length, for you were they, and now
they follow you in war like faithful friends and slaves."
"Love the entire earth, its waters, soil, and stones;
on these I cling to live, for I've no other steed."
"Each day deny your joys, your wealth, your victories, all."
"The greatest virtue on earth is not to become free
but to seek freedom in a ruthless, sleepless strife."
He seized the last rock then and carved an upright arrow
speeding high toward the sun with pointed thirsty beak.

(XV, 1161–74)

Odysseus had hoped to end his life as a "political animal":

"City, I want to hunt no longer now, I long
to bind my harehound mind to your strong virgin walls."

(XV, 1304–5)

But the blind force which ruins his city-state drives him into solitude. At the beginning of his new retreat, the god-slayer utters a cry of complaint and terror:

"Never shall I forgive and bend down to that vain,
that senseless dark which blots the holy light of man!"

(XV, 1450–51)

The sense of the absurd (*absurdum*) is the frightful discovery which consumes Odysseus more than the volcano's fiery rain. From now on, there is nothing for him to do but surrender to his introvert mania:

as his mind marched beyond all sorrow, joy, or love
—desolate, lone, without a god—and followed there
deep secret cries that passed beyond even hope or freedom.

(XVI, 405–7)

[ 105 ]

The fruit of Odysseus' second retreat was *absolute liberty*—the vision, that is, of a godless and hopeless world.[139] The forms of liberty he had hitherto achieved were many and various. To start with, he had rebelled against every "ready made" sentiment or opinion. This "much-wandered" one, who knew "cities and mind of men," has the illusion, on returning to his own country, that he is turning time back. All the values which seem to be immovable in Ithaca have been overturned in the great kingdoms of the world. All must be reconsidered. The liberty he has won by his refusal to submit to sanctified laws is succeeded by a certain aggressiveness, and it smacks of anarchy. It does not bring him peace, and it often produces the reactions of an automaton. The death of the Olympians has not freed his soul, even though it may have emancipated his spirit. The world's mystery enrages him. His psychology is that of a rebel, not a free man. Another form of liberty which he cultivates and proclaims with arrogance is that of dissatisfaction: no type of social life, no office, no exploit can tie him down; the fiery energy of his spirit consumes everything. This is the romantic form of liberty. Social freedom, political freedom do not concern him—one may recall how Nile, the revolutionary, upbraided him. Odysseus finally discovers that freedom sometimes coincides with necessity. He enjoys this knowledge from the moment he sets to work with his companions to build the city-state which is to guard the god. The vision of the final purpose and public approbation do in fact liberate Odysseus' energy and open his heart to human feelings. But it must be noted that never for an instant did Odysseus forget that God was his own creation. His God never attained such transcendent power that he could absorb Odysseus himself and truly liberate him. At the first misfortune—admittedly devastating, but not incurable, as Granite's conduct shows—Odysseus rebels against God, as if God had broken his promise. The world suddenly seems absurd to him: "No master-god exists, no virtue, no just law,/no punishment in Hades, no reward in Heaven" (XVI, 1241–2). Odysseus calls this *void* "complete freedom."

The world is deserted, absurd, unreal. This is the moment for the "free" Odysseus to fashion a world of his own and to "play" (XVII, 99–113, 1263–72)—to fashion and dissolve it: to play the part of God. In Rhapsody XVII, we do indeed see Odysseus mold the air according to his will, fashion five small figures from it and involve them in a dra-

[106]

matic action. In this strange performance, Odysseus follows at least two earlier examples of Kazantzakis himself—one in *Christ* and the other in *Buddha*. In the first, the "Master of ceremonies," with the aid of faith, in the second, the Poet with the help of Almighty Mind, had materialized thought. They had adorned the desert "with women, peasants, gods, monks and noblemen" because they wanted to see "many shades fight, mix, separate, unravel the air" (*Buddha*, in *Theatre*, III, 447). In other words they had exercised in the magical "Asiatic" fashion the ancient and inalienable right of the poet to set the creations of his imagination before our eyes.

But how are we to interpret this temporary change of the hermit Odysseus into a dramatic poet? At the height of total freedom, in the excitement of his nihilism, when he denies all meaning to the world, the only reality he accepts is that of song (by which we must understand art in general—XVII, 1269–72). Insubstantial in its origin and consequently true in its claims, song seems proof against all argument. Absolute in its essence, placed outside time, unaffected by the contagions of the absurd world, song consoles the nihilist in his solitude and answers to his tormenting hunger for forms. It is the ultimate refuge, the only plank of salvation in the void. It is the final opportunity for man to reveal his instinct for order in the face of chaos (XVII, 1201–3) and be delivered of his unexpended powers (XVII, 1179–1219). If, like the Egyptian king, you give up a whole kingdom for a song (X, 688–94), or sacrifice your seven sons to it like Prince Elias (XIX, 1250 *ff.*), do not say you have paid dearly for this "deathless flame":

All flow on toward the sea and drown in that dark stream,
great towns and all their souls submerge, all women rot,
all gold crowns rot, and even gods rot like the trees;
don't cling to them, O Prince, they fade like whirling smoke,
the only deathless flame is man's own gallant song!

(XIX, 1224–28)

In the realm of thought, the poet is all-powerful: his freedom is unlimited (XVII, 1236–55). In the realm of action, total freedom is to deny appearances and to follow your own vision: a typical example of this is Captain Sole (Don Quixote), whom Odysseus meets immediately after Prince Elias (Rhapsody XX). "Don Quixote" rises above the absurd world by proclaiming it to be *unreal.* This perhaps needs some elucidation.

The poet, in his preamble to the epic, declares that the world is a "dream of a dream" (Prologue, 64–68). Odysseus and some of the secondary characters in the *Odyssey* accept this theory in differing degrees. Even though prepared by Euripides,[140] one is startled to find Odysseus wondering whether Helen of Sparta was a body or a shadow (III, 837–39; IV, 1093–96), and even more to hear Helen herself disputing the reality of the world (even though this may be one of her many affectations):

"How can the shallow brain of mortals, O sage man,
separate vapid truth from dream, or mist from mist?

------------------------------------------------------------------------

Was it then I who laughed and wept on Trojan shores,
or but my empty shade, and I in my husband's bed
dreaming of seizures, handsome youths, and gallant deeds?"

(IV, 1111–16)

Kentaur, the most carnal figure in the poem, also has this doubt at times:

"I'm afraid, my lads, that we'll awake one day and find
we're still in Ithaca's bay, dead drunk on its far beach . . ."

(XIII, 1122–23)

These things may of course be said without conviction. But when Odysseus is overwhelmed by the destruction of his city-state and by the death of two beloved companions, his last consolation is to declare the ungovernable world to be a transient fantasy of the human mind:

"There is no master now on earth, the heart is free!
At dawn from my right temple the sun leaps in flame,
sweeps through the great dome of my head all day, then falls
at dusk in my left temple, swollen with crimson blood;

------------------------------------------------------------------------

the mind snuffs out like a thief's lantern, all things vanish."

(XVI, 1208–16)

This final opinion of Odysseus, which is to determine his main reactions until his death, coincides with the poet's idea of the phantasmagoria of the world:

"All in my brains distill to quintessential pith,
a puff of blue-green smoke, the secret of the world!"

(XVIII, 535–36)

Life is a dream. It is not surprising that the dream occupies a special place in the *Odyssey*. The heroes of the poem dream on some fifty occasions—not only the animate characters, but also inanimate things (XX, 17–23; XXI, 77–80)—even Death (VI, 1271). Dreams bear the "unguarded mind" to distant worlds (VI, 775–6; XVIII, 194–97), reveal the future (VII, 10–115; XXI, 1049–1115), fulfill the waking man's privations (VII, 359–60), direct him to strange actions (IX, 786–834), clarify thought or make it visible (X, 507–13, 576–93; XI, 750–808; XIII, 471–84), provide an outlet for repressed desires (XX, 710–1305). The frequency of this theme is doubtless due to the poet's own nature and to his antirationalist upbringing; but it is also due to the intellectual currents of the period which introduced the dream into literature (Freudism, surrealism, the works of Kafka). Each of the references cited indicates a part of the text which would confirm our thesis. But there is one passage of an altogether special significance, and that is the account of Odysseus' nightmare in Rhapsody XX (710–1305). The poet here makes use of one of the terrible themes bequeathed by Freudism to literature: "man's dark longing need to slay [slash] the ancient father and sleep safe in mother's arms" (XX, 979–80). Freudian in texture is also the endless dream of the old hermit who regrets his joyless life (XIX, 662–955)—the kernel of a "last temptation"—as well as Odysseus' cosmogonic nightmare (XXIII, 1069–1136), where man sets out to kill not now his own father, but the "superlative" of the father according to the dream's logic—in other words, God.

We have spoken on various occasions of the poet's anti-rational view and have expressed doubt as to whether his natural predisposition altogether coincided with the spirit of his times. Similar thoughts are provoked by the behavior of wily Odysseus. He too learns from the mouth of a third party that

"Athena's helmet . . . has now been smashed to bits
nor can it ever again contain the whole world's head."

(II, 1338–39)

Later, when he leaves land behind him and sets sail for Egypt, he regards
his departure as the beginning of deliverance from reason and measure:

"Farewell, O balanced virtues and housekeeping cares,
and mind, guardian of fruits, who raises tall stone walls
between the vineyards of God and man and chokes our hearts.
Earth spreads out southward, lads, and the mind plucks a rose,
then hangs it down his echoing ear and bursts in song!"

(VIII, 1009–13)

In a time of interregnum the new myth is still unformed: the mind (the
male) is unable to grasp the shape of things to come; intuition (the female) is swept away by it:

"How often have I not seen maids, like poor night-moths,
leap in the flames to burn when new fires sweep the world!"

(X, 460–61)

The poem on several occasions gives evidence that both the poet and
his creation regard reason as incapable of penetrating the mystery of the
world and that they believe in subconscious and superconscious powers.
When the old witch doctor in Rocky's kingdom in the heart of Africa
makes Odysseus and his band see beyond mountains and forests the lost
Orpheus,

then the much-suffering man mocked at his own proud mind:

----------------------------------------------------------------

and for an hour he envied those exotic powers
with which the old man ruled and marshaled all the winds.

(XIII, 1160–70)

Odysseus in fact envies the magic which fashions and destroys the world,
and does not rest until he himself, after his second retreat, gives himself
to that superrational play (XVII). The encomium which he then addresses to his mind shows how he had desired this power (XVII, 1175
ff.). The crossing of the African continent supplies Odysseus with repeated opportunities for freeing himself from the bonds of reason, for
giving himself to magic and for plunging into the depths of the subcon-

scious. His anti-rationalist spirit is satisfied to the full. At the point of death he again bids farewell to and praises—with the other elements—the mind, ". . . great master-craftsman of the homeless air'" (XXIII, 1002). But of the terms in which he greets it, the most resonant is that of "charioteer":

"O Mind, your four steeds, water, fire, earth and light
strain at the bit and leap, but you hold the reins firmly
and temper savage strength with the brain's prudent thoughts."

(XXIII, 1031–33)

In view of these last words, one is justified in asking to what extent the anti-rationalist message of the times really accorded with the poet's own nature.[141]

A mysterious and unexplored world gives rise to indescribable sensations: where the mind fails, words will certainly not succeed. The poet has then to resort to a mode of expression more primitive than that of words: he makes his characters *dance*. When Pharaoh's emissaries dazzle the barbarians who have invaded Egypt with their verbosity, the latter, dumb for a moment, quickly recover:

"You've burst our brains with all that rant! Draw back, far back,
spread far and wide so that your land may hold us all!
Whatever we have to say we'll stamp in lively dance!"

(X, 1135–37)

If words fail, then they are able "to uncork their minds" (X, 1138) in another way. The barbarians are, in fact, on the lowest rung of knowledge: their minds have "no tongue," few words rattled in their thickset skulls" (X, 1113). But their behavior prefigures Odysseus' own impatience with words and his resorting to dance. Odysseus had already danced in the cemetery at Ithaca in order to commune with his ancestors (I, 684 *ff.*), he had danced with the rebels in the halls of the palace at Knossos in order to prophesy the destruction (VI, 1205 *ff.*), he had danced with Hardihood in their palace prison, "so that their minds might clear, their brimming strength distill" (VII, 254). Later (XI, 1208–77), Odysseus dances beneath Death's sword a mime in which he successively plays the beggar, little orphans, war, widows and invalids, and works himself into a Dionysiac frenzy. Pharaoh, who is terrified by this dance, spares Odysseus' life. But Odysseus is already "transfigured":

[ 111 ]

A wide-eyed, tall intoxication blazed in his head
as his feet whirled him on beyond both life and death.

(XI, 1258–59)

In similar circumstances, Odysseus' companion Rocky also dances a "dance of death" before the cannibals, who have already lighted the fire and cut the spit. Through his movements pass unspeakable love of life and inexpressible despair:

Two wings sprang from his temples, two from his slim heels,
his feet and brains took flight, the stones about him sparked,
his handsome body hissed like flame, fell like a star,
yet kept on dancing boldly on a sword's thin edge.

(XIII, 55–58)

In order to instruct his companions about the new God, Odysseus makes them dance: thus their minds will expand and become capable of receiving "a great secret" (XV, 887). After his second retreat, Odysseus himself, treading now "the peak of power and despair," plunges into the "whirlpool of the dance" and liberates his superrational powers:

"On! Let the heavy beasts awake in memory's cave,
let the black forest of the heart growl as dusk falls;
I dance, and all the tight coils of my head unwind!"

(XVI, 1333–35)

Odysseus' course in the Dark Continent and amid the polar wastes is accompanied by dancing: witch doctors, exorcisers, wild youths and the dying dance—all those who leap the bounds of reason in the pursuit of the absolute. The last dance in the poem is danced by Odysseus' mind: it is the final flash of a dying lamp:

His mind now danced and cackled on the green-haired earth;
glutted with loam, he scorned it, soared on high serenely
and blew to scatter life's toy down the hollow winds.

(XXIV, 1345–47)

The "death and dematerialization" of Odysseus—*per finire!*—are accomplished in a dancer's leap:

. . . the great mind leapt to the peak of its holy freedom,
fluttered with empty wings, then upright through the air
soared high and freed itself from its last cage, its freedom.

(XXIV, 1391–93)

# PART III

# THE POET AND

# THE POEM

One day the nettles asked the rose-tree: "Madam Rose-tree, would you teach us your secret? How do you make the rose?" And the rose-tree replied: "My secret is very simple, Sister Nettles; all winter long I work the earth with patience, confidence and love, and have but a single thought in my head: the rose."

—N. Kazantzakis, *Report to Greco,*
*Nea Estia,* November 15, 1957

[114]

Whom do I write for? Since I am alone.

*—Letter by Kazantzakis from Aegina, October 5, 1938*

It is not the height, but the cliff which is terrifying. The cliff, from which the glance falls into the void and from which the hand stretches up toward the peak.

*—Frederick Nietzsche, from*
THUS SPAKE ZARATHUSTRA

### 1

The first draft of the *Odyssey* was finished on September 22, 1927. Kazantzakis emerged from his arduous task without the slightest physical fatigue, but he was troubled in spirit. His creation had not given him release. A great deal remained concealed within him; and in many ways he had unintentionally gone beyond his original conception. Odysseus had developed without the control of a firm regulating principle, psychophysiological or social, and had even come to dominate his creator, as that "Tulpa," the Hindu ascetic's creation, which Kazantzakis describes in his travelogue *England,* did.[142] On the other hand, the artist, *il fabbro,* was still restless. The hull had been built, but it needed calking, tarring and rigging.

It would indeed be presumptuous to try to give an account of the poet's reactions to his work, were it not for his own testimony—a testimony that recurs throughout his letters during the ten years he was writing and rewriting the poem.[143] Kazantzakis did not always interpret correctly, or he interpreted in a manifold sense, his anxiety about the outcome of his effort. But the anxiety itself was painfully real. It is therefore the commentator's task to search for its causes, particularly when he recognizes them with that inner certitude which comes from having shared similar experiences.

Kazantzakis, on the completion of his superhuman task, might have been like a master mason pausing before the exotic temple built with his own hands; and if we were content with the external aspect of things, that might have been the impression he would have given us. But the enormous epic of the *Odyssey* may, where its inner significance is concerned, be compared not to a temple but to a mountain of ruins. The circle opened by Homer is indeed closed by Kazantzakis; but this is to beg the question, for the circle here is not a shape of perfection, but an image of Nothing. All the values produced by Hellenism from the time when Homer established the form of the Olympians, and to which Christianity added with its message of love and its promise of life eternal, are overthrown in the new *Odyssey*. And not only the values, but even the content of ordinary human life is traduced in the poem. The poet derides every possible achievement and strips bare each human hope. The reader is led from destruction to destruction until he confronts the head of the Medusa. The circle closes. The gods are dead! The desolate world of the *Odyssey* seems pervaded by a premonition of the "atomic" terror of our period.

Kazantzakis did not wish to be a destroyer only. On the contrary: "All my life," he himself declares, "I have tried to expand my mind to breaking point, in order to forge a great idea, one able to give a new meaning to life, a new meaning to death, and to console mankind."[144] Alas! The *Odyssey* does not announce a new myth. The one positive idea it opposes to total nihilism is the affirmation of life. Instead of being led by his consciousness of nothing to a negation of all things, Odysseus feels an insatiable hunger growing within him. "Dionysiac nihilism!" But human existence remains without justification: no last judgment or retribution awaits it. Death is the ultimate reality.[145]

The poet has destroyed a world, overturned all the gods. The only constructive element in his epic is the exaltation of life sensed to the point of lust. Odysseus is driven by a painful hunger, the counterpart to a tragic sense of life (supreme delight has its counterpart in supreme pain at parting). It is as if nature is revealed to him beneath the suspended sign of a stimulating *memento mori*! "Death is the salt that gives to life its tasty sting!" (XVIII, 912) The hero's conduct is determined by that "Mediterranean" sensitivity which Greeks, Latins and Arabs have at various times interpreted and which we find expressed with terrible clarity in the line of the popular Cretan folk song: "They see Death stand against the garden wall."[146] Moreover, the lack of any metaphysical entity to which the innumerable aspects of the ephemeral world may be referred makes Odysseus' thirst "Tantalean." The material he has to consume has no order: it remains without limit.

Kazantzakis was never deceived into believing that the trial of Western civilization was a conscious problem in his own country. The more he became in tune with contemporary European thought, the greater was his divorce from the Greek public. Odysseus among the indolent, unsuspicious elders of Ithaca (II, 631–722) undoubtedly represents a bitter experience of the poet himself. Change of place is equivalent to removal in time. Between Berlin and Athens, the poet went back at least fifty years in time. At the end of his struggle a disheartening feeling of homelessness dominated him. For whom was he writing? The poem was not based on any national reality: the struggle pervading it was inconceivable and indeed meaningless to the national soul. For one generation, at least, the *Odyssey* was to appear as an untimely monologue, foreign and ineffectual.

Kazantzakis did not have the good fortune to be supported by a native intellectual elite. Among the writers of his own generation he was an alien: he belonged to no literary school, he never became a disciple. Nourished more by philosophy than by literature, he converted the latter—like certain other troubled spirits of the century: Péguy, Giovanni Papini, Unamuno—"from an art of style and description into a question concerning the crucial problems of mankind."[147] He had introduced into his country the chill of that "Existentialism" which, twenty years later and after the Second World War, was to be popularized by French literature. Themes which even in Greece were to become common, thanks to Malraux, Sartre and Camus, had already been scattered profusely by Kazantzakis through the pages of the *Odyssey.* Camus, in his *Myth of Sisyphus,* observes that the difference between the classical and the modern sensibility is that the former is nurtured on moral and the latter on metaphysical problems.

Kazantzakis' alienation from the national spirit did not only have the consequences we have described. The poet suffered from his loneliness and was at the same time tormented by a longing for the world he had lost. *Et in Arcadia ego!* He too had once been rooted in the people's world. Although that world was in an undeveloped state, it had a quite definite sense of what was sacred, just, beautiful, decent. While in contact with it, the poet's soul responded to the collective soul, and a broad, well-based reality supported him.[148] The "sin" of learning, travel, the experience of an alienated time had destroyed the harmony. What mythical hero other than the much-wandering Odysseus could represent this amputation of roots?

A homeless person attempts to compose an epic. The contradiction inherent in this proposition is as irresolvable as that contradiction between the affirmation and the renunciation of life which troubles the whole *Odyssey*. The poem in the end could only amount to a monologue. Its assumed objectivity is misleading. Taking place outside historical time, with its hero an Odysseus who has forgotten—except in the recapitulation of Rhapsody II—his Homeric embodiment, it finishes by being the expression of a subjective struggle and sometimes even of pure fantasy. Presented with an acute sense for the concrete, in the majestic scenery of the Mediterranean world, the poet has set up symbols borrowed from at least five different civilizations (Creto-Mycenean, Greek, Christian, Indian and African). The *Odyssey* is like an immense temple built and decorated with the spoils of an invasion and dedicated to an unknown god.

"We are alone, in the little shop we have opened in the desert, and there is no fear of becoming corrupted by the customers."[149] Kazantzakis faced his isolation now with humorous resignation and now with traditional heroism, as if he were besieged. But he had one ideal support —the modern Greek language. He often referred to it in his letters and writings as the "fatherland." "The popular tongue is our fatherland! Only someone who loves our demotic language with such fervor can feel that it does not matter that he has been born, that he wrestles without help amid the ignorance, idleness and indifference of his race."[150] Kazantzakis defended this fatherland fanatically. Any reservation in regard to it on the part of the pedant or the dull-witted he looked upon as blindness or lack of respect. There could be no compromise. Yet there were certain observations which troubled him. I do not of course mean criticisms of his idiomatic use of the language: these merely exasperated him. He knew that he had adopted certain Cretan words, but he considered that the mechanism of his language—the important thing—was subservient to the Panhellenic canon: Syntax, grammar, phonetics follow the common law. The observation which disturbed him did not concern glossology. He himself might indeed have formulated it tacitly. The luxury and superlative use of the language had left him with a doubt: the language had revealed its strange and dangerous power of "surpassing our feelings and impressions, perhaps even of inventing them."[151]

According to Pascal, passion cannot exist without excess. Kazantzakis refuted another criticism directed at his "coarse" language by adopting it. Yes, his words are indeed *pexa et hirsuta*—as Dante would have wished them to be—in the image and likeness of the poet. "Nonetheless, through their excessive 'shagginess' they stick in the throat of the reader and do not pass into his heart!" Criticisms of this nature were made by many people. I do not know whether Kazantzakis was disturbed by this common complaint. But whether he was or not, the *Odyssey,* between the first and the seventh draft, was enriched by thousands of unusual words and its ruggedness was not moderated. Reviewing his work, the poet may have been alarmed by its excessive richness: he had gathered together more words than it seemed humanly possible to gather. Could one mind have produced so many names for sensible and intelligible things? "After five hundred, a thousand years, the Greek language will not be spoken!"[152] With that thought Kazantzakis ended his reflection on the language. His one and only "fatherland" was not the ship to carry him to immortality. So much the better. "What is our goal? To be shipwrecked!"[153]

Versification was another cause of anxiety. Kazantzakis had chosen the seventeen-syllable iambic verse as the meter for his epic "because that followed most closely the rhythm of his blood during the period in which he was living the *Odyssey*." His right to choose such a meter cannot be disputed, even if he had not eloquently explained the compelling reason for his choice. But his difficulties were not fewer on this account. The seventeen-syllable iambic verse—invented by Polylas and used here and there by one or two poets—had not been used sufficiently to make clear all its possibilities. Kazantzakis himself was not a very skillful versifier: his generation had already begun to neglect metrics, so thoroughly cultivated by someone like Palamas. The poet of the *Odyssey* had seriously set himself to the writing of verse only after his thirtieth year, at the time when he became acquainted with Sikelianos. His practice in versification up to the year in which he embarked on his epic was largely confined to the tragedies *Odysseus, Christ, Nikephoros* and *Heracles.*

Kazantzakis never regretted his choice of form, but he had to fight hard before he could master it. He was exploring the mechanism of the seventeen-syllable line long after the first draft of the *Odyssey* had been finished. The two syllables tacked onto the usual fifteen-syllable line—the modern Greek meter *par excellence*—often seem superfluous, particularly when the poet adapts verses from popular folk songs, as is customary in an epic. Kazantzakis, like every poet worthy of the name, aimed at perfection. He aspired to express his "inner tempestuousness" through the rhythm of his verse—to match form and content.

"I cut through all the flooding waves with wide breast strokes."
Δρασκέλιζα μέ ἁπλοταριές φαρδιές τὴν κυματοπλημύρα

(II, 392)

The poet here indicates, through the spacing of the accents and the recurring watery consonants, the breadth of Odysseus' movement and the expanse of water, in the same way as Claudel, thanks to Virgil's line . . . *aut gravibus rastris galeas pulsabit inanis,*[154] "literally participated in the effort of the plowman holding the handle of the plow and heard the hollow noise of the rusty helmets turned up by the share."[155] The Philistine will call this the fantasy of poets. Each time Kazantzakis made such a person the judge of his creation, he experienced acute disappointment. But even the well-disposed reader, accustomed to the regular caesura of the fifteen-syllable line, had difficulties in speaking Kazantzakis' seventeen-syllable iambic with its irregular caesura. At the conclusion of the first draft of the *Odyssey,* the work seemed to the poet like a newborn bear cub that needs licking and re-licking by its mother to give it shape.

The matter and texture of his poem gave Kazantzakis greater trouble. I have already spoken of his desire to dissolve the reason through the use of music. Reading his letters, one can conclude that his poetic ideal was summed up in the theory of pure poetry. This needs clarification. The poet had adopted the aesthetic trends of his period, for which he had been prepared by Bergsonism: he too was a foe of rationalism and recognized the primacy of music. But beneath these contemporary modes he kept very much alive a poetic consciousness formed in the school of Homer, the Bible, Dante and folk songs. From these models he had been taught to admire the heroic molding of the characters, the grandeur of the images, the daring transposition of the abstract to the concrete, the nakedness of the emotions. Whatever the fashion of the times had added to the mighty tree of poetic tradition was but a sparkle and a whisper of the leaves. Meaning was always basically for Kazantzakis more important than sound; in supreme cases, the one was fused with the other.

The epic—and in fact all great poetry—cannot exist without a theme. The great poet expresses the theme in archetypal images, he invents the "poetic situations" which enrich the myth of man. These give poetry its human value: this is what the Poet in Solomos' *Dialogue* must have perceived when, in order to confound the Pedant, he made him consider the farewell of Hector and Andromache, Priam's kneeling before Achilles, Ugolino's frightful meal.[156] This must also have been perceived by Dante, Goethe,[157] or by that anonymous Greek poet who made the mother of Kitsos (a Greek fighter against the Turks) throw stones at the river.[158] Kazantzakis did not wish to fall short of these. The cosmogonic scope of his theme could not but inspire in him the mythical figures and the large compositions treasured in the memory of peoples. He himself had a mass of experiences seeking to be embodied in myths and expressed in forms.

It would indeed have been plain sailing for the poet if modern Greek civilization had been able to embrace the theme of the *Odyssey*. Kazantzakis exploits the modern Greek language and folk songs to the full, but he failed to take them for more than an exaltation of the concrete world. Often indeed the poetical form imposed by folk poetry makes his own voice sound discordant: the limitless and chimerical themes he handles are not to be contained within the world of representations or the range of feelings of the folk singer. Kazantzakis grapples with this contradiction, this antinomy. He expands his sensibility, borrows symbols from primitive myths, inserts in his epic "expressions" from works of art belonging to every age and place.[159] But very few things are actually dictated to him. Myths, symbols and embodiments are all the result of his own choice. A subjective world-view and daemonology could only be represented in a subjective manner.

Kazantzakis recognized these difficulties well enough. He felt deep anguish at the death struggle of a glorious civilization, but he sought to embody this anguish in a myth created *ex nihilo*. The natural way in which the modern Greek language speaks with images, its power of conveying the intelligible through the sensible, continually gave him the illusion of being able to clothe his spirit with flesh. Up to a point he was not deceived in this. But the creation of myths and forms is not brought about through language alone: there is need of a culture to provide the symbols. To explain my meaning with an example opposite that of Kazantzakis: Dante conveys the most abstract thoughts in images; but when the moment comes for mythical creation he finds all the symbols he desires in the Christian myth. The Holy Scriptures, the frescoed churches, the unwritten world of Christian memory—all provide him with forms. When Kazantzakis' imagination seeks support, it encounters a changeable scenery: beasts and birds on the walls of Knossos, monstrous gods in Egyptian tombs, African masks, the polar waste.[160]

When a civilization begins to disintegrate, the breaches are first to be perceived in the domain of art: that is the most disinterested aspect of the social life and those who represent it are the most sensitive people. To realize the truth of this, one has but to consider the aesthetic canon of the Renaissance: for several centuries, it was one of the most cohesive bonds of the European community. From the beginning of our century, modern art, breaking with this canon, presages the death of other values. The destroyers do not suspect what freedom the artist had when the rules of his art were dictated to him. Necessity was not a prison for him, but a form of freedom. The spirit of the civilization which filled him guided his hand without weighing it down. The contemporary artist, who seeks for the elements of his aesthetic among the forms of the past, works without knowing that he does so under conditions of decadence. His eclecticism is his servitude. He may flirt, for instance, with archaic forms, but his archaism is foreign to him, for his own spirit is sophisticated. An experienced eye will detect among his archaized forms an inquiring sensitivity quite alien to the archaic spirit.[161]

Kazantzakis, obedient to the nature of the modern Greek language and his own Cretan origin, desired to be an archaic writer. But he belonged to the baroque.[162] He himself was painfully aware of this: "I must fly from Pergamos to Delphi."[163] But he remained a child of his century, a century dominated by the muse of Claudel, Barrès and D'Annunzio. Kazantzakis would have liked to escape the embrace of this muse, but the will is not sufficient to break through the conditions of history. The spirit of the age imposes the style of the poet, even when he himself believes that he molds it independently. Yearning for the archaic is determined as inescapably as a yearning for the picturesque, its dialectical opposite. And the same is true of the tendency toward the colossal, anti-rationalism, mysticism, nature worship, sensualism.

At the first of the seven stages of his task, Kazantzakis, when the fever had fallen, was faced with another contradiction. What this is may be indicated in the words of the young Solomos: "The difficulty felt by a writer (I am speaking of a great writer) does not depend upon his showing imagination and passion, but in his subjecting these two things, with time and toil, to the meaning of art." Many times already Kazantzakis had judged his own art severely and had mistrusted his liking for color and ornamentation. During the composition of the *Odyssey,* he had to face problems infinitely more complex. He had become more fully conscious of the meaning of art, and the material which he had to set in order was indeed without beginning or end: here was no Ithaca to regulate or put a term to the inventions of his imagination. Ithaca was the journey, as Kazantzakis said in one of his letters, and the object of the journey was shipwreck in the gulf of death.

According to the precept established by three thousand years of epic poetry, the epic narrates the feats of heroes who often have divine blood in their veins. In wars and on journeys they are led by an immutable ideal which gives them strength to overcome difficulties beyond the measure of man. Epic heroes are raised up as models for the people: they teach manliness or sagacity, they inspire daring or sacrifice, they embody the virtues of the race. As the content of epic poetry is heroic, so also is the form: for centuries people responded to the hexameter as the warhorse to the bugle. The sword is the emblem of the epic. It was with a sword in hand that Dante pictured Homer.[164] The epic poem corresponds to man's longing for the ideal, it satisfies his primordial yearning for the gods. The epic scale is suited to gods and demigods. But it does not violate the human: man recognizes himself among the characters and actions of the epic poem.

At the opposite pole to the epic hero we find the *pícaro;* and at the opposite pole to the epic we find the *novela picaresca.* What does the word *pícaro* mean? According to the Dictionary of the Spanish Academy,[165] as a noun, it means a shameless, insolent and dissolute type who lives an unsettled life on the roads of evil; as an adjective it means base, wicked, deceitful, sly, knavish. The word first occurs in Spanish texts of the sixteenth century, and its etymology is obscure. The *pícaros* were usually street urchins, errant boys, scamps, knaves, vagabonds. Living on the fringe of a closed aristocratic society which bred them and later disowned them, they became experts in flattery, lies, trickery and stealing. They constituted a separate class in Spain during the sixteenth and seventeenth centuries. They appeared in literature with the *novela picaresca,* an antiheroic type of writing among whose components are satire, caricature, parody of the idealistic legend, and a reaction against the imaginary tales of knights. Among the first examples of the picaresque novel are *La Lozana andaluza* (1528) of Francisco Delicado, the great anonymous masterpiece *La vida de Lazarillo de Tormes* (1554), and *Guzmán de Alfarache* by Mateo Alemán (1599–1604).[166]

The nihilistic theory, assimilated by an intelligence, may generate the hero; assimilated by an ignoramus, it may give birth to the *pícaro.* St. Paul divides men into spiritual, natural and carnal: even the spirit of God bears fruit in a different way in each person (I Cor. 2–3). The human types of Kazantzakis' imagination consisted of heroes and *pícaros:* heroes who act like *pícaros* and *pícaros* who act heroically. The poet believed that he could hold back the latter and delay their release: "I am impatient for the printing of the *Odyssey,*" he wrote to me from Aegina on October 5, 1938, when the book was already in the press, "to be rid of the weight, to write at last whatever I like, without any purpose or limitation. *Whom do I write for? Since I am alone. 'Hazain pirouit'* (the master is enjoying himself), a Greek baker in Russia used to stick up on his shop when he was going to get drunk. It seems to me that the time has come for me too to write a book entitled '*Hazain pirouit.*' "[167] Who the characters of this book are to be, Kazantzakis tells us in another text: "The characters have suddenly got hold of me, I am having a party: I have started to write novels ... *I have found some old friends, ruffians from the gallows and the stake* [my italics], some other good people whom I love and enjoy myself with."[168]

Turn a *pícaro* out at the door and he will come back through the window. The *Odyssey* is full of them. From the very first rhapsodies, the "old friends," the ruffians, those of flesh and bone, are poured into the poem.

The royal banquet with which Odysseus regales them (I, 1023 *ff.*) symbolizes the dissolution of order and the lighting of fires which takes place when civilizations crumble. "Everything is permissible!" Odysseus himself is to be infected with something of the spirit of his companions: he feasts and carouses with them (II, 933 *ff.*) to the point of shocking the whole island:

A rumor spread from town to town that demons lashed
their king who all night long danced naked in the moon.

(II, 955–56)

The Ithaca that is troubled by the conduct of her king represents the poet's own country: Greece also lives in a different age from that of her epic poet, and is to be made uneasy by his creation.

2

> Christ, Buddha, Lenin—stages in the journey: I had to pass through these, these marked the passage of the mystic bird, these were the goads which helped me to bring forth the Cry.
>
> —N. Kazantzakis, *Report to Greco,*
> *Nea Estia,* November 15, 1957

At the end of the first draft of the *Odyssey,* Kazantzakis must have felt as I have tried to describe: thus his letters indicate and thus I remember him. Be that as it may, a feeling of homelessness dominates him. He is alone. He has no friends, no followers, no audience, no publisher. He is in debt for the money he borrowed for his expenses during the few months in which he wrote the poem (this he writes in a letter), he is extremely poor. He has hardly raised his head from his seventeen-syllable iambics when he has to take on the joyless task of writing several hundred articles for *Eleftheroudakis' Encyclopaedia,* which will provide him with the means of livelihood for some time.[169] "A great man," said Nietzsche, another sufferer, "is harried, pressed and tormented until he is coiled up in his loneliness." Identified with his own Odysseus—how could it be otherwise?—Kazantzakis realizes also another form of isolation: that of the fighter who refuses to admit the equality of his fellow men. The absolute measures he applies to himself may transfigure him, but they may also martyr him.[170]

Like all epic poets, Kazantzakis had seen the spark become a blaze. *"Poca favilla gran fiamma seconda!"* (Dante) "And from one small spark a mighty fire arose!" (Kornaros)[171] In spite of all adversity, Kazantzakis had felt his greatness: he had succeeded in bringing the demon into his life, in involving himself in his personal myth and in building the cathedral of the demotic tongue. He had mastered all his experiences, had cured all inhibition. He had overcome the consciousness of nothing with a huge poetic creation. This raft, which had carried him through the marshes of Helladic triviality, might convey him one day to an enlightened world where man's labor is honored. To escape from the Philistines, the petty politicians, the pot-boilers, the mandarins, the buyers and sellers! To show his loathing for social conformity, the most humiliating of necessities, the most degrading of servitudes! To get free from all this!

His premonition was soon to be realized. A letter from Moscow at the beginning of October 1927 invited the Greek author to the tenth anniversary of the Revolution. "Moscow uttered a cry!" This phrase, which occurs at the beginning of *Toda Raba,* expresses a critical event in the poet's life: Geranos, who speaks for Kazantzakis in the book,[172] had heard the message! "In the old monastery of Apezanes, above the Libyan Sea, Geranos suffers and struggles. He seeks to express and to save his soul with words; to express and to save the souls of the people surrounding him. . . . Moscow! Moscow!—Who is calling? Ah! how he had longed for that departure! Russia, from the days of his childhood on this African island, had seemed to him to be a legendary land, multicolored, snow-covered, limitless. . . . When during the years of Turkish servitude the old Cretans used to get drunk, they would put their fezzes on crooked, enter the Turkish coffee shops and begin to sing, at the peril of their lives:

> Freedom! Freedom!
> I will bring the Moscovite!

And now, at the height of his powers, Geranos suddenly felt within him an old Cretan, his grandfather, with his fez awry, bursting his lungs in singing the same refrain!"[173]

Kazantzakis had had his first experience of Russia in 1919, at the height of the Civil War, when he went to repatriate the Greeks from the Caucasus. Yannis Stavridakis, the beloved companion of his youth, had died there. This death had made Russia seem even more fabulous— a land from which young men do not come back! Three or four years later, while in Berlin, he was seized with a longing for the "Nova Mater": his letters to his first wife bear witness to this. He hoped to see there with his own eyes the Great Breath, which he had visualized in his *The Saviors of God* shattering bodies in order to pass through them. In no other country in the world could one witness so titanic a birth. But, as we said at the beginning of this book, his second visit (in 1925) had not fulfilled his expectations. It had left him frustrated: he had not found the means to satisfy his messianic tendency, he had not even been able to communicate with reality.

A Cretan proverb says: "Where you fail, return, and where you succeed, depart!" Human dignity bids one to leave the memory of a victory behind. In his third journey to Russia Kazantzakis saw the opportunity for a new test. Was he a man of action? Would he be able to make contact with the revolutionary society, with the god-bearing people, and to release his powers? While he was still at work on his epic and without any cause to hope for an escape, he had written to me from Aegina (August 25, 1927): "As soon as I finish the *Odyssey,* my small service, I shall give myself entirely to the problem of how to get to grips with reality and to act. If I live elsewhere, if I find friends outside Greece, I shall triumph. That is to say, I shall do what my nature is capable of doing." His repressed desire for action often appears not only in his letters and in his plots, but also in the style of his language: he had not succeeded in releasing his messianism, but he had preserved its ardor. The drama of Kazantzakis' life up to this time—and even a little later— was that he was setting out in pursuit of his destiny at an age when others have created their work and through it have found release.

His travels up to this period were, above all, in the nature of "trials" of his world-view. He everywhere sought to discern the "Invisible who steps on all things visible and mounts upwards." But he also did not omit to gather images and sensations for his poetry. He had the capacity to adapt himself to all mental climates and to appreciate all countries, from waterless, poverty-stricken Spain to grassy, prosperous, Pepysian England; and the figures of legend sprang up in his imagination in a way that was often far more alive than what he saw with his eyes. He nourished his reverie with reading. His knowledge of languages gave him access to the literatures of many nations, enriching his soul and mind. I think that he caught most easily the spirit of the principal Romance languages, but he was also able to read both English and German. A host of thoughts, shades of expression, shifts of sensibility resulted from this peregrination.

But the journey he now proposed to make was not like the others. It might have a decisive influence on his life. A cry of deliverance and enthusiasm escaped from him when he arrived in the "Red Mecca" (October 27, 1927). He at once recovered his mental poise, lost after four months of unremitting creation; he gazed deeply at the images which had nourished his nostalgia and verified in actual fact memories which had haunted his imagination. The actuality exceeded his expectations. The change of country signified this time a plunge into the future. Between Athens and Moscow, Kazantzakis had leaped forward several decades. He had left behind the moribund West, which for months he had been mentally condemning and criticizing, and he found himself in the crater of a cosmogony. Everything here was fluid, new, charged with the future. Things burned and crackled like lava: no ancient mold could hold them. "Anyone coming from Western civilization with its antiquated metaphysical questions and its foolish intellectual reservations, cannot understand anything—and this irrespective of whether he loves or hates it—of the cosmogony of contemporary Russia." A Spanish poet had also found himself, in his isolation in Andalusia, "without hope, without fear, without faith." He had heard the song of the new siren and had made his way to the north. "A poet," Kazantzakis concludes, "that is to say, a lover of the abyss, surrenders in this way to Russia. . . . But a pastor, Karl Vogl, who had traveled a few months earlier in Soviet Russia, found simpler words: 'What I saw and experienced in Soviet Russia has restored my faith in humanity, which I had lost.' " There is no doubt that the poet and the pastor embody the trials and hopes of Kazantzakis himself.[174]

Nonetheless, he could not cast off his old self. He had come to the revolutionary movement nurtured less by Marxism[175] than by the disparate preaching of revolutionaries and prophets like Charles Fourier,

Auguste Comte, Max Stirner,[176] Ferdinand Lassalle, Frederick Nietzsche, Georges Sorel. The latter's *Reflections on Violence* had supplied Kazantzakis with the theory which made him pass (about 1920–22) from aristocratic nationalism to totalitarian socialism. Moreover, Sorel's utopian spirit and fanatical anti-intellectualism had attracted Kazantzakis. Let it be added that his aversion to the false idealism of bourgeois democracy had been strengthened by the explosive argumentation of the French sociologist. Nor must Bergsonism be forgotten. Loaded with this equipment, Kazantzakis—for all his good intentions—did not really succeed in sympathizing with the Russian cosmogony. He chafed at the way in which the communists acted and thought, was as impatient with their interpretations as he was with their program. The new type of man produced in Russia appalled him. How could a person who despised metaphysics, who was ignorant of the inner life and who mocked at the adventure of love be fitted into the definition of "Man"? How could a race, an intellectual tradition which had produced *The Brothers Karamazov* of Dostoievsky, *A Confession* and *Memoirs of a Madman* of Tolstoi, have sunk to this atrocious materialism, to this utter blindness in the face of ultimate problems? Kazantzakis did not in any way attempt to hide what he felt. As was usual, he revealed his vacillation in a dialogue: Vera Grigorievna, a young student, represents "the narrow-minded and strong Communist, dedicated to action." Kazantzakis himself personifies the "broad and polyhedral thought" of Western man. They cannot reach an understanding. "I rose. I felt that I had been wasting precious time on her for no reason. She held out her hand to me and I realized that this hand came from the opposite shore. I shuddered. There was an abyss between us. What abyss? The Russian Cry!"[177]

Shortly afterward, Kazantzakis saw the celebration of the tenth anniversary of the Revolution. "The festival the day before yesterday was an astonishing sight," he wrote to me from Moscow on November 9, 1927. "More than a million people and troops paraded in the Red Square. All Moscow—with the cannons, the neighing horses, armed workers, wild Asiatic drums, Chinese dragons, Caucasian dances, prancing cossacks—had taken on the appearance of a fearful barrack ground."[178] After a couple of days a pro-Communist World Congress opened. Representatives had been sent from everywhere—there were more than a thousand: "Chinese, Negroes, Indians, Americans, Japanese, all Europe, very few from the Balkans." One Greek: Kazantzakis. The delegates first heard an account of the ten years' work of the Revolution from Rykov, President of the Soviet Government. The second theme of the Congress was then discussed: how a new world war could be prevented. Kazantzakis mounted the rostrum. Rejecting evasions, he gave a message for the workers of the world to the representatives of forty-three nations who were attending the Congress: Capitalist war is inevitable, because the capitalists who are in power have an interest in making war. There is only one thing to do: to prepare for social war. When the capitalist war comes, it must be turned into a social war.[179]

"They told me you were a mystic," Panait Istrati, also invited to the Congress, said to Kazantzakis the next day, "but I see you've got your feet well on the ground."[180] Who was Panait Istrati? Thirty years ago, that question would have been unnecessary. The Greek-Roumanian writer, whom Romain Rolland had introduced to the literary world of France and who had charmed the European public with the legend of his vagrant life and his stories, was then in his heyday. He was forty-three years old and had published the "Stories of Adrien Zograffi" and "Life of Adrien Zograffi" (Zograffi being none other than himself) in a series of volumes, and had already begun to "reap all the fruits which every author dreams of today—fame, money, women." At the very height of his renown, "in one of his articles in L'Humanité, full of indignation and disgust, he bade farewell to Western civilization, rotting in dishonor and injustice, and took refuge in a new land, where he could live and work—Russia."[181] These last words must be taken literally. Istrati had in fact decisively broken with Western civilization in order to embark on a new adventure, to search (he also!) for a new destiny. "Marxian theory and official communism have not narrowed his mind at all," adds Kazantzakis. There is no doubt about it: they were made to be "brothers"!

All his life, Kazantzakis had wanted to find brothers and companions. He had hoped to cure his diffidence in some common work. He longed to realize a manly ideal, a pure friendship between men, a brotherhood inter pares. "O voi che siete due dentro ad un foco!" (Oh you who are two in one fire!) These words—with which Dante has Virgil address the inseparable shades of Odysseus and Diomedes—Kazantzakis had sometimes wished to hear in the company of a beloved friend.[182] He had tried the experiment in various forms, once with Anghelos Sikelianos (in 1914 and 1915), at other times with Yannis Stavridakis (when they were living at Zurich during 1917–18 and when they went to the Caucasus in 1919), with Costas Sphakianakis (when they had lived together at Kifissia in 1921) and with Takis Kalmouchos (when they traveled together to Egypt and Sinai during the winter of 1926–27).[183] In the summer of 1927, as I have already mentioned, Kazantzakis had endeavored to start his coenobium at St. John the Hunter.[184] But he had met only with failure and delusion. This unfulfilled longing he had embodied in the mythical friendships of Rocky and Granite, Kentaur and Orpheus, heroes of the *Odyssey*. But the substitution did not of course satisfy him. Now Fate had set a new companion in his way, unexpected and strange, and yet one who possessed the much-desired qualification of being able to smooth out all the difficulties in the journey they were to undertake together on the morrow of their acquaintance.

On November 17, 1927, Kazantzakis, Istrati and some other guests of the Soviet Government left Moscow by train for a tour of the Caucasus.[185] The two friends broke away from the group, shut themselves into a compartment and talked; they never tired of listening to each other. "How did this multicolored bird fall into my hands? What piece of good fortune is this?" Kazantzakis asks.[186] "I realized at once," Istrati confesses, "that I had to do with someone in many ways a great deal stronger than myself."[187] The merchandise which these two Anatolians had to exchange consisted of tales and ideas. Enthusiasm gave them hallucinations. "Friendship, pure mirror where illusion is mirrored!"[188] The snow-covered plains stretched out to the right and the left of them. They alighted at the large towns: Kharkov, Rostov, Baku, Tiflis, Batum. There were receptions, addresses, visits to factories. "The journey came to an end. Russia shone immortal now in our minds: it was as if we had traveled from one end of our soul to the other."[189]

Throughout the tour, Kazantzakis and Istrati made ceaseless plans. The journey intoxicated them. "I must, by whatever means, find a way of living far from Greece . . . I do not know whether I shall go back to Paris or whether I shall return to Moscow and establish myself there" (Kharkov, November 17);[190] "I am touring the Caucasus, my eyes are full once more, the *Odyssey* grows, my determination to act is being strengthened. The likelihood of my staying here increases. . . . The decision is ripening, it is still fluid, but in a few days it will take a definite shape" (Caucasus, November 20); "Probably I shall come to Greece with Istrati and go back with him to Moscow" (Baku, November 21); "I have decided to return to Moscow and to go thence to Kiev, where I shall stay with Istrati, and then we will leave for Greece together on December 23. I shall look out for a house for us and try to settle here, giving an abrupt turn to my life. I shall deny myself many joys which still hold me through personal necessity, I shall give a vigorous, *farouche jusqu'au bout* expression to my life. The time which passes here is heavy-laden with precious substance, with responsibility. Without knowing it, they live here the major problems which interest us, they realize them spontaneously" (November 22); "My life must assume a decisive tension in Russia" (Tiflis, November 25); "We leave Tiflis this evening for Batum; from there, via other cities, back to Moscow" (Tiflis, November 27); "My life is changing . . . I am coming, I am descending slowly down to Athens" (Kiev, December 10, 1927).[191]

Four or five days after Christmas the two friends reached Athens. To give me notice of his return, Kazantzakis sent me, wrapped in a red cloth, the mask of Nietzsche which for years now had hung over his door. He had surrendered his old idol to a younger person. Our acts are symbols. On the day of his arrival in Moscow, he had hastened to pay his respects to the tomb of Lenin. On leaving Russia two months later, his mind was made up: he would turn his back on his old life and try his luck in a friendly venture.[192] A beginning was made in Athens: he introduced his companion to the Greek public with an article in the *Proia* (December 31, 1927); he published a series of articles on the Soviet Union in the same paper (January 8, 1928 *ff.*); with Istrati he spoke to the Athenians at a large meeting in the Alhambra Theatre.[193] For several days the Athenian press had to deal with the two agitators. An article by Istrati,[194] some incendiary statements made after visiting the Sotiria Sanatorium, brought the scandal to a head. The Aliens Department gave Istrati to understand that his presence was not desired in the country of his father. A temporary compromise became necessary: Istrati went to live at George Nazos' house in Kifissia, where he started to write the novel *The Thistles of Baragan,* for which his French publisher had been asking him for some time.[195] Kazantzakis returned to

Aegina to continue the writing of the articles for *Eleftheroudakis'*
*Encyclopaedia*.

For two or three months, Kazantzakis found "calm, the sea, the mountains—and himself" once more.[196] But Istrati had returned to Russia
and was awaiting his companion. The plan of common action was not
yet settled: they were to meet as soon as possible to decide what to do
with their lives. Kazantzakis left again for Russia on April 19, 1928.
After four days, he landed at Odessa. Some ill omen perturbed him: "A
great misfortune will overtake me. Let it happen as it will. I am even
ready to die."[197] The same evening he left for Kiev to meet Istrati. There
might be a new life before him. Not even he himself yet knew his limits.
He hoped that the foreign country would release the powers frustrate
within him, would reveal something different from what he had in his
heart. With the myriad godless fighters who achieve deliverance through
history, perhaps he too would recognize his place in the collective drama.

Kazantzakis could not conceive any form of activity other than traveling and writing. Istrati by nature favored the indefinite and the empiric:
he proposed that they learn Russian, become acquainted with leading
figures, converse, listen, wait: submit themselves unconsciously and
gradually to the methods and ways of behavior dictated by their new
faith.[198] The difference in approach of the two companions reflects a still
deeper difference: in temperament, in upbringing, in habits. At the
same time, an unconfessed disagreement became apparent: Istrati both
said and believed that he had found a fatherland in Russia; he wanted to
live and die there. Kazantzakis, although he had said the same, had
never truly believed it. The plan which developed under these conditions was that they should undertake a great journey through all Russia
and together write a series of articles for the world press, extolling the
struggle of "Crucified Russia," the Redeemer of the human race. These
articles were later to be produced in three volumes entitled *Following
the Red Star* (this too an allusion to the birth of the new Redeemer).

Istrati left for Moscow to arrange permission and means of travel.
Kazantzakis stayed on in Kiev to write a scenario commissioned by the
Soviet cinema on the subject of the Greek War of Independence and
entitled *The Red Kerchief*. The two friends met again at the beginning
of June in Moscow, and lived together in a "datsa" (a wooden country

house) at Bekovo, in the middle of a fir wood, forty kilometers out of the capital. Kazantzakis began to write a second scenario, with the title *Lenin*—which had the outline of the later *Toda Raba*—and some articles on contemporary Greece for which he had been asked by *Pravda*. Their itinerary was drawn up: the Volga, Astrakhan, the Caspian, Azerbaidzhan, Georgia, Armenia, Turkestan, Siberia ("and, if we can, Peking and Japan":[199] Kazantzakis had not given up his longing to know the world, even if this lay outside the orbit of the Red Star). The Soviet Government presented to the two pilgrims—and to the two female companions who were to accompany them—a round-trip ticket, valid for all the railways and ships in the country.[200]

Kazantzakis' temporary sojourn at Bekovo is connected with an important event in his spiritual life, one which I have already indicated: his turning toward total nihilism. It is strange but none the less true that it was in Russia, where the new world was being built, at the start of a journey that was to end in a hymn of praise, that Kazantzakis formulated the frightful conclusion of his spiritual development. "I am correcting *The Saviors of God*," he wrote to me from Bekovo on June 11, 1928. "I have added a small chapter: 'The Silence'—a bomb which shakes the whole *Saviors of God*. But it will burst in the heart of a few people." The text is in fact enriched with an eschatological prophecy: "Fire will surely come one day to purify the earth. . . . One day the entire Universe will become a single conflagration."[201] It is enriched also with a proclamation of total nihilism. The beatitudes of *The Saviors of God*, which conclude the confession of faith in the first edition, here change their meaning completely: "Blessed be all those who free you and become united with you, Lord, and who say: You and I are one. And thrice blessed be those who bear on their shoulders . . . this great, sublime and terrifying secret: THAT EVEN THIS ONE DOES NOT EXIST!"[202]

Not to see here evidence of a real spiritual struggle, the daring and terror of a thinker, would be a great mistake. Kazantzakis must have cried out like Nietzsche when the fearful idea of Eternal Return was revealed to him: *Lux mea crux!* The terrible illumination had consumed him. "Slay me in the light!" cries Homer's Ajax to Zeus. Heroism is always one and the same. At the same time, Kazantzakis' world-view rose round him like a wall: "My life becomes more and more dense, savage and solitary. The day will soon come when I shall be like a rock where

[ 134 ]

—as a mystic nun of the Middle Ages so well expresses it—only martins can build their nests."[203] The feeling of solitude was never more acute. A journey which Kazantzakis made with Istrati as far as Murmansk, "the utmost rock of Russia," two thousand kilometers north of Moscow, filled him with cosmic terror: there "a people is living in the most in-human wilderness, worshiping a ferocious god (we saw his rages, in a museum, full of thick, black blood), and every morning they lift up their hands to the East and utter this one prayer: Do not kill me!"[204] Kazantzakis' fellow traveler did not share his terror: "He sometimes has tragic shudders, but he forgets them at once and returns to his food, his coffee, his cigarette and easy conversation." "I am silent—it is my only refuge—and I suffer alone. . . . Many frightful things enter my mind. . . . More and more I despair and grow in strength. . . ."[205] "Bitterness, savagery, passion for the wilderness, scorn of hope, silence, pass through me."[206]

I shall not attempt to explain Kazantzakis' intellectual fever or his harshness to himself. I shall merely repeat that here perhaps is revealed the psychology of a person who cannot make contact with reality and whose impotence turns to impatience, to the point of wanting to obliter-ate the world of appearances: "Ah! When shall I start *Buddha,* who is all eye, who plays with shadows, who knows that all things are transient creations of the intricate human *appareil?*"[207] But behind appearances does there exist a metaphysical unity, a real Being? The conclusion of *The Saviors of God* had given the answer. Is there at least an ethical world? Moralists sell the temporal as eternal.[208] Nothing exists except an inconceivable and continually renewed energy. Man out of conceit identifies himself with it, rides with tragic joy the cataract bearing him towards the abyss. In these frightful aphorisms the reader may recognize something of the "hammer philosophy" of the "destroyer of idols"—of Nietzsche when he had reached his final paroxysm (1888).

In the meantime, preparations for the journey were continued. Kaz-antzakis set down (in French) the Introduction to their travel book, and Istrati countersigned it.[209] He had not yet measured the gulf which separated him from the inhuman theory of his companion. Kazantzakis was more aware of it: "My companion has misgivings, he does not dare face the whole journey, he wants to get out of it. I am afraid he is going to stop halfway and that I shall go on alone. Even the fieriest men are inert and material. I am impatient to be left alone." As usual, Kazantzakis prepared himself by reading a pile of books, "rammed a sixth of the earth into his head."[210] On August 28, Kazantzakis, Istrati, Eleni Samios and Bilili Baud-Bovy left Moscow for the south, with Nizhnii Novgorod as their first halt. From there they traveled down the Volga to Astrakhan, where the river joins the Caspian Sea, stopping on the way at Kazan, Samara, Saratov and Stalingrad, and reaching Astrakhan on September 16. During the last ten days of September, they left for Azerbaidzhan (Tiflis on September 25). Thence they took the famous Vladikavkaz road, landing up at Borjom. There they had a month's rest, during which time Kazantzakis wrote twenty articles.[211] "I am going to send most of them to *Nouvelles Littéraires,* but do not know whether they will publish them, as for them they are revolutionary; here in Russia they are regarded as *mystiques.*" The journey continued (November 4) into Armenia as far as Mount Ararat: Erivan, Esmiadjin. Back to Tiflis. A little later (about November 10), they set out for the Black Sea; they stopped at Sukhumi and stayed at the old seaside monastery of New Athos, now a "rest house." Kazantzakis wrote a second set of some twenty articles: "I don't know what has happened to the first twenty articles I sent" (December 1, 1928). At the end of December they set off again for the north, intending to stop at Moscow and to go as far as the Arctic Ocean (for the second time) "to see the black day and the aurora borealis."

During his previous Russian journey (November–December, 1927) from Moscow to Batum, at the beginning of his friendship with Istrati, Kazantzakis' letters always touched on the same subject: Action! The New Life! On his new "pilgrimage," the prevailing theme is the *Odyssey.* His presentiments about dedicating himself to the revolutionary movement had gone. His one remaining refuge lay in poetic creation: Lenin gave place to Odysseus.[212] "I should like to see all Siberia, to see much land, much water, people and animals, and then shut myself away for months and years in creative immobility" (Kiev, May 10); "I am impatient to start work quietly on the *Odyssey* once more" (Kiev, May 17); "I must travel through all Russia to gather images, movement, color for the *Odyssey.* Otherwise, my stay here has no great point" (Kiev, June 2); "I am working well and sometimes write disconnectedly a few verses of the *Odyssey*" (Bekovo, June 19); "The White Nights have given me great happiness—blue, luminous, *mystiques*. . . . All this joy must illuminate the *Odyssey*" (Leningrad, June 25); "I am impatient to end my two-year Russian service and to start the *Odyssey* again" (on the way to Murmansk, beginning of July); "It broadens and enriches the brain and eye of Odysseus. All this: ports, Lapps, white nights, frozen oceans, reindeer, will be yoked to the verse" (Murmansk, July 20); "I am impatient to make the journey, but am much more impatient to finish it and to start work on the *Odyssey*" (Moscow, July 29); "I am happy and excited and everything seems good to me because in the background I behold the sea of the *Odyssey*" (Moscow, August 15). "All I see and live: people, colors, wastes, rivers, have only one purpose within me: to become the *Odyssey*" (Astrakhan, September 21); "I hope I shall be able to live quietly on top of some high mountain—Pyrenees or Engadine—and to rewrite the *Odyssey*. . . . When this journey is over, with what joy I shall plunge myself into absolute solitude among the snow! Like a silkworm that has eaten all the leaves of the mulberry tree, I feel my body transparent, filled with precious substance, all silk" (Sukhumi, December 1); "I still don't know whether the articles I sent to Europe will be published. . . . They are simple *impressions*. The substance of my journey will all go into the *Odyssey* alone. More and more I feel a fearful harshness within me, clarity, obstinacy, silence. When I am alone, I think I shall feel a *frisson* of terror before myself. Ah! to be alone on a high mountain and hold all the earth I have seen in my hands!" (New Athos, December 6, 1928)

Odyssey! Odyssey!—that is the prevailing theme. How much was Kazantzakis' return to his old self responsible for making Istrati tire of the journey? Did the independence and vitality of his friend exhaust him? Did his merciless world-view oppress him? Undoubtedly all this contributed to the crisis through which Istrati passed when, a little later, they reached Leningrad. An old friend of his, Victor Serge, and his family had been unjustly treated by the Soviet bureaucracy (this was a forewarning of the inhuman treatment that the Trotskyites were to suffer). Istrati was roused into a frenzy. He ran up and down staircases, he hammered on doors, shouted, insulted. All in vain. Victor Serge was first isolated and then exiled; his wife went mad, his child was left in the streets, his father-in-law starved to death. This was the famous "Rusakov Affair." During the first phase of the crisis, Kazantzakis seems to have

[ 137 ]

remained true to his own nature: Serge's personal tragedy, which had so unsettled Istrati, affected Kazantzakis too as a man, but it did not provoke in him such violent reactions, still less did it darken the face of Russia for him. "Then Panait went out of his mind, and shut himself up in his house in Moscow and wept and cursed as if he had rabies! . . . And as he thinks Kazantzakis is unmoved—the dirty egoist—he hates him, hates him with all the power of his soul."[213]

The two fellow travelers parted "without shaking hands."[214] Istrati returned to Paris, where he ordered the newspapers and periodicals which were to publish their articles to throw them into the waste-paper basket.[215] In the murderous depths of winter, Kazantzakis continued his journey through Russia alone. The two women who had been with them also wanted to return home. The new exploration required the spirit of a conquistador: from Moscow to the Arctic Ocean; from the Urals to the Pacific Ocean through Siberia; from Moscow to Turkestan—three immense journeys. Kazantzakis was a prisoner of railway timetables: he had neither the means nor the permission to travel in any other way than by train. One can follow, with astonishment, his itinerary on the map. Leningrad-Petrozavodsk-Kem-Murmansk (January 20–24, 1929): "The planet is frozen and you feel the *frisson* of the total destruction which is to come." On February 5 Kazantzakis crossed the Urals and entered Siberia: "Alone, calm, very happy indeed."[216] Perm-Sverdlovsk - Omsk - Novosibirsk - Krasnoyarsk - Irkutsk (February 9): "Frightful cold, they sell milk with a knife, the river Yeniseysk, frozen with all its waves, is full of troikas and people." The journey continues: Chita-Khabarovsk-Iman, a short stay on the Manchurian border (February 16): "Now I understand this clearly: what interests me is not man, nor earth, nor heaven, but the flame which devours man, earth and heaven. It is this flame which I must grasp, express. Only then shall I go beyond all previous stages."[217] On February 18, 1929, Kazantzakis arrived in Vladivostok: "I have reached the last stage, set a hard victory as my target. Obstinacy, inhuman love, scorn for men, faith and silence. Today is my birthday and I am calm, quite alone, and I see the Pacific Ocean with its green frozen waves before me."

Kazantzakis set off on his return journey, stopping at various towns which he had missed on his way out. "But my mind is already completely focused on the *Odyssey*. My Russian venture is at an end" (February

20). In the second week of March he re-entered Old Russia: Vologda-Yaroslavl-Rostov. "Tomorrow I shall be in Moscow, in the hope of getting the permit I need to go to Bokhara and Samarkand. I want to be free from these two names and cities which have troubled my mind since childhood." In the meantime, summing up his trans-Siberian journey, he notes the precious things it has given him. Above all he puts "the great, fertile, divine inner *silence*." The spring is coiled again for creation: "During my life I have often been silent for months on end; but this Siberian silence came when it was due, after the vain, superficial talk about trivial problems of the 'companion.' I am glad that for weeks I have kept my mouth closed, unsullied by any word" (March 10).

On March 26, 1929, Kazantzakis entered Turkestan without permission. "Joy, freedom, solitude, silence, sweetest spring in the heart of Asia." The traveler raves with enthusiasm. Samarkand, Bokhara! "Ah! how marvelous this world is, what souls, what faces, what happiness to tread the ground, to cross over the earth and to have two eyes!" (March 27) "Bokhara will remain in my mind forever. It pleases me because all the houses are low, mud-built, without any color, without ornament. And suddenly from out of this mud rise the huge multicolored mosques glittering in the sunlight. Everyone has been sacrificed to raise this unexpected lofty madness. In the midst of this mud, God rages with the love of the eternal, the multicolored, the luxurious, drinking and disdaining the muddy roots around him—houses and men. When the wind blows—and while I was there it blew strongly and hotly—the houses are broken to bits and are scattered in the air and wrap like incense round the green flaming cupola. Ah! how the sight of that ruin and that flame delighted me! I held a piece of bread and a large melon and sat on a stone at the foot of the mosque and ate them. On another occasion, in Spain, I thus had enjoyed fruit—grapes then, and bananas—and bread. But here it suddenly seemed to me that I was completely at home, so much so that clearly and all at once I realized that I was 'happy,' that I sat at the root of my soul with all Bokhara spread out like entrails within it" (April 9). "In a few days," Kazantzakis concluded, "I leave Russia; I have whatever I wished to see, hear, learn, enjoy."

## 3

From this seed, from this son, my fate would be decided.
—N. Kazantzakis, *Report to Greco,*
*Nea Estia,* November 15, 1957

Kazantzakis left Russia on April 19, 1929, stayed for about three weeks in Berlin, and by May 10 was settled on a mountain in Bohemia, the Erzgebirge.[218] His longing to be alone on a mountain had been fulfilled. But the time had not yet come for him to sink himself into the *Odyssey.* A publisher in Berlin—where Kazantzakis had given a lecture on the Soviet Union on May 6—had given him the hope that he would publish a book of his recent impressions; and Kazantzakis began to write *Toda Raba,* in French. The work was accomplished in thirty-two days, but, realizing that a reputation as an author is not usually established with a single book, he also went ahead with a novel, which he called *Kapétan Elia:* it occupied him till the end of August.[219] In the meantime, the *Kölnische Zeitung* published some of the articles Istrati had repudiated. The Parisian magazine *Europe* accepted the travel notes from Egypt and Sinai, *Les Nouvelles Littéraires* the impressions of Palestine and Spain: the correcting of the French translation of these also took up time. Negotiations with French and German publishers made Kazantzakis wild with impatience. "Ah! When shall I once and for all be rid of Russia? *Odyssey!* Nothing else."[220]

That summer was critical for Kazantzakis' inner development. The first piece of writing he undertook in French reconfirmed his breach with his native land and indicated how foreign to his own people was the world that he wrote about. In fact, from the first he had been a disturber of the carefree atmosphere prevailing among the Greek intelligentsia. Each time he returned from the world's centers of disturbance, he gave the impression of someone who has barely escaped from a fire, who belonged to another time. The fever which had inflamed some of his contemporaries—André Malraux, Arthur Holitscher—had consumed him also; he too had seen "Asia in eruption."[221] The style of his diction was a proof of it: it abounded with declamations, reverberated with prophecies. His heroes—incarnations of his own polyhedral consciousness[222]—were terrified by their own premonitions. A sense of the

Second Coming—now, in the atom age, become general—was from that time, thanks to Kazantzakis, present in the Greek intellectual world.

Cut off from his fatherland, defeated in his attempt at action, the shift from Lenin to Odysseus cost Kazantzakis dearly. The non-attachment of nearly half a century here came to an end. Exclusive dedication to art promised him moral harmony, but Kazantzakis suffered at this junction like a novice who abandons worldly things forever. "*Odyssey! Odyssey!* My whole heart and strength are concentrated there. Everything else is ephemeral; it shines today, tomorrow it darkens, disappears. The perfect verse is the only salvation of the soul."[223] This passage is like a confession of faith. But it is followed by a cry of pain: "Indescribable bitterness, despair with clenched teeth, calm, disdainful, which laughs when it sees someone, because it does not condescend to share earth's burden with anyone . . . Here I live on the mountain, and sometimes the deer come outside the house and I watch them and hardly keep back my tears. Joy, despair, serenity—all of them together—and I do not know what to call this intricate and united heartbeat."[224]

Kazantzakis used to proclaim the superiority of poetry over action, but I do not think that he has ever finally decided to which of the two primacy belongs. As he himself admits, terrible doubts still tortured him. For Kazantzakis, action would mean the discovery of God. Refuge in poetry meant that the void had not been filled. The declaration that no metaphysical or moral idea is loftier than poetic creation is an attempt at self-consolation: we noted this when following Odysseus' desertion by the gods and his temporary dedication to art (Book XVII). But he never gave evidence of real inner harmony. If Kazantzakis had been sure of the outcome of his poetical effort, he would certainly have found peace at once. His faith in art would have sprung from an ontological certitude, having no need of proof. Man's form-creating demand would have appeared to him as a metaphysical reality: he would have been able to say, like Malraux, that the answer of the human race to the gods on the Day of Judgment would be a people of statues. Alas! Kazantzakis was imprisoned in his nihilism, and his prison had only one skylight: art. He had to trim his wings to escape through it.

To trim his wings. But he wanted his flight to be so light that a voice could be heard: a God took the weight from him. "I marshaled all my recollections, I retraveled all my journeys, I recalled all the great spirits to whom I had lighted candles in my life, I sent my blood wave by wave to nourish the seed within me, and I waited. I fed it on the precious honey I had gathered sucking all my life at the sweetest, the most venomous flowers."[225] The process he here describes no doubt goes with the creation of every long poem. But at the same time it reveals the nature of Kazantzakis' inspiration, its spiritual and psychological cause: the poetic act amounted to an endeavor to master the countless experiences of the poet and to save them from formlessness. Kazantzakis' lengthy travels—physical and spiritual—and their termination before a blank sheet of paper remind me of some Cretan monks who, with a small box of sacred relics, harrowed all Christendom, from Egypt to St. Petersburg, and gathered offerings in order to rebuild the church of their monastery. Everything collected on the journey was fitted, stone by stone, into the church. In the end, the sensible world seemed unreal: reality was the building.

"The second draft," Kazantzakis told me in a letter, defining his program of work, "will be enrichment, change, addition, but mainly attention to the verse."[226] "The verse is wretched; it all needs remolding, working over, flexibility, simplicity," he declared on another occasion.[227] He made odd corrections, "still skirmishing," and waited till October 1, 1929, before joining battle. "Each morning I awake I feel a frightful indignation and grief; but as soon as I set to work, I am lost and forget everything. . . ."[228] The struggle I tried to describe in the first part of this section had indeed overtaken Kazantzakis. Grandeur and servitude! The only thing he did not intend to change was the spirit of the poem. On the contrary: Odysseus' world-view was to be adapted to the poet's final revelation. He who struggles is the *fabbro*. For the first time, I think, he fully understood how to handle the seventeen-syllable iambic verse and saw the beauty of which it was capable. "I hardly use any of the old verse."[229] His ambition was to give his verse the "elasticity and simplicity of a folk song." His industry now also seemed to be inexhaustible: "I am in a splendid fever, as I was in Aegina. Here (in Gottesgab) it is frightfully cold, all snow, quietness. The house is altogether good, life is ordered like that of a plant."[230] Book after book was gone through without a pause. He planned to work from Book I to Book XI and then to go to the Congo to collect African impressions and panoramas, only starting Book XII after that. But his progress carried him away. He had finished Book XI by the beginning of December and had got to Book XV by the end of the month. At the beginning of February, he had started on Book XX ("here I am renewing even the *trame*"). On March 3, 1930, after five months and three days,[231] he finished the second writing of the poem.

The first and second drafts have not been preserved except for some fragments which he enclosed in his letters to me. It is consequently impossible to gauge the full extent of the improvements the poet made. But we can recognize the views of the polar wastes which he used, the cosmic terror, the experience of total solitude and silence, the exaltations and disappointments of his companionship with Istrati. A unique experience of life, still warm, has passed into the poem. At the same time, the new form of the poet's world-view, the idea of ultimate nothingness, has been fused with Odysseus' actions. Kazantzakis himself, judging his work, declares: "I correct every day, and the difference is astonishing" (September 12, 1929). "The second draft is immeasurably superior to the first" (February 3, 1930). "The *Odyssey* has turned out better than I thought" (April 4, 1930). The fever of work and the satisfaction of something well performed gradually set him at ease: "I feel that I am a good man and that tomorrow morning I have work. All this gives me a serenity, a rhythm so human, simple and fertile that I say I may even be happy" (September 25, 1929). "Frightful snow, blizzards, the house cut off by the ice, and within the deepest unworldly calm: I consider that to work on a high, snow-covered mountain is one of man's sweetest joys" (January 4, 1930). "I am in such a nervous state, so 'superabundant' spiritually, that I dare not turn on the tap to tell you of the fevers through which I pass—all wonder, fullness, fertility, and sweetness. Rarely have I been so 'ripe,' so remote from any pettiness as during these months" (February 3, 1930). At last he had achieved moral harmony: the Sunday of the Creator.

The poet now belongs to the poem. He had scarcely finished the second draft when he was impatient to begin the third. "But I must first glance at Chinese and African poetry and at two or three books by Frobenius." As he had not undertaken the journey to Africa, he would make up for it by reading. "The third draft already disturbs me, I have a mass of changes, new views, a stronger and at the same time deeper atmosphere. This song must not be read; but a rhapsodist, an African

[ 143 ]

*Dialli* must declaim it day and night at the sea's edge during a great festival. Thus it will assume a warmth, a *sans façon*, something spontaneous, far from the work of the office or of pedantry. It still needs simplicity, a working and a reworking at the abstract ideas, until it becomes a legend, an image and action."[232]

To give the abstract a concrete form was in fact the poet's great concern. In its origin, the *Odyssey* was an intellectual conception. It needed to be interwoven with feeling. Logical analysis had to be neutralized, the interpretive procedure effaced. The idea had to be made perceptible, to be dissolved like salt in water, to taste brackish without being apparent. A transubstantiation had to take place. "Think loftily and feel deeply," Unamuno counsels. No doubt poetry is nurtured on thought and sense. But its original source lies in the tragic union of the poet with reality, in the impetuous seizure of both the sensible and the intelligible by the whole nature of man. A world is revealed, a world is born: the language expands in order to receive the revelation without the intervention of logical thought. Anything else is an agony.

Kazantzakis' passion for the modern Greek language—the treasury of sensible things—for books on natural history such as those of Brehm and Fabre, for folk songs, for primitive legends, for travel, is explained by his desire to give the abstract a concrete form. One has only to read *The Saviors of God* and then Book XIV of the *Odyssey* to see clearly the poet's effort to achieve the desired transposition. From one draft to the next Kazantzakis sought to gather the material for this alchemy, the metals and fuel for his furnace. It is not surprising that he did not like living in large cities. There nature is thrust outside the walls, and the uprooted people often speak the inhuman language which Camus puts on the lips of Nada. People are to be found in the great cities who have lived without ever beholding the dawn. "I have been in Paris for some days now," Kazantzakis wrote to me on April 19, 1930, "where I do not feel any delight. . . . I can only spend a few days in these centers of a superficial, inane civilization and then I go back to the eternal elements —the earth, vegetation, cows, solitude. Only these elements correspond with what interests me." "Time is my only hope," he adds, "and nothing more precious remains to me. . . . Now I must exert myself, grow savage, isolate myself, in order to achieve my purpose."

Fortune was soon to be kind to him: his life "returned to its natural course—to solitude, to the fertile day, the quiet, nourishing night." From mid-July till mid-October 1930, Kazantzakis lived at Nice, the town loved also by Nietzsche, and from Christmas 1930 till the middle of May 1931 in Aegina. He had spent the month of November in Crete. All that time he was preparing himself for the third draft, studying how to remold the poem and saving up in order to live during the months of complete dedication again to the *Odyssey*. He worked on, as usual, without a break, but at writing foreign to his true nature ("contests of Eurystheus" he calls such work in one of his letters). At Nice he translated or arranged the children's books—some forty volumes—brought out by the two Athenian publishing houses of Eleftheroudakis and D. Dimitrakos. On Aegina, he half finished a French-Greek dictionary commissioned by Dimitrakos.[233] In the intervals between this exhausting labor he reread Frobenius, gathered a new treasury of modern Greek words, planned (without success) a brief journey as far as Biskra, on the borders of the Sahara.

For the last ten days of June 1931, Kazantzakis was in Paris. He had gone there to see the Colonial Exhibition—a presentation of the exotic world subject to the West—arranged in the Bois de Vincennes. He had a longing "to fly to Africa or to India, to touch a tropical atmosphere, to breathe the heavy tropical scents, to see the southern constellations, before plunging once more into the seventeen-syllable waves."[234] His desire remaining unfulfilled, he had resort to a substitute: "For the *Odyssey* it is indispensable."[235] With the booty he collected he retired once more to the mountain which would wrap him in silence. Near the Tyrol, midway between Venice, Salzburg and Vienna, at Turraherhöhe, at an altitude of 1750 meters, was a small house which friends who knew his ways had recommended. There he hoped to settle. He climbed up to it, but did not stay. "I saw that I should not find a better house than my old one at Gottesgab. So I returned with joy to the house in the wood and was quiet. Calm, sunshine, fir trees, scent of new-mown hay— and before me once more the sea of the *Odyssey*. I move in on July 1."[236]

While still on Aegina he had planned the third draft: "isolation, elaboration, verse by verse, syllable by syllable."[237] One would have thought it would have taken him years. But "the demon inside me presses." His letters record the stages of his progress.[238] By July 17 he had already completed three books. A month later, he was at Book VIII.

On September 8, he was at Book XI, on October 5 at the end of Book XIV, on the 31st of the same month at Book XVIII. On November 17 he was at Book XXII, and on December 4, 1931, he finished the third draft. Six months' work! "How fearful it would have been if I had died before doing this third draft. What mistakes, what roughness and precipitation there was in draft two. Surely—I hope—I shall be saying the same thing about draft four, and so on. But I am still in the dramatic and epic element; in a later draft, perhaps in the fifth or sixth, I shall flood these solid elements with the watery, vague, wavelike element of lyricism. We shall see."[239]

The impressive spectacle of Kazantzakis sailing the "Great Mediterranean with the horizontal lines"[240] must not take all our attention: we must glance at his inner life. He is alone, celebrating his happiness. He is not mistaken: solitude is the climate for creation. Even poets like Solomos, whose nature was different from that of Kazantzakis, valued it greatly: "There is no doubt that nobody lives well except alone. Always from my early childhood I have been impressed by the lame god, whose mother threw him down from heaven and who lived at the bottom of the sea and worked without anyone's seeing him and without hearing anything round his cavern but the sound of the infinite ocean."[241] But solitude often means loneliness, as when it is not self-chosen but is the consequence of a nature different from that of others. "The note from the young Jewess you sent me moved me very much. It was like a warm hand stretched out to me in my loneliness. Now I begin to understand, from personal experience, Nietzsche's emotion when someone once climbed up to his mountain and said a kind word to him."[242]

Kazantzakis' solitude had yet another consequence: he had no help from anyone. It is very moving to see, from his letters, his extreme gratitude for the smallest object he received: a book, a paper. He was continually deprived of things he should have been able to find at his own front door. Indeed he had to learn to live like a hermit—but not to have the books he needed? More distressing is the lack of any encouragement: for years and years he struggled without hearing a word of praise. "I am as lonely as the hangman," Michelangelo, another tormented soul, once cried: this feeling is expressed by the elect throughout the centuries. Kazantzakis also was deprived of the help he might have received from a teacher: his letters are full of appeals and questions about this or that. For a point of verse technique, for the translation of certain terms and expressions, in the many difficulties which arose during his work, Kazantzakis had to turn to someone younger than himself. "I am facing an immense problem alone," wrote his "parallel," Nietzsche. "It is a forest where I am lost, a virgin forest: *Wald und Urwald.* I am in need of a help. I need pupils, I need a teacher. How sweet for me it would be to obey!"

In the depths of his loneliness, Kazantzakis deliberately split himself into two in order to have someone to talk to: he recalled his dreams, "the dense, many-colored, rich vision of the night"; he listened attentively to catch the voice of his subconscious. Like the archaic man that he was by nature, he attached a great importance to dreams and sought guidance from them: we noted what a part they play in the *Odyssey.* On the other hand, his loneliness lessened his sense of reality. Kazantzakis slipped into an imaginary world, taking it for the highest form of freedom: "As soon as I finish the third draft of the *Odyssey,* I shall write the *En fumant*—a completely *fou* work. For I shall know it will never be printed."[243] On another occasion he considered writing something similar: "If I had time, I would like to write a play where time and place and causality are conquered as if men were *piccoli:* all daring, insanity, essence."[244] At the same period he planned a *Buddha,* another fantasy: "The 'Buddha' with the seven *Credos,* where *The Saviors of God* will be fitted like a stone."[245] In the end, the construction of the *Odyssey* absorbed all his material: "The further I proceed with the *Odyssey,* see what deficiencies, what lacunae it has, and what struggle is still needed before it is launched into time, the more I understand this very simple fact: Happiness lies in giving your soul to a great beast to devour!"[246]

The third draft of the *Odyssey* was finished during the first days of December 1931. But Kazantzakis did not stop revising till the beginning of May 1932. It took him another seventy-five days to copy out the poem.[247] At the same time he wrote four scenarios: *Buddha, Mohammed, Don Quixote, A Solar Eclipse.* This may seem strange. But it was a continuation of his recent exercise in this type of work and it was another attempt, unfortunately ineffectual, to solve the problem of his livelihood. In March 1932, while he struggled in uncertainty, Kazantzakis received a great shock: he lost his mother: "I hold myself in firmly so as not to cry out. Yet I know that only if I shouted like a wild animal would I find relief."[248] With this blow still fresh, he reached Paris on June 1, 1932, and went to live—with Eleni Samios, who had also been with him at Gottesgab—in a little flat in Boulogne-sur-Seine.[249]

That summer, stirred by the admiration for Dante which he shared with one of his neighbors, he started translating the *Divine Comedy*. It is not an exaggeration to say that Kazantzakis absorbed the very spirit of the "loftiest poet." Certainly, he had always honored him; but full assimilation only took place during the work of translation, when the nightmarish and yet seraphic vision passed through Kazantzakis' mind and was clothed in the dress of the Greek language. Dante's poem affected him deeply, nourished and strengthened him as the Eleusinian "Kykeon" the neophyte. When, shortly after, the Cretan called the Florentine his "Leader," the word must be taken in its full sense: Dante was indeed for him *il duca, il segnore, il maestro*. He embodies the ideal of poetry and is the supreme victor over a most harsh fate.

Uncertainty about his livelihood, not to say indigence, made Kazantzakis leave Paris on October 3, 1932 to try his luck in Spain: he had made an adaptation of the Italian comedy *Calandria*, by Cardinal Bibbiena (1470–1520), and hoped to have it played at some Spanish theater.[250] He had similar hopes for the scenarios *Don Quixote* and *Mohammed*. His expectations in the end came to nothing, but the journey proved useful to him in another way. The temple Kazantzakis had built and continued to decorate could hold all the booty he could capture and all the offerings made. The mind of the builder, moreover, was enriched and instructed. To enlarge the temple was the purpose of every voyage. On his first visit to Spain (1926), the *Odyssey* was no more than a premonition: the spirit could wander at will. Now that the poem was under way, Kazantzakis' vision searched a narrower field, but it had gained in intensity: "For the first time I am *seeing* what I saw before. Am I inattentive, or does my mind develop, change, and all change with it?"[251] I spoke in Part I of this book of the impact the statues from Pergamos and beside them the *Delphic Charioteer* made on Kazantzakis when he saw them in the Cast Museum at Madrid. "Entirely virginal" is also the feeling given him by El Greco:[252] "Another wonder which I am seeing as it were for the first time is the golden 'St. Peter' of the Sacristía" (in the Escorial).[253] As with Dante, Kazantzakis was carried from the work of art to the soul of the creator. He wished to make El Greco, too, a guide and a confessor.

This old master had personified the soul's ascent. As the war song says about his native Crete, he too was "girded with flames." Whatever he depicted soars upward as if drawn by a heavenly magnet. Not one of his figures is asleep, all keep watch. They symbolize a longing for deliverance, a thirst for God, the supremacy of the soul over the flesh. Their creator did not belie them. He too burst forth like a fountain from the total bondage of his race, assimilated the spirit of three civilizations (this being the number of the languages he spoke), wrestled alone on a rock "for the ultimate prizes." His life was a heroic sortie, a glorious victory. If, generally speaking, artistic creation is a lone struggle, El Greco's work is the triumph of a single, homeless person over destiny: darkness has here been fought with an indomitable flame.

Many things may help to strengthen the mind, to stimulate life's energy. Kazantzakis found his old friend Juan Ramón Jiménez, met García Lorca and Valle-Inclán, plunged into books. "A young professor of philosophy at the University [it was Cardenal] has recommended to me the most *daemonische* works of Spanish literature. . . . I am hoping to use them for the *Odyssey*" (Madrid, October 19). "Here in Spain I feel *mon climat* better, here, I think, I could work. This race has vigor, joy, tragedy, warmth, eyes all aflame, splendid figures—like Greco, I feel myself among brothers" (Madrid, November 2). "I am reading Spanish poetry, I am translating many poems, I go to the 'Ateneo' and look through books, I am entering the Spanish soul, which I find continually to be more deeply related to my own than any other. Garcilaso, Fray Luis de León, Góngora, Ruiz, San Juan de la Cruz, Quevedo, disturb and move me. Perhaps this will do my life good" (Madrid, January 21, 1933). "Modern Spanish lyric poetry interests me and perhaps it will be useful in my work. In translating, I enter into various lyric spirits which, though narrow and confined, yet have a laconic sensitivity which pleases me" (Madrid, February 6, 1933).[254]

Dante's shade had not deserted Kazantzakis in Spain. The wanderings of the living man had also an air of exile. One November day in 1932, a poem with the beat of Dante's eleven-syllable line came to him. It is "Dante" (or, more exactly, "The Death of Dante"), first of the Cantos which Kazantzakis was to write.[255] The assimilation which I indicated above is here made manifest. The "Leader" too is scorned, unjustly treated, proud, obstinate, vindictive. He is champion of the popular tongue, the divine poet:

> Ah, how fresh speech and wealth of tongue
> O'erflows the breast and makes it glad!
> And how the people's brooding bird
> Will hatch the word that like a swan
> Enters the peaceful lake of verse!
>
> (lines 64–68)

And the poem he created, triumphing over all adversity, is an eternal monument:

> Lofty temple in the dews of eve
> Glittered all moist the exalted song!
> Demons had borne it up from Hell,
> Dark roots, but now of purest down
> It raised toward light's holy springs
> The ripened flower of bitter strife.
>
> (lines 133–138)

Kazantzakis was encouraged in his struggle by recollecting the great saint of poetry. But another blow, the death of his father, made him "cry out" once more. "I got your telegram [from Crete]. I left at once, overcome by an inexplicable horror. I felt the need to tire myself, to exhaust my body, in order to find a little relief. It was not love, something deeper, more animal, as if a great piece of my body had fallen to the ground, as if horrible roots were drawing me into the earth, before my time."[256] The man-beast whom Kazantzakis had feared all his life and had regarded as deathless had collapsed. He had symbolized, while he lived, the roots, the original beast: the mud of which the son was destined to make spirit. Father and son had made a fantastic couple—one part dense flesh, the other powerful wings—like those winged lions set to guard the gates of Assyrian palaces, or the lion of St. Mark which Kazantzakis had seen carved on the Venetian ramparts of Herakleion. All his life the son had struggled to raise the beast up on his wings: suddenly it had fallen to earth and the two parts had separated. To recover from the shock, Kazantzakis "left at once." The journey he undertook was 2,000 kilometers long: Salamanca-Valladolid-Burgos-Saragosa-Valencia-Alicante-Elche: "almost without eating, without sleeping, with exhausting nightmares . . . The sea at Alicante did me a great deal of good, the sun, the sweetness of the earth, *lying on the hot sands*."[257]

The major experiences of the poet between the third and fourth drafts affected him strongly: "If time were mine, I should climb a deserted African mountain to rewrite it all [*The Odyssey*] from the start; perhaps it would give me relief" (Madrid, October 18). "I am impatient to get back again to the red-hot atmosphere of solitude where alone I can breathe. . . . The fourth draft of the *Odyssey* glows in my mind, it is beginning to possess me, my spirit has become like a field and the seasons of sowing and reaping come and go in regular periods. The fourth draft alone interests me, neither the third nor the fifth, and my eyes rove uneasily and inquiringly, like those of a cat about to give birth" (Madrid, November 26). "I must preserve all my strength for the *Odyssey*. The fourth draft is terribly rich, deep, sweet, wild and fresh in my blood" (Madrid, February 6, 1933). "Now one thing only: solitude, solitude, quietness, a pencil, paper, a piece of bread, olives, some fruit, nothing else. These are the great materials, the primary divine materials" (Madrid, February 23, 1933). "Where can I place all the new things I have to give it? But let us put them in now and take them out in the sixth draft" (Madrid, March 7, 1933).

The day of Kazantzakis' departure from Spain drew near. He went to Toledo to bid farewell to the other "Leader," who years later was to receive the "Report" from his warrior.[258] "As I walked in the narrow streets, a host of voices, words, verses fell upon me. From then on I could think of nothing else" (Madrid, March 14, 1933). The canto of Greco, still nebulous, is forming. Kazantzakis "works it out in his mind, finds scattered verses" (March 15) but does not set them down in writing. The "sweetest shock"—to quote Valéry—came to him a few days later in Paris.[259] "I feel myself full, like a bee. As soon as I find a hive, a sheltered cavity, I settle and produce the honey" (Paris, March 26, 1933). El Greco, in Kazantzakis' poem, also symbolizes the fight against man's obtuseness and the final victory: King Philip II rejects the "St. Maurice," the most spiritual of the pictures, dismisses the painter "from the temple of his dreams"—that is, from the Escorial which he aspired to decorate. There is no refuge but the heavenly Jerusalem, the sphere of autonomous artistic creation. The poem concludes:

> The unseen height of earth rose up;
> Within him an archangel's breast
> To the pure peak compelled him on,
> To untamed freedom's lonely cliff,
> To this world's most lofty stage,
> To heavenly Crete, the hidden fatherland.

(lines 161–166)

While writing the canto of Greco, Kazantzakis had already turned for home. Two lines make it evident:

> Turn to the sun, towards Crete turn,
> Freedom and solitude to find.

(lines 131–132)

Instead of Crete, it was to be Aegina. Kazantzakis reached its harbor on April 12, 1933. There a companion awaited him and a small house on the edge of the sea.[260] "Happy is he," says Goethe, "who without hatred withdraws from the world, clasps a friend to his bosom and with him enjoys that which men neither know nor even suspect, that which passes through the heart's labyrinth by night." After a delay of some years and in an unexpected fashion, Kazantzakis realized his old desire for the coenobium, the "Phalanstery" of which Nietzsche had dreamed. He had now only to bless his good fortune and to turn his attention to the *Odyssey*.

There are no "letters to a friend" this time through which to follow the poet's inner history. Reminiscences will have to take their place. Kazantzakis had found once more the ideal home in Aegina. Spring, solitude, a new house. Soon came the figs and the grapes, the cool sea, sleep beneath the stars. Many times in his life he had dared to be happy: in creation, in travel. He was so now, bursting with health and with the inner richness he had gathered. The room where he lived was on the upper floor. It had windows on three sides and a door and a balcony to the west. He settled down to work before dawn: he had a small paraffin lamp on his table until the light of dawn fell on his paper. A village woman—Pagona, daughter of Christos Baltas—left his breakfast (a cup of milk, wheaten bread and fruit) on the doorstep. He lunched with his companion. Work in the afternoon. An occasional plunge in the sea. At night, sweet conversation . . . It was indeed happiness. Kazantzakis allowed it to absorb him as he paced alone on his balcony. Sometimes the monologue would be heard down below:

On life's peak where roseate blows
Liberty's unsullied air,
And where, a nightingale divine,
Poetry pours out her heart
Like music from immortal flute,
A diamond fort you raised . . .

The lofty verses dedicated by Mavilis to Polylas do indeed express the felicity Kazantzakis had found.[261]

The poet began the fourth draft of the *Odyssey* on April 23, 1933;[262] full of exhilaration, he finished it on July 24, three months later. This time, the third and fourth drafts are side by side in the manuscript given by the poet to his companion, and hence a comparative study is possible.[263] One could see to what extent Kazantzakis' recent experiences affected the new draft—his bereavements, Dante's poetry, Spanish literature, scenes and monuments; one could mark the development of his poetic art, appreciate the increased richness of language. In my mind remains the image of an ascetic who, without stirring from his seat, scatters his thoughts and visions generously; of a tree which, firmly rooted, yields shade, fruit and scent.

As soon as he had finished the fourth draft, Kazantzakis began to correct his translation of Dante. What but total dedication could absorb him? He did not expect anything from anywhere; he cultivated a sense of freedom whose only content—in the words of Benedetto Croce—was freedom. In this self-sufficient sphere where there is no room for payment or reward, justification for the toil lies in the purity of the purpose. It is the privilege of the lone man that his own conscience is his final judge. In a world of unbelievers and cynics whom no virtue can disarm, Kazantzakis had to be both believing and innocent in order to preserve his faith in the holiness of the "highest hope." But often he awoke like a somnambulist before a precipice. He was seized with giddiness. Then

[ 153 ]

he gave one the feeling that the *Odyssey* was for him like an unreal island which with rigorous struggle he had formed in chaos and which a breeze could scatter.

In mid-September, Kazantzakis was left alone. His companion had gone to Crete to do his military service, Eleni was still in England. The eloquent testimony of his letters begins once more: "Now that I am alone, I have grown wild, I work frightfully hard, I write notes for 10-12 cantos a day . . . [264] If for a minute I am without intensive work, I feel such bitter, pure, illusionless despair that I am afraid I will die" (Aegina, September 29, 1933). In the same letter, a few lines down, Kazantzakis concludes contradictorily: "Here I feel that I am completely happy . . . I see the sea, the absolute calm, all time, as though it were my garden where I can go and cut the fruit." There are only a few sudden breaks to the happiness of total dedication. He was living a form of the absolute, with uninterrupted time and unlimited stretches of solitude: it is not surprising that at times he was frightened, like a camel driver lost in the desert. "Weeks go by without my uttering a word," he says in another letter (October 20): he was also living another form of the absolute, the silence of the hermit.

But the void demanded to be filled. Since no god visited the hermit, the god-bearing heroes of thought and deed were brought into action. In order to increase his inner tension, Kazantzakis invoked "all the great spirits that he had reverenced in his life." Letters of this period reveal who his heroes were: Dante, El Greco, Genghis Khan, Psycharis, St. Theresa, Lenin, Don Quixote, Mohammed, Nietzsche, Buddha, Moses. From November 1932 till July 1934, he was to devote a series of cantos to these, one for each. He called them "bodyguards of the *Odyssey*"; it would be impossible to find a more expressive title. A verse from "Ghenghis Khan" makes their role even more clear: "Help me, advance guards of the human race!" cries the Mongol war lord on the eve of a great enterprise, and he brings before him the shades of Buddha, Christ and Mohammed.[265]

From the titles of the poems alone one can see that Kazantzakis was here giving expression to new and old experiences. Dante is the poet who offered him his flesh and spirit in the Host of the *Divine Comedy*. Greco, St. Theresa and Don Quixote embody his recent experience of Spain. Lenin personifies the bloody resurrection of Russia. Struggles and exaltations of former years are crystallized in the remaining cantos, those of Mohammed, Nietzsche, Buddha, Moses—the mystagogues— and of Psycharis, who represented his passion for the modern Greek language. A detailed analysis of the poems would reveal Kazantzakis' intellectual preoccupations on the morrow of his writing of the fourth draft and would show his private cure for his sense of powerlessness and isolation: in some of the cantos spiritual vitality conquers all adversity, in others the persecuted heroes take refuge in the heavenly Jerusalem, and in others still the heroes become punishers and avengers. Dionysiac pessimism is a common characteristic of all the poems: "Without hope I fight on: it pleases me!" ("Genghis Khan," line 131)[266]

Kazantzakis himself wondered what the motive-cause was of this poetic creation: "Where the devil do I find this savage power to sing over such furnaces? This persecution of fate and total abandonment and desolation on earth gives me such power and repose and fertility that I realize that inside me there is someone else at work, like Death, with his fez awry! It is either some ancestor or some descendant, certainly not me" (Aegina, November 20, 1933). The next day in another letter he again sought for the cause of his creative fever: "I am very *troublé*: if for a moment I stop battling with some difficulty, my blood chokes me. My father at such moments—for he had such moments, identical though on a different level—would take a thick glass in his fist and, with an easy movement, squeeze it to pieces. Thus he would give himself relief. I do the same, using other glasses. . . . If we do not turn the poison into honey," he concludes, "we are lost; because all, all except the creator's heart, is poison."

Eleni arrived in Aegina on December 26, 1933. Kazantzakis' loneliness was sweetened. The fourth draft was added to here and there: "Now that Eleni is copying out the *Odyssey*, I am looking at it again: there is no end to it! Corrections, new images, come to me at every line, 'fresh waters' spring up; each word is a brilliant stone sparkling in a new way when I strike it" (January 1934). In the meantime, in order to earn some money Kazantzakis wrote two primers for the lower grades and submitted them to the Ministry of Education in Eleni's name (February-April, 1934). At the same time he went ahead with the publication of the Dante translation at the printing house of Apostolos Melachrinos in Athens. The printing brought the two poets, who were old friends, into regular contact. Once the epic poet risked showing the *Odyssey* to the lyric writer. "Melachrinos, when he saw it, looked at me with indescribable irony. He made as if to open it, put his hand on it, but withdrew it at once, as if it were a box full of scorpions. If I am able to print it, I shall make 44 copies. And that is a lot. But we still have time—ten years" (Aegina, June 25, 1934). It is not surprising that in this climate Kazantzakis, writing the canto "To Himself," composed the following:

> Patience, my soul, until the grape
> Of vengeance slowly ripens,
> And to the lips comes sparkling wine.

(lines 85–87)

In the same poem, seeking his soul's final desire, he formulates a wish—as a dilemma:

> Ah, would it were my lot once more
> · to mix with all my brothers,
> To tread the loaded grape of earth
> With those who thirst, who hunger!
> Ah, would that earth had handleholds
> That, hung on my mind's hooks,
> High might I raise her up with me
> Into the azure heavens!

(lines 159–66)

The desire for action, it will be noted, has not yet been completely rejected.

In the interlude between the two drafts Kazantzakis lived his struggle more intensely. He tested his strength, prepared for the new leap: "I long for a great journey," he wrote to me from Aegina on August 8, 1934. "I must fill my eyes once more, must break easy habits, must gather firewood for the fifth draft. China, Africa, America—*tengo ganas!*[267] Perhaps some illness would do me good, or a great bitterness ... I am in a state of vague unrest and preparation, in an inner musical uncertainty, a shadow is hanging over me, giving everything other shapes and intense blackness. Sometimes I suffocate, I cry out: 'Enough!' "[268] "When is the fifth draft going to be written?" he asks a few days later. "Only when something special happens in my life, good or bad—let me hope, a long journey. It is the only fruitful method to make me shift all this load and give it some sparkle and levity. The soul is hungry and finds nothing more in Aegina. But how is it to browse on other rich pastures? Ah! China, India, Africa, America!"

Fate heard him. It sent the illness to Eleni, but he himself lived in extreme anxiety from August till the end of November: "I went through a great trial and difficult moments." A little later, fate sent him the journey also. "My head is beginning to fill again," he writes to me from Suez on February 22, 1935, on his way to Japan and China. "I have a silent joy and long to see what will come out of this new raid. A *vision*, a new color, a new jolt to the *Odyssey*? We shall see." "I read, write, see, collect whatever I can. Colombo and Singapore have given me great joy. *La Croix du Sud* is wonderful" (Hong Kong, March 16); "Wonderful temples, statues, colors, stone lanterns. . . . 'Good is this earth . . .' "[269] (Nara, Japan, March 27); "My head is full at last" (Tokyo, April); "Much richness and variety have filled my mind and I shall have to arrange everything in two or three circles in order to give it some coherence. . . . The fourth circle will be the inner elaboration of all this material, the reforming and transubstantiation that my mind struggles to give it, so that it serves my purpose—the *Odyssey* . . . I am impatient to be lying once more before the sea at Aegina and to begin the holy life. To take up again the first line of the *Odyssey* and to start" (Tokyo, April 21, 1935).[270]

His wish was once more granted. The pirate returned to his hideout with the loot from Japan and China. In a letter from Aegina (end of June, 1935), he writes: "I have found happiness and joy. Solitude is to me what a woman is to the warrior; sea, sun, quietness, the day endless, I sleep out on the balcony, all the stars above me, I awake at daybreak, the sacred toil begins, I think over the *Odyssey*, read about China, cook, do not speak, do not see anyone, the time is full of substance."[271] Kazantzakis first of all sought to set in order the treasure he had collected: he wrote his impressions of the long voyage and published them in the Athenian newspaper *Akropolis*: they were to end as a new travelogue.[272] Before he resumed work on the *Odyssey*, he wrote some more schoolbooks, called in builders to repair his house in order to receive Eleni, bought the site where he was to build his "cocoon," and opened a well.

The sights of Japan and China continued to work within him. The aesthetic law of the Far East—its elliptic, substantial style—had stimulated him. Dangerous fermentations were taking place in his mind: "Without willing it, and at violent lucid intervals, I meditate on the *Odyssey*. I am tempted to turn it upside down" (Aegina, July 16, 1935).

He began the fifth draft toward the end of autumn: "Fifth draft, winter 1935," Kazantzakis had written to me in one of his notes. Exactly how many months he worked on it and what he sought to do is not clear from his letters. But he was absorbed until the beginning of spring. On April 11, 1936, he announced some new works: "I have finished a novel in French, *Le Jardin des Rochers,* and have sent it to the German publisher who commissioned it. It will come out in German in the autumn. . . .[273] These last days, I have begun another novel in French, *Mon Père,* about Crete (August, 1896)."[274] On April 17, he gave more details about the *Garden of Rocks:* "I used a lot from the articles [on Japan] and put in nearly the whole of *The Saviors of God.*[275] It is a double journey, internal and external. For that reason I thought of calling the book: *La Double Marche.* But later I saw that the *double marche* is the means, the road, and the *Jardin des Rochers* is the goal. Afterwards, as a sequel, I am going to write the *Klosterfelsen* (*Monastère des Rochers*), and third the *Schulefelsen* (*École des Rochers*), and fourth simply *Felsen: Rochers.*"

*The Garden of Rocks* is in part a travel book, with the difference that the author raises his journey to a spiritual level, introduces imaginary persons and is involved in action with them; it is also a novel, with the narrator as the main character. The subject, as Kazantzakis says in his letter, is the double journey of the hero: through his adventures of heart and mind he attains a heroic conception of duty; from episode to episode in his trial, he describes his ascent in the language of ideas. Double march! It ends in the "Garden of Rocks," a garden without flowers, trees or water; but its rocks are an image of the free soul, a soul without illusions, without hopes.

The narrator's principal trial lies in the passion inspired in him by a young Chinese girl, daughter of the venerable mandarin who is his host. Their love is the lofty and desperate love of romanticism: the lovers suffer together to the end, but their passion remains unfulfilled. It is as if a sense of guilt has numbed their limbs. Finally the man deliberately renounces happiness in order to dedicate himself to spiritual exercises; the woman allows herself to be carried away by the Revolution, likewise fulfilling her duty—the duty of subjugating self to a super-personal aim. The lovers' parallel journey toward their sacrifice is marked by a passionate analysis of their feelings: erotic intoxication, exaltation, secret remorse, distress. The hero's attraction for a woman of another race fills him with voluptuous trepidation. His excitement is stirred by the sight of an ancient civilization, by his participation in exotic rites, by tender and sublime experiences. The millenaries and the present, the monuments and the fruits of the earth are reduced to a taste of ashes; happiness is presented in its most refined and sensual forms; death lies in wait like a serpent among the rose gardens and like poison in the dishes of a banquet.

Where did Kazantzakis conceal all this tenderness? Where had he learned this refined artistry? It is the miracle of the poet's protean power that he can enter every world. The *Garden of Rocks* beside *Kapétan Michalis* is like a Tanagra figurine beside an archaic statue. The French language which Kazantzakis here used was undoubtedly the most suitable in which to express the fantasies of the Far East: its spirit had increased and refined his own. The style is gentle, discreet, without strong contrasts; at the same time it is penetrating, versatile, lovingly turned toward the civilization it is interpreting: an old-fashioned writing, somewhat self-contented, thin now and then and yet unbroken, like a filigree. Certain pages recall the *Jardin des Supplices* by Octave Mirbeau, others —how could it be otherwise?—*The Saviors of God:* they do not merely recall but repeat, in another language, passages from it. Here the language becomes warmer, more vivid, fired as it is by the spirit of the original. He flirts with the French language like male with female or rustic with courtier. The hero's double journey—through the world of the senses, the world of the spirit—is served by two voices.

Still further activities, both literary and itinerant, are to fill the gap before the sixth draft. Ten more cantos are scattered like signposts between summer 1936 and spring 1937: "Shakespeare," "Leonardo," "Toda Raba," "Hideyohi," "Alexander the Great," "Christ," "Eleni." The dilemma (concerning ways of deliverance) formulated by Kazantzakis when he dedicated a canto to "Himself" appears again here: sometimes a canto expresses the idea of a creative liberty out of time or place ("Shakespeare"), and sometimes the desire for social revolution ("Toda Raba").[276] At the same time the old themes are repeated: that of the desperate fighter who expects no reward, whose loneliness is not to be healed ("Hideyohi"); that "all human things are vanity," life is the dream of a dream, the prize for the most glorious contest is a fleeting perfume, a distant melody ("Alexander the Great"); "God" wrestles within man, the spirit devours the flesh, the Pure passes over the hair's-breadth bridge set up by the Evil One ("Christ").[277]

The journey to Spain (his third) tore Kazantzakis from his solitude and from his papers. The journey this time was neither for recreation nor was it an intellectual raid. Spain was embroiled in the Civil War: "A beloved friend has been wounded and I am hastening to see him." The fratricidal struggle tested Kazantzakis deeply: two world-views were at war. There is no doubt that heroism was a virtue to be found in both camps: it belongs to the Spanish race. The frightfulness of war, murderous passion, can provide material for nonpartisan writing. But Kazantzakis felt the need to examine his conscience and determine his "spiritual longitude and latitude." "The simplest pattern I have found is this: up to 1923 I was a nationalist, all emotion and fire. Dragoumis was the shadow I felt beside me. From 1923 to 1933, approximately, I belonged, with the same emotion and fire, to the Left Wing (never Communist, as you know). The shadow I felt beside me, vaporous, was P. Istrati. Now I am passing to the third—will it be the last?—stage: I call it freedom. No shadow of anyone. Only my own, long drawn out, deep black, ascending . . . I know that ideas are inferior to a creative soul. I become more and more *amoral, anidéal,* not in the negative but in the positive and deep sense of these words—which are negative only to barren, unfeeling, cold spirits. . . .[278] Thus armed—that is to say, stark naked—I am making the first critical *expérience* of my new liberty: I am going to see bleeding Spain" (letter, October 12, 1936, from the ship *Ousoukouma,* near Gibraltar).

What did Kazantzakis gain from this new voyage? This can be gathered from the articles he published in the Athenian newspaper *Kathimerini,*[279] which later formed the second part of *Travelogue-Spain* bearing the title "Viva la Muerte!" These are some of Kazantzakis' most beautiful pieces of writing. He had bitten into the flesh of things. Throughout this adventure, the usual cry—"I am collecting images and sensations for the *Odyssey*"—does not occur once. Now the furnace tempers him completely. He saw his most frightful premonitions fulfilled, reason torn to shreds, passion carry men this way and that. The bloody experience cut into him deeply, reached his most hidden tissues. "Thus armed—that is to say, stark naked" (also bloodstained, I may add), he started on the sixth draft. This time the poet had to prune his overgrown garden: "The sixth, last but one, draft of the *Odyssey* had 42,500 lines: to cut out the nine thousand lines (limiting the poem to the 'sacred' number 33,333) was a painful business: as if I were cutting living flesh."[280] The task took him the whole winter and the spring of 1937.[281]

There were to be seven drafts, according to Kazantzakis' original program. The time was approaching when he would give his ship to the sea. An excursion to the Morea in September 1937[282] enabled him to collect further material for the *Odyssey*. The antique world which awoke within him (Corinth, Epidaurus, Mycenae) inspired the tragedy *Melissa*, which he wrote in December of the same year.[283] Behind the ancient myth and its decoration sounds the desperate, the utterly desperate cry of the poet. The world's kingdoms cannot cure man of his loneliness. Glory is unreal, thrones are barren wood, descendants are savage enemies. The fate of the race of Periander is shown to be even more frightful than that of the sons of Atreus. The archaic king of Corinth kills his wife and slaughters his first-born son—from excessive love. He wishes to perpetuate his race and himself cuts off his only scion. Man wrestles with the night, death rules life. Everything is absurd, a flame devours man, reducing him to ashes. No one knows why.

In this frame of mind, Kazantzakis started on his seventh draft. It took him from May 1, 1938 till the end of November of that year. In the same year he began printing the work. An art-loving woman—not Greek—had undertaken the expense of a monumental edition of 325 copies.[284] Up to the last moment the poet corrected, added and cut. At last he finished it and took a deep breath. Like a shipbuilder, he had built his craft, calked, tarred and rigged it. Whatever was within his power he had put into it. It only remained for him to launch it: *Habent sua fata libelli!* Christmas 1938. The time had come for the *Odyssey* to set forth. Who better than the poet himself could give us the image of his triumph?

His dragon crew were hard at work, pushing with pride
their new ship slowly down the heating logs with care
while the scared piper drenched them to prohibit fire.
Just as they braced their shoulders for the final heave,
their captain rushed in time to join them, spread his hands,
shoved hard, pushed off the virgin keel into the waves . . .

(II, 1469–74)

# EPILOGUE

Insensate care of mortals! Oh, how false the arguments
which make thee downward beat thy wings!

One was following after law, and one aphorisms,
one was pursuing priesthood, and one dominion by
violence or by quibbles,

and another plunder, and another civil business, and
one, tangled in the pleasures of the flesh, was moiling,
and one abandoned him to ease;

the whilst, from all these things released, with Bea-
trice up in heaven, thus gloriously was I received.

—Dante, *Paradise,* XI, 1–12
(Carlyle-Wicksteed translation)

$T$*he first and second parts of this book were written during the summer of 1957: Kazantzakis was still alive. I wrote the third part in the spring of 1958, when his eyes had closed forever.*

*A book's first critic must be the author himself. But I do not wish to hide the fact that from the moment I started writing I mentally submitted each line to the judgment of Kazantzakis. My desire was to finish it and to read it to him; it would not have been the first time I had done this with works I had written. His pride had from the first approved of the independence of my views: the object of my study, both for him and for me, could not be other than the truth.*

*I had first told him of my intention of setting down my testimony of his life and work in spring 1950. He at once gave me his blessing: "God grant me before I die to be worthy of such joy. I should like much to know, before I die, whether my birth was worth the trouble." Seven years later, when he had finished his* Report to Greco, *which I took to be an autobiography, I wrote to tell him that I was shortly to start writing my book. "I am more interested in what you write about me than I am in what I write about myself," he replied, "and I am glad that I shall still live to read it" (Antibes, February 12, 1957). I then told him that I was anxious lest the* Report *be published before my book: my conclusions would lose their value if they seemed but to follow his own assertions. He hastened to reassure me. He was then receiving treatment at Freiburg, preparing for the fatal journey to China. "I shall not publish* Greco [*that is,* Report to Greco] *before: I shall await you with longing.*

*You are the only man in the world who can judge me and whose word will have unspeakable value for me. God give you strength, and give me life so that I may see what you write" (April 4, 1957). If Kazantzakis had such confidence in me, the reason is that he himself knew what he had given me of himself during the thirty-one years of our friendship. "How the thirty-one years have passed! Like a glass of cool water!" These words concluded the same letter.*

*I started to write the third part of my book some months after my Master had been laid to rest. I was able to finish it on June 2, 1958. I had tried not to alter the tone, even though my heart enjoined a new kindness. The only concession I made to the beloved shade was to let him speak more often through his letters: their testimony after his death seemed to me invaluable.*

> Is not this the duty of the heart? Did not God fashion it for this, to revive the beloved? Revive him!
>
> —N. Kazantzakis, *Report to Greco,*
> page 331 of the original.

*End of June 1958. Propitious circumstances have brought me to Antibes. I have left my manuscript in Athens with my friend Emmanuel Kasdaglis, who has willingly agreed to supervise the printing during my absence. I am determined now to read* Report to Greco *and to seek for verification of my conclusions. I have finished my work and I do not intend to change it. But I am anxious to check it. Kazantzakis himself will once more be the judge.*

*I am sitting in his study, sad and yet at peace. The things around me are still warm with his presence, like a garment he has just taken off. They are all familiar to me. I knew them in his house in Athens when I first met him, and later in Aegina, Gottesgab and Antibes. Time has added but little. The ascetic does not hoard up treasure: his pitcher filled with water is enough for him. What is entirely new is a wall of books: writings of Kazantzakis, translated into some thirty languages—the dream of his life realized.*

*Here in his house, I am often alone. Eleni is occupied with the work to which she also is dedicated. The silence is great, the hour sacred. A tap drips, wood creaks. Now and then the wind passes like a bird's flight through the vine hanging outside the window. Kazantzakis lives within me. I know that he is buried in the soil of Crete: my own eyes saw his remains lowered into the grave. But every instant my heart revives him.*

*When at evening we stop work, Eleni and I talk about him. Tears fill her eyes as she counters her fate. From his most daring ideas down to the least detail of his daily life, we recall the man himself: the harmony is unbroken. Dedication, endless toil, disinterested struggle . . . I never tire of hearing her recollections of the last years. Kazantzakis had grown beyond materiality. He had known that which he had never before encountered and for which he had sometimes wished: the trial of illness. He had become like Prospero: a good, holy spirit. An odor of sanctity issued from him.*

*I continue my recollections alone. Like a dream which we lose when we awake, only to find it again in sleep, so are my memories of Kazantzakis. Where are we together? In Arcadia, Aegina, Antibes? The soul keeps what it loves ever present. Time is reversed, the past is interwoven with the present, history burns with a scent like that of incense. Is this total knowledge? Is this complete participation? Last night I had a dream: before me a fountain played, it leaped up with vigor and pride, as if trying to surpass its own power. Seeing it, my eyes were refreshed. They watched it endlessly, not wishing to lose sight of it. Suddenly, without any gradual lessening of its vigor, the fountain fell, like a bird shot in flight. I awoke. "The symbol of the life which has gone," I said to myself.*

*Under that sign, the impartiality of my opinion seems a sin, a betrayal of the heart. I want to forget the path I have taken, to resign myself to that sweet warmth which enfolds me on all sides and wakens hidden life within me. What did I seek in my book? Truth for others. My own truth is this total union with a person. I had been encircling a monument; suddenly I had found the door and had entered. My final knowledge covered me like the wing with which the bird covers its head when it sleeps.*

*For about twenty days I did nothing but read* Report to Greco. *Kazantzakis has here made a myth of his life. "Poetry and Truth." He has confused the dates, put ideal order into his struggles, given harmony to his life. Imagination has given him whatever life denied him. The* Report *is not an autobiography: it is the chronicle of the fight with the daemon, the mythical preparation for the* Odyssey. *It is an ascent affording a magnificent view, the total conception of the world. Whatever*

[ 167 ]

*Kazantzakis wrote or did after the* Odyssey *is omitted from the* Report *of the soldier to the general: the poem was the mission of his life. Kazantzakis has noted in a book found among his papers: "Secondary works: (a list of his books follows).* Obra *(i.e.,* Work*):* ODYSSEY.*"*[285]

*What I have maintained is thus confirmed by Kazantzakis himself: the* Odyssey *is the crowning glory of his life. The fountain reached as far as that. In the* Report *he bears witness to the difficult course that led him to Odysseus: "Christ, Buddha, Lenin—stages in the journey." In the* Odyssey, *this course is raised to the level of poetry. My book—if I may be allowed to relate it to its cause—is the Commentary: an attempt to find parallels between the poet and the new Odysseus, both hunters of God.*

*I write my thoughts down without egoism or modesty. What constrains me is respect and love: I listen to them with all the attention I can. I have left every sound behind me, as all my life I have wanted to do. The silence of this cell is the last lesson that Kazantzakis has left me. Offices, certainties, customers—how foreign and remote! A blank sheet of paper: let that be our destiny, that our final judge. No one will cry, "We have triumphed!" There is no victory, the struggle is endless.*

*A pain tenses my heart. That head was still full of seed. Sketches of the books he planned were found in his notebooks: an* Akritas *(the "New Adam," as he called it, an epic counterpart of the* Odyssey*); the* Third Faust; *the* Atomic Heart; *and several others. Kazantzakis dreamed of his rebirth, he aspired to make the Ascent again: to raise—like the master masons of the Middle Ages—the spire of a still loftier cathedral, sister to the first. He saw his salvation in extremes.*

*But behind the worlds that his spirit molded during the last ten years of his life, illness was at work. I had met him in 1948 and in 1953: his body was being destroyed. The nine books he wrote during that period are evidence of the power of his soul, but they had also weakened his body.*[286] *It was as if the wounded fighter had accepted a challenge. He turned his back on everything he had achieved up to 1948, retaining nothing but* Zorba the Greek. *He leaped anonymous and naked as an athlete into the arena: he won world-wide recognition. If he had not achieved his victory, he would have died without consolation. Was not this then a promise of rebirth? He hoped up to the last moment. He had transposed traditional heroism to the realm of the spirit. Could it be that the gods would desert him? In the* Report *he does not hide his premonition of the end: "The sun has set, the mountains have darkened, the ranges of my mind still have a little light on their peaks, but holy night is falling, it rises up from the earth, it descends from the sky. . . ." But could the surety he had gained, the wisdom, the honesty sink into darkness? Absurdity of man to disregard death! Absurdity of death to reap the ripe man!*

*The journey to China was the last that Kazantzakis was to make: "I see the world through the eye of an elephant." And he adds: "Nevermore!" An airplane carried him, sick, from Japan to Denmark across the North Pole. They touched for a short while at Anchorage, on the top of the globe. Did Kazantzakis think of his Odysseus? Odysseus had known deifying death on the snows of the Antarctic, at the South Pole. Now, as one of Kazantzakis' friends observed, there was an identification of the fate of the poet and that of his creature. Kazantzakis and Odysseus set out toward Immateriality from the poles. Both had desired to exhaust this world, and to look down on it from the highest watchtowers.*

*Antibes, July 11, 1958*

# Notes

NOTES TO PART I

1. Kazantzakis both feared and admired his father, the "wild beast"
as he called him, while he loved his
mother, a "holy woman" (the description is again his), and suffered
for her. He attributed the ambivalence of his will to the disparity of
the blood contending within him
(letter from Antibes, April 1950).*

2. Idas: pen name of Ion Dragoumis,
Greek diplomat, politician and man
of letters (1878–1920). Dragoumis
played in Greece a role similar to
that played by Maurice Barrès in
France. He was the victim of political assassination.

3. An association of progressive writers, educationalists and politicians
founded in Athens in 1910 for the
purpose of bringing Greek education up to date and introducing the
popular language into the schools.
It published a monthly bulletin.
Kazantzakis was one of its found-
er-members.

4. Venizelos, Eleutherios (1864–
1936): Greek politician of Cretan
descent who embodied the national
aspirations of the Greeks. He gov-
erned Greece on several occasions
and led her to great and victorious
military undertakings which resulted in the liberation of thousands of Greeks from the Turkish
yoke.

* Wherever in these notes or in the main
text I cite a letter of Kazantzakis, I refer to
a letter sent to me. I usually add the place
and date of origin. Where the letter has been
sent to another person, I give his or her
name.

5. Mavilis, Lorenzo (1860–1912):
Greek poet from Corfu and a member of parliament. He was killed
in the First Balkan War, in which
he was fighting as a volunteer.

6. Palamas, Costis (1859–1943):
Greek poet and prose writer from
Patras. He is regarded as the out-
standing intellectual figure of his
generation in Greece. He published
twenty collections of poetry, a great
number of critical essays, one short
story and one play. In his two long
poetical works, *The Dodecalogue
of the Gypsy* and *The King's Flute,*
he expressed the spirit and ideals
of contemporary Hellenism.

7. Sikelianos, Anghelos (1884–1951):
Greek poet from the island of Lev-
cas. He published lyrical poems and
tragedies. In four collections of
poems with the general title *Consciences,* he sought to grasp the
spirit of his country and his race
and to interpret his own destiny as
poet and mystagogue. With his
American wife, Eva, he founded
the Delphic Festival (1927).

8. Letter of Kazantzakis from Gibraltar, October 12, 1936.

9. *Nikephoros Phocas* appeared as a
book in 1927, *Odysseus* and *Christ*
in 1928—all three in Athens. (*Odysseus* was first published in the
Alexandrian periodical *Nea Zoi* in
1922. Kazantzakis had signed it
with the pseudonym A. Geranos.)

10. Prologue to the novel *Zorba the
Greek* (Athens, 1946).

11. In addition to his original literary
works, Kazantzakis also produced
a notable series of translations,
which he undertook for some years

[ 171 ]

as a means of earning his living. The following is a list of the translations for the period 1911–15: William James, *The Theory of Emotion*; Nietzsche, *The Birth of Tragedy*; Nietzsche, *Thus Spake Zarathustra*; Eckermann, *Conversations with Goethe*; Laisant, *Education on a Scientific Basis*; Maeterlinck, *Le Trésor des Humbles*; Darwin, *On the Origin of Species*; Büchner, *Power and Matter*; Bergson, *Laughter*; Plato, *Alcibiades 1, Alcibiades 2*; Plato, *Ion-Minos-Demodocus-Sisyphus-Cleitophon*. All were published by the publisher George Phexis, Athens.

12. It is worth noting that the eviction of the Greeks from the Caucasus fed Kazantzakis' imagination when he wrote the novel *The Greek Passion* (or *Christ Recrucified*).

13. Kazantzakis hesitated to recognize his life's purpose. Perhaps this explains his frequent change of pseudonym: Akritas (as columnist in the Athenian newspaper *Akropolis* in 1906 and as correspondent for the Athenian newspaper *Neon Asti* in 1907); Karma Nirvami; Petros Psiloreites; A. Geranos; Nikolaï Kazan (in the foreign editions of *Toda Raba*).

14. Galatea Kazantzakis, *Men and Supermen* (Athens, 1957), pp. 137–41.

15. While still a child, Kazantzakis' Odysseus raises his fists to the sky and cries: "O God, make me a god!" (*Odyssey*, XIV, 210–12). Kazantzakis is here drawing on a personal experience, as he himself confessed to me.

16. Letter from Berlin to his first wife (*Letters to Galatea*, Athens, 1958, pp. 141, 150).

17. "I am leaving, I am traveling," Kazantzakis wrote in August 1922 to his first wife, "not a journey of recreation, you understand. Fearful struggles go on within me. I think I shall die if I stay for long in one place. I must move in order to find something of myself, to forget the frightful command I have given myself and which I cannot fulfill" (*Letters to Galatea*, p. 69). Kazantzakis stayed in Vienna from the end of May until the end of August 1922. From September 1, 1922 until mid-January 1924 he was in Berlin. His stay was interrupted by several short journeys within Germany.

18. From *Letters to Galatea*, pp. 106, 120, 122, 123.

19. Kazantzakis' impressions of Russia were first published in the Athenian newspaper *Elevtheros Logos* between November 20 and December 27, 1925. A second series, inspired by his new journey to Russia (October–December 1927) was published in the Athenian newspaper *Proia* from January 8, 1928 on. Later a selection from the first and second series of articles appeared in book form with the title *What I saw in Russia,* 2 vols. (Athens, 1928).

20. Kazantzakis' impressions of Palestine, Cyprus, Spain and Italy were published in the Athenian newspaper *Elevtheros Typos*. His impressions of Egypt and Sinai were published in the Athenian newspaper *Elevtheros Logos*. A selection from these articles constituted a book entitled *Traveling: Spain, Italy, Egypt, Sinai* (Alexandria, 1927).

21. Thus Kazantzakis himself describes Nietzsche's appearance in *England* (Athens, 1941), p. 182.

22. Eleni Samios was then in Paris.

She had met Kazantzakis in 1924. In the same year they had spent a few days (August 18–28) on a coast of southern Crete, and in September 1925 they met for one week on Amorgos. In the spring of 1926 they made the journey to Palestine and Cyprus together with two woman friends. On that journey Kazantzakis gave Eleni the Hebrew-like name of Lenotschka Dybouk which we find in the dedication of the *Odysseus* (1928). July 1926 they passed together on Mount Pelion. They met again in Russia in 1928, and from then on were never separated except for short periods. Kazantzakis testified at every opportunity to his love and gratitude to the "brave, devoted and proud companion." "To Eleni," he wrote to me from Antibes on May 4, 1957, "I owe all the daily happiness of my life; without her I would have died many years ago."

23. Nikos and Galatea Kazantzakis (the latter of the Alexiou family) lived together from 1910 to 1924. During those fifteen years Kazantzakis was frequently absent from his home. He toured Greece with Sikelianos (1914–15), he stayed in the Mani working in a lignite quarry (1915), he traveled to Switzerland (1917–18), to the Caucasus (1919), to Crete, France, Germany (1920–21), to Austria and Germany (1922–23), to Italy (1924), etc.

24. Stavridakis, Yannis: Greek diplomat of Cretan descent, childhood friend of Kazantzakis. He served as Greek consul in Zurich, where he gave Kazantzakis hospitality for about a year (1917–18). Together they undertook the repatriation of Greeks from the Caucasus. Stavridakis died during this operation.

25. See note 2.

26. Plato, *Ion*, 534 b.

27. Letter from Antibes, May 4, 1957. Many indications of Nietzsche's influence on Kazantzakis are to be found scattered in the latter's articles from Paris in the Athenian newspaper *Neon Asti* in 1907–9. Particularly worth noting is Kazantzakis' article on Nietzsche in the Athenian newspaper *Elevtheros Typos* on August 22 and 26, 1926, for the 26th anniversary of his death. Equally important is the "canto" that Kazantzakis dedicated to Nietzsche (the periodical *Nea Estia,* Athens, August 1, 1938). If in sketching Kazantzakis' character and in interpreting the significance of his behavior we continually refer to Nietzsche, this is chiefly because Nietzsche was the first Martyr: "A nature like that of Nietzsche must have known, leaping forward a generation, the wretchedness which we now know; what he endured, alone and misunderstood, thousands endure today" (Hermann Hesse, *Der Steppenwolf,* Prologue).

28. Letter from Gottesgab, October 31, 1931.

29. It is worth noting that Kazantzakis' frustrated messianism found outlet in the *Odyssey* (Book XIV), and later in his novels: in Manolios in *Christ Recrucified,* in Jesus in *The Last Temptation,* in Francis in *The Poor Man of God,* etc.

30. Kazantzakis, "H. Bergson," in the *Bulletin of the Educational Society* (Athens, 1912), pp. 310–34.

31. Apart from his doctor's thesis *Quid Aristoteles de loco senserit* (1889), Bergson had up to 1912 published *Les données immédiates*

*de la conscience* (1889), *Matter and Memory* (1896), *Laughter* (1899), and *Creative Evolution* (1907). In 1907–9 Kazantzakis had taken a course given by the philosopher from his Chair in the Collège de France.

32. See Nicolas Berdiaev, *Le Sens de la Création, un essai de justification de l'homme* (Desclée De Brouwer, Paris, 1955).

33. See *Odyssey*, XVI, 144–53.

34. See Galatea Kazantzakis, *Men and Supermen*, p. 176.

35. Wagner's theory was known to Kazantzakis (see *England*, p. 175, *cf. Odyssey*, XVII, 1263–72, VI, 256, etc.). "We have art," says Nietzsche also, in *The Birth of Tragedy*, "in order not to die because of the truth."

36. Letter from London, July 23, 1939.

37. Letter from Madrid, October 11, 1932.

38. "In the succeeding drafts I shall give every attention to the versification and to something still more difficult: to freeing every word and expression from 'intellectual' content; only emotion, substance, music. Absolute simplicity, with simple imagery, clear, visual" (letter from Gottesgab, November 17, 1929). "I am in the dramatic and epic element; in a later draft, in the 5th or the 6th, I must flood these solid elements with the watery, vague, wavelike element of lyricism" (letter from Gottesgab, July 17, 1931).

39. Henri Bremond, *La Poésie Pure* (Grasset, Paris, 1926), p. 22. "Do you know anything more tedious than the *Iliad*?" Valéry once asked Gide. And Gide replied: "*La Chanson de Roland*" (André Gide, *Journal*, Bibliothèque de la Pléiade, Paris, 1941, p. 1325.)

40. E. R. Curtius, "Barrès, 'critique créateur,'" in the periodical *La Table Ronde* (Paris, March 1957), pp. 88–91.

41. Let it be noted that Kazantzakis had been inspired by the herald of the "Worship of the Ego." Through Ion Dragoumis, who had admired Barrès and had known him personally during the latter's visit to Greece (1900), Kazantzakis came into closer contact with the work famed above its deserts at the beginning of the century.

42. "While very young I loved the French romantics: Rousseau, Chateaubriand, Musset, Lamartine, Hugo . . ." (letter from Antibes, May 4, 1957).

43. Letter from Astrakhan, September 21, 1928.

44. "Now I am getting ready to embark on the *Odyssey*. And as I get used to the idea, I feed insanity, *Notre Dame*, with geometrical logic, and with abundant learned food. I brought a pile of books, I read, I take notes, *je réforme, déforme* whatever falls into the mill of my mind: I am getting ready" (letter from Gottesgab, August 20, 1929).

45. Aegina, April 14, 1936. In an open letter (in the periodical *Neo-Ellenika Grammata*, Athens, March 25, 1939), Kazantzakis elucidated his theory about good and evil. There are, according to him, four stages through which man may pass: "1. Good and evil are enemies. 2. Good and evil co-operate. 3. Good and evil are one. 4. And that one has no existence." According to Kazantzakis, those who realize these four stages of initiation are—in this order—the fighter, the sage, the saint and the "super-saint" (the perfectly delivered).

46. See *England,* 1941, p. 173.
47. See *Odyssey,* XIII, 905–12.
48. See *Odyssey,* XIII, 1174–78.
49. "From Siberia, after terrible labor, I have the following fruits: the vision of the inhuman snowy wastes (like the desert of Sinai; but the desert is more inhuman and more in harmony with my heart)" (letter of Kazantzakis from Old Rostov, March 10, 1929).
50. In *Nikephoros Phocas.*
51. In *Christ.*
52. In the *Odyssey,* Book XVII.
53. See *Odyssey,* II, 169–74; II, 405–28, etc.
54. Letter from Kiev, May 25, 1928. The remark he cites is from a critical article on *The Saviors of God* and on *Nikephoros Phocas* which I had published in the Athenian periodical *Anagennisi,* December 1927, p. 177 *ff.*
55. "I thirst for myself," Nietzsche had exclaimed when he saw that his professional duties as a philologist absorbed all his time.
56. Sir Edmund Whittaker, *Le commencement et la fin du monde* (Albin Michel, Paris, 1953), p. 109.
57. Compare with the passage from the *Buddha*: "In a small star, in a narrow strip of earth which they call China, in a foot's length of soil, rose a water-worm, which they call Yang-Tse."
58. From *Buddha.*
59. From *Buddha.* (*Cf. Odyssey,* XXII, 1465–76.)
60. Eckermann, *Conversations with Goethe,* Third Part, September 26, 1827.
61. W. B. Stanford, *The Ulysses Theme* (Blackwell, Oxford, 1954), p. 211 *ff.*
62. See Daniel Halévy, *La Vie de Frédéric Nietzsche* (Paris, 1909), pp. 78, 89, 91–93, 269–70. The similar endeavor of Georges Duhamel and of his companions in the Abbey of Créteil is well known. The idea of founding a "mystical order" and of establishing it in an isolated castle (at Lough Kay in Rosscommon) is met with also in Yeats' *The Trembling of the Veil,* Book III (See Colin Wilson, *The Outsider,* V. Gollancz, London, 1958, p. 223, where there is an eloquent extract from Yeats' text). Well known also is the "Castalia," the "Pedagogic Province" visualized by Hermann Hesse in his novel *Das Glasperlenspiel:* a monastery where daily bread was secured for a spiritual aristocracy and where celibacy and the anonymity of works were obligatory.
63. Sphakianakis, Costas (1890–1943): Greek composer of Cretan descent, influenced particularly by Byzantine music. He was a friend of Kazantzakis.
64. Papanastasiou, Alexandros (1876–1936): Greek politician from Tripolis. He was on one occasion Prime Minister and on several occasions Minister.
65. Letter from Antibes, July 5, 1951. It is impossible not to recall the lament of Odysseus when he buries his co-fighter Clam (*Odyssey,* VIII, 817–20).
66. Solomos, Dionysios (1798–1857): national poet of Greece. He was born in Zante and died in Corfu. In his poems he sung the War of Independence which brought freedom to Greece. He is considered to be one of the noblest poetical figures of the nineteenth century.
67. Virgil (*Georgics,* Book II, 473–74).
68. "When and where does a classical national writer appear?" Goethe once asked. And he answered: "When he finds in the history of

his nation great events and their consequences in a felicitous and significant unity. When he does not seek in vain for greatness in the souls of his compatriots, for depth in their feelings, for strength and consequences in their actions. When he himself, saturated in the national spirit, feels, with the genius which lies within him, that he is capable of loving the past in the same way as the present."

69. O. V. de L. Milosz: *Poèmes* (Fourcade, Paris, 1929), p. 91: "Cantique de la Connaissance."

70. "What will you do with so many words?" an Athenian of society will ask. I could reply: "Do you remember the wild flowers that Shakespeare needed in order to weave Ophelia's wreath or to embroider the river bank where Titania slept?"

71. And Valéry: "You receive the anonymous and middle language, you give it back resolute and unique." (*Tel Quel,* Gallimard, Paris, 1941, I, p. 193.)

72. Fabricator of the "inhuman" language in every land is the Bureaucracy. Albert Camus puts an example of such inhuman language into the mouth of one of his *dramatis personae,* Nada (*i.e.,* Nothing): *L'État de Siège* (Gallimard, Paris, 1948), pp. 122–23.

73. Eckermann, *Conversations with Goethe,* Part III, January 2, 1824.

74. Eckermann, *Conversations with Goethe,* Part I, April 14, 1824.

75. Here one may recognize, through antonomasia, Tolstoi, Ibsen, Péguy, Claudel, Pirandello, Gide, Mallarmé, Valéry, Loti, D'Annunzio, D. H. Lawrence, Huysmans, Barrès, etc. (See R.-M. Albérès, *L'Aventure Intellectuelle du XXè*

*Siècle,* La Nouvelle Édition, Paris, 1950.)

76. Glynos, Demetrios (1882–1943): Greek educator born in Smyrna. Was one of the founders of the "Educational Society" (see note 3).

77. Two names became known when Kazantzakis dedicated books to them: Rahel Lipstein (*What I saw in Russia,* 1928) and Elisabeth Alexander Lange (*Christ,* 1928). To these must be added at least three others: Itka Horowitz, Dina Matus, Rosa Schmulewitz. These three, and Rahel, were Polish Jewesses.

78. *The Saviors of God,* after a short preface, proceeds as follows: The Preparation, The March, The Vision, The Action, The Silence, and the concluding Credo.

79. These citations and those immediately following are taken from the text published in 1927 and not from Kimon Friar's published translation of the revised text of 1945.

80. I have reproduced the complete "confession of faith," for it was shortly to be entirely altered by Kazantzakis himself, and we shall need it in order to compare it with the new text.

81. Polites, Photos (1890–1934): Greek man of letters, critic and producer of the Greek National Theater. He was the first to give life to this theater, and he created a distinguished tradition.

82. See note 54.

83. Kazantzakis frequently named Nietzsche and Bergson as his teachers. He also indirectly recognized his debt to Arthur Schopenhauer (or, more exactly, to his work *Die Welt als Wille und Vorstellung*). Schopenhauer's pessimism was,

after the example of Nietzsche, overcome in Kazantzakis' case by the heroic affirmation of life, by the acceptance of a struggle without reward. He is not the only one among our contemporaries who has been a herald of energy in the darkness of pessimism. Many of Kazantzakis' passages remind one of Malraux, Sartre and Camus.

84. Below is given the time taken for each draft of the *Odyssey,* according to information given to me by Kazantzakis himself in a letter of May 4, 1957:

1st draft: Books I–VI:
Crete, Winter 1925.
1st draft: Books VII–XXIV:
Aegina, May 20–Sept. 22, 1927.
2nd draft: Books I–XXIV:
Gottesgab, October 1, 1929–March 3, 1930.
3rd draft: Books I–XXIV:
Gottesgab, July 1–December 4, 1931.
4th draft: Books I–XXIV:
Aegina, April 23–July 24, 1933.
5th draft: Books I–XXIV:
Aegina, Winter 1935.
6th draft: Books I–XXIV:
Aegina, Winter and Spring 1937.
7th draft: Books I–XXIV:
Aegina, May–December, 1938.

85. Letter from Aegina, August 25, 1927.
86. Letter from Madrid, October 10, 1932.
87. As Virgil takes the end of the Homeric *Iliad* (the capture of Troy) as the starting point of his *Aenead,* so Kazantzakis takes the end of the Homeric *Odyssey* (the slaughter of the suitors) as the starting point of his own *Odyssey.* But if this is a similarity or analogy, there is a great difference between the compassionate, magnanimous, justice-loving and pious Aeneas and the god-slaying, destructive, hardhearted, daemonic Odysseus of Kazantzakis.

88. Papanoutsos, Evanghelos: Greek educator and historian of philosophy, born in Piraeus in 1900. He is regarded as one of the leading intellectuals of modern Greece. He produces the periodical *Education and Life.*
89. Jean-Paul Sartre (in *Situations I,* Gallimard, Paris, 1947, p. 99 *ff.*) has made an analysis of Camus' *Stranger* in the sense which I have here developed. The presence of the "Stranger" in contemporary literature and in the modern world has been studied methodically by Colin Wilson in his book *The Outsider* (V. Gollancz, London, 1956) which the author has presented as "an inquiry into the nature of the sickness of mankind in the mid-twentieth century." An outsider (a "stranger"), according to Colin Wilson, is one who has a consciousness of chaos, one who dares to look the truth in the face. Naturally, Colin Wilson's perspective does not include modern Greek literature, although the latter has produced several works in which the "sick man of the century" suffers and struggles.
90. W. B. Stanford, *The Ulysses Theme* (Blackwell, Oxford, 1954).
91. *Inferno,* XXVI, 139–42. Kazantzakis translated the *Divine Comedy* in 1932, worked over it in 1933, and first published it in 1934 ("Kyklos," Athens).
92. Dante developed a tradition cultivated by Pliny and Solinus, the Roman grammarian.
93. *Paradiso,* I, 34: "A mighty flame follows a tiny spark."
94. *Poems of Tennyson, 1830–70*

(O.U.P., 1950), pp. 182–83: "Ulysses." Stanford with great acumen points out (p. 202 *ff.*) the influences that appear in Tennyson's poem.

95. Kazantzakis had also defined the desperado: "A desperado is: he who has absolutely nowhere to stand, who does not believe in anything, and who in his unbelief is dominated by rage" (see *Spain*, Athens, 1957, p. 156).

96. Hans Egon Holthusen, "The Zero Point," in the periodical *Confluence* (Cambridge, Mass., September 1953), p. 25. In addition, for the significance which the dissolution of the "Myth of the Great Idea" had for the Greek mind, see the three articles by G. M. Theotokas, "The Most Acute Crisis of our Times," in the Athenian newspaper *To Vima*, September 21, 23 and 24, 1958.

97. Kazantzakis had in fact already in 1909 heard "the sign of the earthquake destined to overthrow modern society and civilization, of which the foundations have been shown to be rotten makeshifts" (*Nietzsche and the Philosophy of Right*, p. 8).

98. Revelatory are Kazantzakis' letters to his first wife from Germany. In one of them he tells her of the conference of the "Reformers of Education." One of their leaders, Oesterreich, had impressed him: "An ascetic figure, thin, forty-five years old, tall, wild and very poor. He wears tattered clothes made from *peau de diable,* and when he speaks, he forgets that he is speaking about schools and begins violently and with hatred to attack the whole disgusting state of modern social life" (Oct., 1922). "I have written and finished yesterday the *Ascetic* [*The Saviors of God*]. . . . Let this world be destroyed, cease to exist any longer. That is the first duty . . ." (March 1923). "Destruction, destruction, destruction! All today's misery and shame must go" (April 1923). "What is contemporary life? The end of a civilization, the creation of a new civilization" (April 1923) (*Letters to Galatea*, pp. 101, 170, 171, 182). See N. Kazantzakis, "The New Pompey," in the periodical *Anagennisi* (Athens, 1926) pp. 76–80. The text is worth study: it is a comment on *The Saviors of God*.

99. Proofs of this temporary and peculiar conversion of Kazantzakis are to be found also in the Letters to his first wife and at the same time in the original form of *The Saviors of God*: although "post-Communist," it contains something of the theory of the class-war.

100. See *Nietzsche and the Philosophy of Right*, pp. 17–18, 28, etc.

101. Oswald Spengler developed his theory in his work *Der Untergang des Abendlandes*. The first edition of Vol. 1 was published in 1918. Vol. 2 appeared in 1922. In 1923 the enlarged and definitive edition was published in Munich.

102. Spengler, *Der Untergang des Abendlandes* (1923) Vol. I, pp. 144–45.

103. The *Prologue to the Persian Letters* was first published in 1926 with the title *Au Sujet des Lettres Persanes*. This important text has been republished several times (see Paul Valéry, *Oeuvres,* Bibliothèque de la Pléiade, Paris, 1957, Vol. I, p. 1709). The *Regards sur le Monde Actuel* was first published in 1931. The second edition appeared in 1936 (Stock, Paris).

104. Cavafis, Constantine (1868–1933): Greek poet from Alexandria. He wrote poems in a "hellenistic" style, distinguished by the strangeness of their versification and their language and pervaded by a sense of decadence. He is honored greatly both in Greece and in the West, where he has become known through successful translations.

105. Vlastos, Petros (1879–1942): Greek intellectual and writer. He wrote poems, short stories, critical essays and a dictionary of the demotic Greek language. He lived mostly in India and England.

106. In accordance with the significance given to these words by Albert Camus with his books *Le Mythe de Sisyphe* (1942) and *L'Étranger* (1944). I ought to add that long before Camus, Hermann Hesse had investigated the significance of the "Stranger" in his novel *The Wolf of the Steppes* (1928).

107. "Everything is permissible": in accordance with the terrible phrase that Dostoievski puts on the lips of Ivan Karamazov. Compare, by contrast, the behavior enjoined by the word of God: "All things are lawful unto me, but all things are not expedient: all things are lawful unto me, but I will not be brought under the power of any" (I Cor., 6:12–13). See Albert Camus, *Le Mythe de Sisyphe* (1950), p. 94.

108. The passages from Novalis and from Luther are cited from H. E. Holthusen (see note 96).

NOTES TO PART II

109. A broad and very intelligent summary of the *Odyssey* by Kimon Friar, the translator of the epic into English, has been published as a supplement to his monumental translation (Simon and Schuster, New York, 1958). Every praise is due to this translator who has most successfully re-created the Greek original, surmounting incredible difficulties of both language and style.

110. *The Odyssey* is written in 24 rhapsodies (books), one for each letter of the Greek alphabet. The titles given to the rhapsodies are due, not to the poet, but to his translator, Kimon Friar. The titles I have proposed in the Greek original of my book are not the same, but I have adopted Friar's titles in the present edition in order not to confuse the English reader. The differences are not important, but I wish to mention here the titles I proposed for the 24 rhapsodies (books): I, Odysseus' Return; II, The New Departure; III, Odysseus in Sparta; IV, The Rape of Helen; V, Odysseus in Crete; VI, The Bull Orgy; VII, The Conspiracy; VIII, The Burning of the Palace; IX, Odysseus in Egypt; X, War in Egypt; XI, Imprisonment and Rebirth; XII, The Exodus (rhapsody of the Desperadoes); XIII, Rocky's rhapsody; XIV, Asceticism; XV, The City-State (or the Utopia); XVI, Destruction of the City-State; XVII, The Absolute Freedom; XVIII, The Rhapsody of Buddha; XIX, The Rhapsody of Prince Elias; XX, The Rhapsody of Don Quixote; XXI, The Rhapsody of Jesus; XXII, Odysseus in the Polar Village; XXIII, The Last Voyage; XXIV, Death and Dematerialization.

111. The idea is Goethe's (see Stanford's *The Ulysses Theme,* p. 192).

112. This strange metamorphosis of Death occurs in a Cretan folk song.

See Anton Jeannaraki, *Kretas Volkslieder* (F. A. Brockhaus, Leipzig, 1876, p. 145).

113. "My work is the purification of unspeakable struggles and joys, written in blood. I have tried for many years to save what I could of my soul. So that when I die men know how much I too have loved and felt for life and how I have gazed upon and touched the sea, the soil, woman; and so that they learn that I was not a beast or a stone but a man with warm flesh and an insatiable soul" (letter to Elias Venezis from Aegina, December 30, 1938, published in the periodical *Neo-Ellenika Grammata,* Athens, January 7, 1939).

114. The poet on two or three occasions had summarized the development of his hero from Beauty to Virtue, and from there to the Thirst for Truth and to Freedom: see *Odyssey* XVI, 1083–93, and in particular XVII, 55–101.

115. The second edition of *The Saviors of God* (1945) appears to follow directly the world-view of the *Odyssey* (1938). But this appearance is deceptive. The first (unpublished) form of the *Odyssey* (1927) was based upon the world-view of *The Saviors of God* of 1927. Finally the poem—after seven drafts—followed the development of the poet's thought as we know it from *The Saviors of God* of 1945. I should emphasize that the Myth of the *Odyssey,* in its general lines, had already been shaped in the first draft.

116. The quotations from the *Odyssey* and all references to that poem are all taken from Kimon Friar's translation. I am greatly indebted to him.

117. Spengler calls the organic necessity of fate the "logic of time" and he opposes it to causal necessity, the "logic of space": "Whatever we grasp with the mind has a cause; whatever we live with an inner certainty as an organism has a past" (Spengler, *op. cit.,* Vol. I, p. 199; *cf.* Vol. I, pp. 154–55).

118. Kazantzakis, "A Comment on the *Odyssey,*" in *Nea Estia* (Athens, August 15, 1943), p. 1031. For the relationship of Odysseus and Helen in the poets of antiquity and of recent times, see Stanford, *op. cit.,* p. 210 and pp. 227–28.

119. It may not be superfluous to remark that most of Odysseus' erotic caresses take place before witnesses.

120. See also II, 1000–15, where Granite's history is related: he had killed his brother for a woman about whom they were quarreling, but he refused to touch her.

121. See the facsimile of a letter written by Kazantzakis in 1952 from Assisi to the writer Max Tau: Nikos Kazantzakis, *Rettet Gott!* (Donau-Verlag, Wien-München, 1953, p. 48). This theory was applied in a typical way in his novel *The Last Temptation.* It is Nietzschean in origin.

122. Paul Claudel, *Mémoires Improvisés* (Gallimard, Paris, 1954), p. 59.

123. As is known, the vitalistic teaching pervades André Gide's *Les Nourritures Terrestres* (1897).

124. See also XXII, 15 *ff.*; XXII, 168–72; XXIII, 260–66.

125. See XIII, 1213–14 and XV, 664–65.

126. The charred sentinel of Pompey was one of Kazantzakis' favorite symbols.

127. Polylas, Jacob (1826–1898): Intellectual and politician. A friend of

Dionysios Solomos, he published the poems of the latter found after his death, and added a prologue and notes.

128. See III, 477–79; V, 588–634; VII, 221–47 and 977–91, VIII, 847–48; IX, 380–94; X, 206–19; XI, 885–92; XIII, 471–84; XIV, 1063–68 and 1093–1125; XV, 515–23, 808–23, 899, 910, 916–20, etc. I know no nontheological text in which the word "God" recurs as frequently as it does in the writings of Kazantzakis.

129. In a notebook found among Kazantzakis' effects is the following note in his own hand: "Odysseus' religion in the end became unshakable, so that no idea or act could any longer destroy it—precisely because it was supported on the Void: neither God, nor hope, nor eternity. Each moment was immortal, and he had no need of any other immortality. He lived each moment intensely, qualitatively."

130. "In the Report to Greco I make a confession . . . and there I speak of the four main stages through which I have passed, and each of those stages bears a sacred name: Christ, Buddha, Lenin, Odysseus" (letter from Antibes, February 12, 1957).

131. "In the final books Odysseus meets the great leaders of souls—entirely changed of course: Buddha, Faust, Hamlet, Don Quixote, the Poet, Christ—and gives me the opportunity to put into contact and to contrast Odysseus' soul with all of them" (letter from Gottesgab, February 3, 1930). In one of Kazantzakis' manuscripts I came across the following note: "Faust sought to find the essence behind appear-ances. Hamlet is entangled in appearances and writhes. Odysseus rejoices in appearances and, rejoicing, creates the essence." I must add, however, that I have not been able to recognize Faust and Hamlet in the Odyssey. (The hermit in Rhapsody XIX reminds one very distantly of Faust, but the lord of the tower in Rhapsody XX does not seem to me to have the characteristics of the Danish prince.) Evidently Kazantzakis finally abandoned the idea of contrasting them with Odysseus, although his original conception was not altogether lost.

132. See X, 448–49, 494, 517, etc.; XI, 661–66, 727–38, 830–1015, 1343–50.

133. A comparison of Odysseus with Christ is also found in the Laus Vitae (1903) of D'Annunzio, in the first poem of the collection. Kazantzakis wrote the following in connection with the great importance Christ had in his spiritual life: "Christ tormented me from my childhood years—that union, so mysterious and so real, of man and God, that Sehnsucht, so human and so superhuman, for a reconciliation of God and man on a higher level than one can desire. When I grew up, I wanted to free myself from that persistent idea with a work of art: at the age of twenty-five [?] I wrote a tragedy in verse, Christ—Christ after the Crucifixion, when the Magdalene and the disciples re-created him in their hearts, and gave him the new immortal body, resurrecting him. But that tragedy did not liberate me: at the age of forty-five I was again compelled to confront Christ in my epic, the Odyssey, dedicating

to him an entire rhapsody; but that did not liberate me either. Later I made a fresh attack: I wrote *Christ Recrucified,* and immediately after, *The Last Temptation.* But in spite of all these desperate efforts the subject remains for me inexhaustible, because the mystery of the struggles of man and God, of the flesh and the spirit, of death and of immortality, is inexhaustible" (*Rettet Gott,* between pages 48 and 49, reproduction of a letter in French in Kazantzakis' own hand). Christ has a further significance for Kazantzakis. He personifies, as do Buddha and Lenin, the universal power of the human word. "The word of Christ, the word of Buddha, heard but by some thousands of Jews or Indians—has it not shaken the whole world?" (Jacques Pirenne, *Les Grands Courants de l'Histoire Universelle,* Neuchâtel, 1950, p. xi. From statistics, issued by UNESCO we learn, moreover, that from 1948 to 1955 Lenin has been translated 968 times; the Bible is second (*Le Courrier de l'Unesco,* Paris, February 1957, p. 8).

134. Odysseus considers himself to be more a "robber" than a "shepherd" (the expressions are from Nietzsche).

135. During the German occupation of Greece, Kazantzakis translated Machiavelli's *The Prince.* The manuscript was found among his effects.

136. I mean the *Utopia* of Sir Thomas More (*De optimo republicae statu deque nova insula Utopia,* 1516). Kazantzakis, if I am not mistaken, had the old English translation of Ralph Robinson in his library.

137. At the foundation of the ideal City, Odysseus beseeches the sun: "let the crawling worm sprout upright soaring wings!" (XV, 431). Later he calls his city the castle of the son, of all brave sons "who shall surpass their fathers and set their prow for God" (XV, 564). These Nietzschean ideas (see *Zarathustra,* Prologue § 3, and Part II § "On Self-surpassing") are formulated in an early work of Kazantzakis, *F. Nietzsche and the Philosophy of Right* (Candia, 1909): see pp. 51–52, 81–82, etc. For the hierarchy of the citizens, see pp. 52–62, 82–83, etc. One recalls here also the social hierarchy dreamed of by Schopenhauer and adopted by Nietzsche.

138. Kazantzakis' idea of making Odysseus carve in rock the commands of God is perhaps due to the memory of the "Stone of Nietzsche": on a rock of Sils-Maria there is a slate where one can see engraved a quotation from *Zarathustra: "Oh Mensch! Gieb Acht! Was spricht die tieje Mitternacht? . . ."* Kazantzakis himself had carved his name and the date of his ascent (1927) on the Sacred Peak of Sinai: there is a photograph of the inscription.

139. I cannot help thinking of the Caligula of Albert Camus. Drusilla, his beloved sister, dies; Caligula discovers the absurd fact that "Men die and are not happy." All values are destroyed at once. Caligula attains complete freedom, and vows to exercise it to the full: "Today and for all time to come, my freedom no longer has bounds." See Albert Camus, *Le Malentendu, suivi de Caligula* (Gallimard, Paris, 1947, pp. 111 and 119). And Robert de Luppé, *Albert Camus* (Éditions Universitaires, Paris, 1952, pp. 102–4).

140. See Euripides, *Helen,* lines 703–7.

141. The poet has made the mind and the will of Odysseus the means of his elevation. The process is strangely studied and deliberate: I am afraid the supernatural world is presented "from without."

## NOTES TO PART III

142. *England* (Athens, 1941, pp. 100–1).
143. "I hasten to finish the *Odyssey* in order to begin it" (letter from Aegina, August 11, 1927). "I hardly use any of the old verse" (letter from Gottesgab, November 15, 1929). "My heart is still heavy, a ball of worries and despairs and unconfessable sorrows. . . . The heart has not been liberated; that means that within me have remained a host of emotions, flashes, bitternesses which have not been expressed, have not taken flight, relieving my burden" (letter from Gottesgab, October 18, 1932).
144. Kazantzakis, "When the seed of the *Odyssey* took root within me," in *Nea Estia* (Athens, November 15, 1957, p. 1644); *Cf.* Kazantzakis, "A Comment on the *Odyssey*," in *Nea Estia* (August 15, 1943, pp. 1028–29): "In times of interregnum, a spiritual undertaking may either look backward justifying and judging the old civilization that is destroyed, or look forward and struggle to prophesy and formulate the new civilization. Odysseus struggles looking forward."
145. From very early on Kazantzakis had mocked every hope of future life, every promise of reward after death, as is demonstrated by his youthful writings *Comedy* and *F. Nietzsche and the Philosophy of Right* (pp. 28 and 45).
146. Anton Jeannaraki, *Kretas Volks-lieder* (F. A. Brockhaus, Leipzig, 1876, p. 119).
147. R.-M. Albérès, *Miguel de Unamuno* (Éditions Universitaires, Paris, 1957, p. 8).
148. This nostalgia later led Kazantzakis to the writing of novels in which he tried to relive the world of his youth.
149. Letter from Gottesgab, April 7, 1930.
150. *England,* pp. 98–99.
151. Miguel de Unamuno, *Niebla* (1914; Espasa-Calpe, Buenos Aires, 1947, p. 97).
152. "If all the lines are successful, my soul is saved for the little time that the Greek language will be spoken" (letter from Gottesgab, June 17, 1929).
153. *The Saviors of God,* translated by Kimon Friar, Simon and Schuster, New York, 1960, p. 59.
154. *Georgics,* I, 496.
155. Prologue to the *Anthologie de la Poésie Mexicaine* (Nagel, Paris, 1952). For the assimilation of the word to the object it expresses, see the striking examples which Giovanni Papini has selected from the *Divine Comedy: Il Dante Vivo,* chapter entitled "The Expressive Power."
156. Solomos, *Dialogue* (Collected Works, ed. L. Polites, Athens, 1955, Vol. II, p. 26).
157. See Eckermann, *Conversations with Goethe,* Part I, January 18, 1825. (Goethe, while discussing the translation of Serbian folk songs by T. Robinson, formulates his poetic theory.)
158. C. Fauriel, *Chansons Populaires de la Grèce Moderne,* I, 98.
159. I give some examples: The Aphrodite of Milos (III, 297–300); Mycenaean seal stone (III, 1021–25); "Dionysos' sailing," vase painting

of Exekias (V, 158–62); the "Venice" of Tintoretto (V, 511–33); Persian miniature (V, 547–50); Mycenaean daggers (V, 840–42); wall paintings of Knossos (VI, 274–78; 302–13); the "Vase of the Winnowers" (VII, 753–55); the "River Nile," the colossal Alexandrian sculpture (IX, 272–73); the beast-shaped gods of Egyptian sculpture (IX, 387–94); Egyptian reliefs with king and captives (X, 274–81); Egyptian frescoes in tomb (XI, 1098–1131); prehistoric frescoes in cave (XIV, 98–103); the "Tyche of Antioch," statue of Eutychides (XIV, 1293–94), etc.

160. One could compare, in the same way, the *Odyssey* of Kazantzakis with the *Odyssey* of Homer.

161. In certain archaizing statues of the Hellenistic period, for example, one can observe the so-called "folds from the chest" cutting the vertical folds of the Doric peplos. The archaizing sculptor is willy-nilly a realist: he sees the breaks in the cloth due to folding, and he copies them. Without copying, the archaic sculptor produced the form out of his spirit and from the conditions of the material.

162. An explanation of the term "baroque" may not be out of place. Sometimes it signifies an aesthetic category and sometimes a historical style (see Pandelis Prevelakis, *General Introduction to the History of Art,* Athens, 1934, pp. 37–38, and particularly, Eugenio D'Ors, *Du Baroque,* Gallimard, Paris, 1935). One of D'Ors's reflections (1918) will make it clear to the reader how the baroque type ramifies in historical forms (in other words, how the baroque spirit pervades historical periods): *"L'après guerre" sera une rechute*

*dans la "Fin de Siècle." Comme la "Fin de Siècle" dans la "Contre-Réforme," comme la "Contre-Réforme" dans le "Franciscanisme," le "Franciscanisme" dans l' "Alexandrisme," l' "Alexandrisme" dans l' "Orient." Comme l' "Orient" dans la "Pré-histoire."* (*Du Baroque,* p. 29. See also p. 161, where the writer gives, according to the system of Linnaeus, the table of the *genus Barocchus*.) The reader may remark that Kazantzakis was attracted by all the above embodiments of the baroque.

163. Letter from Madrid, October 11, 1932, *cf.* note 37.

164. *Inferno,* IV, 86–88.

165. Real Academía Española, *Diccionario Manual y Ilustrado de la Lengua Española* (Madrid, 1950), under the word *pícaro.*

166. Maxim Newmark, *Dictionary of Spanish Literature* (Philosophical Library, New York, 1956), under the words *pícaro* and *picaresque novel.* As a revival of the *novela picaresca* in contemporary literature I would cite *Tortilla Flat* of John Steinbeck and *Zorba the Greek* of Kazantzakis.

167. I should add that Kazantzakis' inherent heroic humanity also sought expression at least as much as the *picaresca.* After the *Odyssey,* Kazantzakis, as is known, cultivated the novel and the historical theater: he always wanted to dedicate himself to dramatical works like those of Shakespeare, Schiller or Kleist.

168. From an unedited text, which Kazantzakis sent me in a letter from Antibes (November 6, 1948). He intended it to form the prologue to his novel *Christ Recrucified,* but he abandoned it at the time of publication (1954).

169. During the last week of September and the first ten days of October 1927, Kazantzakis wrote articles for the *Elevtheroudakis Encyclopaedic Dictionary* and at the same time worked over the selection from his travelogues which was to form the volume *Traveling—Spain, Italy, Egypt, Sinai* (Alexandria, 1927).

170. Odysseus speaks to himself (XIII, 742–44):

*"Haven't I told you more than once or twice, you fool,*
*to use your hard hand gently, for men break in two,*
*but you still stubbornly think the world can reach your height."*

Cf. XIII, 768–76, 830–39, and *Japan-China* (1956, p. 96): "I believe unshakably in the inequality of men."

171. Kornaros, Vicenzo. Cretan epic poet living during the sixteenth or seventeeth century, author of the *Erotokritos,* a chivalresque poem of ten thousand lines, in five parts.

172. I recall that he had signed his tragedy *Odysseus* in the *Nea Zoi* of Alexandria (see note 9) with the pseudonym A. Geranos.

173. Nikolaï Kazan, *Toda Raba (Le Cahier Bleu,* No. 14, Paris, 1934, pp. 5 and 16). *Toda Raba* was written in French, and was first published in the periodical *Revue des Vivants,* Paris, 1931.

174. Newspaper *Proia,* Athens, January 9, 1928. The articles of Kazantzakis in *Proia* (December 31, 1927, January 8, 1928, etc.) contain valuable indications of the significance which the third journey to Russia had in his life. Inestimable testimony also are his letters to the author.

175. Kazantzakis once himself confessed to me, in 1927 or 1928, that he had not read *Capital.* He found Marx's theory unbearably rationalistic. Kazantzakis' attack on historical materialism in the columns of the periodical *Anagennisi* (1927) is well known.

176. The new Odysseus had adopted many ideas contained in the work of Max Stirner, *Der Einzige und sein Eigenthum* (1845).

177. The newspaper *Proia,* Athens, January 8, 1928.

178. The delirium is continued in the description he composed for the newspaper *Proia* (January 9, 1928). "Childish tears," he said, sometimes hid the disturbing sight from him.

179. See the newspaper *Proia,* January 10, 1928.

180. Kazantzakis, *Russia* (Athens, 1956, p. 236). For Kazantzakis' meeting with Istrati there are many first-hand witnesses: Kazantzakis, "Panait Istrati," *Proia,* December 31, 1927; Kazantzakis, *Russia* (1956, pp. 233–45); Panait Istrati, "A Traveler," prologue to the Greek edition of *Toda Raba* (Athens, 1956); pages from Istrati's book, *Vers l'Autre Flamme* (Rieder, Paris, 1929), which had first been published in *Monde,* the weekly periodical of Henri Barbusse, on July 23, 1928; Eleni Samios, *La Verdadera Tragedia de Panait Istrati* (Ercilla, Santiago, Chile, 1938). This last book is an account of the journey of Kazantzakis and Istrati in Russia. More will be said of this journey below. For the sake of brevity, I shall henceforth refer to the book as *Samios.*

181. Kazantzakis, "Panait Istrati," *Proia* (December 31, 1927).

182. He had quoted them in the dedi-

cation he made to me of a copy of his *Divine Comedy* (1934). The verse is from *Inferno* (XXVI, 79).

183. Kalmouchos, Takis (b. 1895): Greek painter of progressive tendencies. He traveled with Kazantzakis in Egypt and Sinai.

184. "Three or four times in his life, Geranos had allowed himself to be caught up in this quixotic and lofty fever: friendship. Mad dreams, austere joys, woman, seemed a pleasant nothing. Earth contracted, happy, before the love of two male hearts. After a bit, the fatal turn was traced, the parting came, violently or soundlessly, humiliating." *Toda Raba* (Athens, 1956), p. 118.

185. See *Russia* (1956, pp. 245–51).

186. *Ibid.*, p. 246.

187. *Toda Raba* (1956), pp. 10–11; see also pp. 11–13, where Istrati gives an account of their journey to the Caucasus.

188. Line of Juan Ramón Jiménez.

189. *Russia*, p. 251.

190. The citations that follow are from letters of Kazantzakis to the author.

191. The following is the timetable of the journey, November 17, 1927: Kazantzakis leaves Moscow for the Caucasus with Istrati and the other guests (Arthur Holitscher, Helen Stöcker, the Professor Kouchinsky, the Belgian Dr. Soeur, the Japanese poet Akita, the Argentinian writer Quintana). The same evening they reached Kharkov. November 20, Rostov; November 22, Baku; November 24, Tiflis; November 27, Batum; November 29, Poti; November 30, Gangri; December 1, Novorosisk; December 2, Rostov; December 3, Moscow; December 8, Kiev; December 20, Odessa; December 22, departure for Greece;

December 26, Salonika; December 30, Athens.

192. "At the moment we are taking the boat from Odessa to Greece," the two companions had announced, "we salute you as your children, Union of free peoples! We who send you salutation are two people —two men, two friends, two fighters united in one soul—Dioscouri inspired with longing for the new life" (Samios, pp. 27–29).

193. Kazantzakis' lecture took place on January 11, 1928, and was published in *Anagennisi*, 1928, pp. 193–98.

194. "Between the dying West and the East that is being born," in the Athenian newspaper *Elevtheron Vima* (January 12, 1928).

195. *Les Chardons de Baragan*. Istrati's publisher was the Parisian Rieder.

196. Letter from Aegina, February 3, 1928. He continues: "How superficial, out of my nature, the rumpus in Athens, the 'Sotiria' (the sanatorium) and the inquiries and the pseudo-daring of the Communists!"

197. Letter from Odessa, April 23, 1928.

198. From a letter to Istrati: it recapitulates the latter's proposals (Samios, p. 120).

199. Letter from Murmansk, July 20, 1928.

200. Samios, p. 35.

201. *The Saviors of God* (1960), p. 128 (see *Odyssey*, XXIII, 932–36).

202. *The Saviors of God* (1960), p. 131 (see p. 49 of the main text where I have reproduced the first form of the concluding Credo).

203. Letter, on the way to Murmansk, July 1928.

204. Letter from Moscow, July 28, 1928 (see *Odyssey*, XXII, 755). The feeling of cosmic terror was often cultivated by Kazantzakis as one

capable of linking him with the primitive mentality. This feeling was a consequence of his atheism and his anti-rationalism: neither God nor reason could interpret or tame the world.

205. In the same letter.

206. Letter, beginning of July 1928 (on the way to Murmansk). In another of his letters, from Moscow, June 19, 1928, Kazantzakis confessed: "Sometimes here I am overcome by such agony that I am at a loss to explain later how my body could endure. Each day I verify more deeply that something inhuman exists in me. Someone within me changes human desires and tendencies into something dark, harsh, insatiable and desperate. Istrati is a man—a good man—he cannot sense it."

207. Letter from Kiev, May 25, 1928.

208. See *The Saviors of God* (1960), pp. 108–9.

209. See this strange text in *Toda Raba* (French original, 1934, pp. 140–146): Azad (*i.e.,* Istrati), who listens to Geranos (Kazantzakis) reading it, is shaken. His eyes cloud with tears, he clasps the hands of his friend: "I do not understand all of it, but I feel my whole soul in the rhythm of your words: pain, hope, struggle." The text was also published by Samios, pp. 98–104. A letter Kazantzakis wrote from Moscow (July 29, 1928) gives us exact information: "By the 10–15th of August we are leaving for the great journey. We have already made agreements with German, English, French, Dutch, Spanish and Russian papers and periodicals to send articles. Today I wrote the first, which will be published later, as an Introduction, in the *Nouvelles Littéraires*. Luckily I wrote

all of it, and so it will be for all the articles. Istrati leaves me entirely free and is glad to sign."

210. Letter from Moscow, August 15, 1928. On the eve of their departure, Kazantzakis wrote, within a week, another scenario: *St. Pachomius and Company*. In the same letter: "It is very sober, visionary, anti-clerical. It was accepted at once."

211. "Panait, not being able to write, asks Kazantzakis to do the work of both of them. Every morning Kazantzakis opens his door, he calls him in and begins to read him the latest production. Panait is pleased, the savage rhythm of the African corresponds to his inner flame, he claps his hands: 'Bravo, bravo, ogre! Bring it here for me to sign'" (Samios, pp. 97–98).

212. "Christ, Buddha, Lenin, the three great beloved corsairs of my life, had not disappeared, but shone in the twilight of memory like hieroglyphics of lofty bygone significance" (*Report to Greco, Nea Estia,* Athens, November 15, 1957, p. 1640). The psychic state here described by Kazantzakis had been formed after the first journey to Russia in 1925, when he began the writing of the *Odyssey*. But, as we saw, "Lenin" came to the surface again when Kazantzakis' messianism suffered a relapse. The conclusive conversion to "Odysseus" takes place now.

213. Samios, p. 168. Eleni Samios gave an account of this unsettling affair in her book: see particularly pp. 157–70. For Istrati's apostasy, see his books *Vers l'Autre Flamme* and *Soviets 1929* (Rieder, Paris, 1929). Both seem to have been written by Victor Serge, as he himself confessed to Eleni Samios. As is known, in the polemic against

Stalin, Victor Serge openly took part (when it was convenient) with the *Fate of the Revolution:* he followed in the steps of Trotsky and his *Revolution Betrayed*.

214. Samios, p. 171.

215. According to Eleni Samios, the breaking of the partnership and Istrati's proceedings with the editors of the newspapers in France, Holland, Sweden, etc., had taken place before the "Rusakov Affair" (Samios, p. 158). Some articles had, however, already been published in Amsterdam (letter of Kazantzakis from Leningrad, January 20, 1929).

216. Letter from Siberia, February 5, 1929.

217. Letter from Iman, February 16, 1929. Kazantzakis continues: "In Russia I again felt it perfectly: Russia does not interest me at all, nor does justice, comfort, or the virtue of man; I am only interested in the flame that burns men with those popular, low, transient baits —justice, comfort, and virtue."

218. The place is called Gottesgab: it is in Czechoslovakia, close to the German borders at a height of 1100 m. There Kazantzakis worked on the second and third drafts of the *Odyssey*.

219. The text (also in French) was not published.

220. Letter from Gottesgab, May 28, 1929. In the end, Kazantzakis' travelogue was not published by the Parisian periodicals.

221. Holitscher's book *Das unruhige Asien*. As I noted above, Kazantzakis had traveled with Holitscher from Moscow to Batum in November 1927.

222. See the preliminary disclosure of the writer in *Toda Raba*.

223. Letter from Gottesgab, June 16, 1929.

224. In the same letter. Kazantzakis' struggle had begun earlier. While his letters from Russia show him firmly turned toward the *Odyssey*, his resignation from action caused him deep suffering: "Terrible questions of doubt and bitterness torture me; my life is lost, I have given nothing of what I could and should have given—I lose myself arranging letters of the alphabet, I give my heart paper to eat—as if it were a goat" (letter from Astrakhan, September 21, 1928).

225. From the *Report to Greco,* in *Nea Estia* (Athens, November 15, 1957), p. 1638. The reader will doubtless remember here the discussion on the "creative critic" in Part One of this book. The psychology of an artist belonging to the baroque will also be perceived: his longing is boundless.

226. Gottesgab, September 25, 1929. He adds: "The third draft [1930–31] will be attention to the essence."

227. Gottesgab, September 12, 1929.

228. Gottesgab, September 25, 1929.

229. Gottesgab, November 15, 1929.

230. In the same letter. Eleni was with him.

231. "I fight as I can not to hurry, but the *daemon* within me hurries" (letter from Gottesgab, February 22, 1930).

232. Letter from Gottesgab, April 7, 1930 (see the Prologue to *The Odyssey*).

233. Kazantzakis compiled half the dictionary—from *A* to *K*. The author of this book was to write the rest.

234. Letter from Athens, April 17, 1931.

235. In the same letter.

236. Letter from Gottesgab, end of June, 1931.

237. Letter from Aegina, May 4, 1931.

238. "I write to you thus as if I were traveling and noting the stations" (letter from Gottesgab, August 17, 1931).
239. Letter from Gottesgab, July 17, 1931.
240. In the same letter: *"La grande Méditerranée de vers horizontaux."*
241. Linos Polites, *Solomos in His Letters* (Athens, n.d.), p. 30.
242. Letter from Gottesgab, September 8, 1931. The "note" to which Kazantzakis refers was a short letter sent to him by a French student, a girl who had read *Toda Raba* in the *Revue des Vivants.*
243. Letter from Gottesgab, September 8, 1931.
244. Letter from Gottesgab, July 17, 1931.
245. Letter from Gottesgab, December 6, 1931.
246. Letter from Gottesgab, October 31, 1931.
247. This valuable manuscript constitutes a volume of 1,984 pages. Kazantzakis gave it to the author.
248. Letter from Gottesgab, April 9, 1932.
249. Avenue des Moulineaux, 93.
250. Negotiations had begun while he was still in Paris. In Madrid he was a guest at the house of his friend Timoteo Pérez Rubio, Assistant Director of the National Museum of Contemporary Art, in the Plaza del Progreso, No. 5. During this time, Eleni was in England.
251. Letter from Madrid, October 18, 1932.
252. Letter from Madrid, October 18, 1932.
253. Letter from Madrid, October 22, 1932.
254. A large part of these translations was published in the Athenian periodical *Kyklos* in 1933 and 1934. Kazantzakis' introductory notes and translations have the general title "Contemporary Spanish Lyric Poetry": they make a small anthology of poems by Juan Ramón Jiménez, Antonio Machado, Miguel de Unamuno, Pedro Salinas, Moreno Villa, Federico García Lorca, Rafael Alberti, etc.
255. Kazantzakis' *Cantos* are poems of about 150–180 lines each, in *terza rima,* celebrating great "leaders of souls."
256. Letter from Madrid, January 5, 1933.
257. Letter from Madrid, January 5, 1933. I have italicized the words which seem to me especially significant.
258. Kazantzakis had been considering his last work, *Report to Greco,* since 1931, as his letters witness.
259. Kazantzakis left Spain on March 22 or 23, 1933, went to Paris, where he stayed ten days (rue Erlanger, No. 17), and reached Greece on April 10, 1933.
260. Kazantzakis was a guest for a week in his old quarters, the cottage of Paul Hanos, now occupied by the author. From April 19, 1933, the two friends lived in the cottage of Mary Pandos, at "Livadi." Not far from there Kazantzakis later built his "cocoon": the foundations were laid on March 4, 1936.
261. Kazantzakis sometimes recited to himself. His repertoire was very limited. It included mainly some opening lines of sections of the *Divine Comedy:* "O insensata cura de' mortali . . ." (*Paradiso,* XI, 1 *ff.*); "S'io avessi le rime aspre e chiocce . . ." (*Inferno,* XXXII, 1 *ff.*), etc. There is no need for me to point out that the passages he remembered were deeply in accord with his own spirit.
262. The first ten days of his stay in

Aegina were occupied in copying out the articles which he had written on Spain: they were published in the Athenian newspaper *Kathimerini* from May 21 to June 3, 1933.

263. See note 247. Kazantzakis asked the author for the manuscript of the *Odyssey* in order to work on the fourth draft.

264. I mean the notes in the Greek edition of the *Divine Comedy*.

265. The "bodyguards of the *Odyssey*" in the end numbered twenty: to be added were Shakespeare, Leonardo da Vinci, Toda Raba, Hideyohi, Alexander the Great, Christ, the poet's female companion and others.

266. All the *Cantos* were published in one volume in 1960, in Athens.

267. Spanish: I desire, I have longing.

268. An inscription on a drawing attributed to El Greco.

269. *Odyssey,* Prologue, line 4.

270. The following is the timetable of the journey to Japan and China: February 22, 1935, Suez; March 16, Hong Kong; March 24, Kobe (Japan); March 26, Osaka; March 27, Nara; March 30, Kyoto; April 5, Tokyo; April 22, journey from Tokyo to Kobe; April 24–28, journey from Kobe to Tientsin (China); April 29, Peking; May 4–6, journey from Peking to Shanghai.

271. Kazantzakis stayed alone in Aegina. Eleni was in France; she returned in the early part of August.

272. Kazantzakis' articles on Japan and China were published in the Athenian newspaper *Akropolis* from June 9 until October 19, 1935. They were first published in book form in 1938, in Athens, with the title *Traveling: Japan–China.*

273. The Leipzig publisher Grethlein had asked for the novel. When he read it, he could not find words enough to praise it: but it was not published under the Hitler regime. The book was published only in Amsterdam (1939) and in Santiago in Chile (Ercilla, 1941).

274. It is obvious that this is the first sketch of *Captain Michalis* (published in the U.S. as *Freedom or Death,* Simon and Schuster, New York, 1956).

275. I would like to pause at this statement and to observe once more that in most of his works—and particularly in the *Odyssey*—Kazantzakis was giving a sensible form to the world-view of *The Saviors of God.*

276. It is worth noting that Toda Raba, returning from war, goes to make reverence at the ancestral graveyard. He drenches the dead in the blood of a slaughtered animal, dances on the graves, summons the spirits to be present at his orgy: all this had been done by Odysseus in mild Ithaca (*Odyssey,* I, 595 *ff.*) in a way that is reminiscent more of African rituals than of the libations of the Homeric hero.

277. It is also worth noting that the canto "Christ" contains the idea of *The Last Temptation,* which was written in 1951.

278. According to Kazantzakis, Shakespeare represents this state of "freedom" in *The Tempest.*

279. *Kathimerini,* October and December 1936, January 1937.

280. "A Comment on the *Odyssey*," in *Nea Estia* (August 15, 1943), p. 1029.

281. To this period (1936–37) belong two pieces of writing: the verse translation of Goethe's *Faust* and

an original theatrical work with the title *Othello Returns*.

282. The following is the timetable of the tour of the Morea: September 4, 1937, Patras; September 8, Mistra; September 16, Monemvasia; September 17, Sparta; September 19, Argos, Mycenae. During the journey, Kazantzakis visited Chlemoutsi, Megalopolis, Karytaina, Tripolis, etc. (see his impressions in *Kathimerini*, November 7–December 21, 1937).

283. It was first published in *Nea Estia* (1939), and circulated as a reprint. It is included in *Theatre—Tragedies with Ancient Themes,* which was published in Athens in 1955.

284. The generous lady was Joe MacLeod. Kazantzakis presents her to us in his *England* (1941, pp. 229–35), and he honored her by dedicating to her the first edition of the *Odyssey*. The poem was printed in Athens in an impressive volume.

## NOTES TO THE EPILOGUE

285. The notebook carries the inscription "Gong." The entry is on the two pages before the last, and must be dated to 1940: the last text mentioned in the catalogue of subsidiary works is *Julian*.

286. *Sodom and Gomorrah* (1948); *Christ Recrucified* (1948); *Theseus* (1949); *The Golden Apple or Christopher Columbus* (1949); *Captain Michalis* (1950); *The Last Temptation* (1951); *The Poor Man of God* (1953); *"He wants, he says, to be free: kill him!"* (otherwise: *The Fratricides*, an unpublished novel, 1954); *Report to Greco* (1956–57).

## ABOUT THE AUTHOR

PANDELIS PREVELAKIS *was Director of the Department of Fine Arts of the Ministry of National Education in Greece from 1937 to 1941. Since 1939 he has been Professor of the History of Art in the National College of Fine Arts, Athens. He is the author of more than twenty books—novels, criticism, plays and verse— many of which have been translated into English, French and German.*

*Mr. Prevelakis was for many years a close friend of the late Nikos Kazantzakis.*

## ABOUT THE TRANSLATOR

PHILIP SHERRARD, *author and scholar, is at present Assistant Director of the British School at Athens.*

[ 192 ]